Geoffrey Wellum was born in Walthamstow. Aged seventeen, he joined the RAF on a short-service commission in August 1939 and served with 92 Squadron throughout the Battle of Britain. He is now one of the last surviving members of The Few. He is contacted regularly to make television and radio programmes.

First Light

GEOFFREY WELLUM

PENGUIN BOOKS

PENGUIN BOOKS

UK | USA | Canada | Ireland | Australia
India | New Zealand | South Africa

Penguin Books is part of the Penguin Random House group of companies
whose addresses can be found at global.penguinrandomhouse.com.

First published by Viking 2002
Published in Penguin Books 2003
Reissued 2009, 2018

001

Set in Monotype Bembo
Printed in England by Clays Ltd, St Ives plc

ISBN: 978-0-241-98434-5

This book is dedicated to all fighter pilots

The time will come, when thou shalt lift thine eyes
To watch a long-drawn battle in the skies.
While aged peasants, too amazed for words,
Stare at the flying fleets of wondrous birds.

England, so long mistress of the sea,
Where winds and waves confess her sovereignty,
Her ancient triumphs yet on high shall bear
And reign the sovereign of the conquered air.

Stanzas composed in the style of Thomas Gray,
Elegy Written in a Country Churchyard

Contents

Illustrations

The author and publishers are grateful to the following for permission to reproduce photographs: 4, 22, 23, Lesley Kingcombe; 5, 11–13, 25, Allan Wright; 6, 8–10, 14–21, 24, 27, 28, Imperial War Museum; 7, RAF Museum, Hendon; 26, Cecil Beaton Archive (photographs from *Winged Squadrons* by Cecil Beaton).

Prologue

The co-pilot of the Catalina flying boat came aft to the crew's rest room where I, a worn-out Spitfire pilot, reclined on one of the let-down bunks, feeling cold and miserable. Smiling, he handed me a steaming mug of hot sweet cocoa and the thickest and largest corned beef sandwich I had ever seen.

I am on my way back home to England from Malta and, as the Catalina drones through the night sky somewhere between Gibraltar and Plymouth and fortified by the cocoa, I ponder the last three years.

It seems like an impossible dream. Did I really find myself in a front line fighter squadron within ten months of leaving school? Did I fly through and survive the Battle of Britain before I had reached the age of twenty? It appears I must have done.

Thirty-five years later I am sitting at the dining-room table in my small cottage. The french windows are open and the sound and smell of the steady summer rain create a peaceful atmosphere. Before me on the table is a pencil, sheets of foolscap and an old exercise book containing some reflections I jotted down at odd times during those momentous early days of the Second World War.

Without realizing it, I pick up the pencil and start to write. Something seems to guide that pencil as my hand moves back and forth, back and forth across the paper. The daylight fades. I switch on the lamp and continue until finally my hand stops. The writing has totally relaxed me. I must write some more one day when I think about it and before memory fades further with advancing years. I kept no diaries, so I'll just have to put all that I've written into some sort of order and call it a manuscript.

1. Ab Initio

While men depart of joyful heart
Adventure for to know

Rudyard Kipling,
'The Song of the Dead'

There are some days in the early spring when the weather is such that, no matter where you are, either in town or country-side, England is at her best and it's good to be alive. I notice that it is just such a day as I emerge from the underground at Holborn, turn left and walk down Kingsway.

The morning sun is already warm and rather comforting, which helps to allay somewhat a feeling of apprehension that has been building up within me for the past couple of hours.

I am seventeen and a half years old and, I suspect, a rather precocious young man. It was some six months ago when I first wrote to the Air Ministry. I was leaving school within a year and very much wanted to fly an aeroplane, so could they give me a job, please? It must have been a frightening prospect because they certainly took their time replying, but eventually I received a response in the guise of an enormous and rather complicated form together with a covering letter.

The writer informed me that he had been directed to reply to my undated communication – always a communication, never a letter – enclosing an application form for completion in due course and he ended by saying that he was my most obedient servant. I remember thinking what charming manners and how polite the Royal Air Force must be to everybody.

So, one evening after junior prep, the members of the VIth Form descended on my study to hold a meeting. The object was to reflect upon and hopefully complete the application form by the simple process of discussing and then taking a vote on the answer to each question. In return I was to supply suitable refreshments for the duration of the discussion. Simple!

The whole meeting was a great success and the answers to the many questions really superb. Duly completed, the form was returned to the Air Ministry a few days later. 'Don't appear to be in too much of a hurry,' they said.

Weeks of silence followed. The Air Ministry had just laughed and torn it up. Then, one day, the headmaster summoned me to the presence.

'I have had an extraordinary letter from the Air Ministry, who require me to say something nice about you and so purge myself. Do you think I dare?'

'Yes, sir, of course; without question.'

'Really? Why on earth should I? And in any case, what could I possibly say?'

'Well, sir, you must have done the same thing before for many others and I'm certain it cannot be the first time that you have been faced with the dilemma of perjury.'

'In that case, I suppose I'd better think something up, but I was rather hoping that you would be here for the cricket season. I gather you have been invited to captain the first XI. That can't be right, surely, can it?'

'I'm afraid it is, sir. You see, lots of people left after last year and we'll be hard up for chaps this summer.'

'Obviously.'

'I shall be able to stay without too much trouble as I'm

under age at the moment. You have to be at least seventeen and a half before you can join the RAF.'

'Let's see, how old are you at the moment?'

'Seventeen, sir.'

'All right, I'll see what I can do.'

He gave me a pat on the shoulder as I left him, which I thought strange.

Not all that long afterwards I received a letter from my father which informed me that he also had been in receipt of an Air Ministry communication. It appeared that what this said, in effect, was that if my dad wanted to get rid of me all that badly, would he please give his consent to my joining the Royal Air Force, if invited to do so, by signing the attached document.

It would seem that Father complied by return of post.

A further period of silence followed before yet another communication arrived, this one inviting me to attend a selection board to be held at Adastral House, Kingsway, at 10.00 hours on Wednesday 20 March 1939 in connection with my application for a Short Service Commission in the General Duties Branch of the Royal Air Force. This writer was also my obedient servant.

And so, this sunny morning finds me walking down Kingsway. I look at my watch. I'm in plenty of time, although it won't hurt to get there a little on the early side. Do I really want to join the RAF and become a pilot? I suppose I'm doing the right thing? Still time to turn round and go home. I take my time and stroll quietly onwards. It would be nice to be able to fly.

I am fully aware that the next hour or so could well be a turning point in my life. Throughout my comparatively short time on this earth I have had an awareness of the dramatic as it occurs, an awareness of the passing of time; that time, once behind you, can never return or be retrieved.

As a boy of eleven, I went as a boarder to Forest School in Snaresbrook. I realized even then that infant days were over and a phase of life was behind me; another milestone was being reached. It is all so relentless that I wonder if life is mapped out from the day that you are born. Is everything pre-ordained? Maybe I'm a bit of a fatalist.

Assuming I am accepted by the RAF, next term at school will be my last. I shall have my study, VIth Form privileges and a young third former to do any job that I can't be bothered to do for myself; I'll be a little tin god. Better make the most of it – as an acting pilot officer on probation I shall be on the bottom rung of the ladder again and a lower form of life will not exist.

Businessmen complete with briefcases and copies of the *Daily Telegraph* hurry by me as I walk. Heads down, intent on another day at the office, the same sort of day as yesterday and no doubt a very similar day tomorrow. Finance, rates, banking, profit margins, insurance, shipping, broking, business lunches and, for the most part, boredom; a stereotyped curriculum. I look at the small fluffy white clouds contrasting against the blue English sky. I'd rather fly, if they'll have me.

Adastral House. Thanks in part to the businessmen, I have no hesitation. I cross the threshold and pass through the large important-looking doors into another world. The first step is taken, a decision is made.

A commissionaire comes up to me before there is time to stand around looking obvious.

'I'm here for an interview with the selection board for pilots in the RAF.'

'Third floor, Room 21.'

Room 21 is an unimposing and austere waiting room. Two commissionaires are present. I enter and approach one who looks a kindly sort of chap. He speaks before I have time to introduce myself.

'Selection board?'

'Yes.'

'Name?'

'Wellum.'

He consults a list. 'Mr Geoffrey Harry Augustus Wellum?'

'Yes, I'm afraid so.'

'Right you are, Mr Wellum, just take a seat. You won't be kept waiting all that long once they get going. I'll be here to tell you where to go when you are called.'

Well, at least they seem to be organized. I sit down to wait and by ten o'clock some twenty would-be aviators are assembled. One person, of course, makes conversation – there is always one. He speaks non-stop in spite of the fact that nobody is really listening, or indeed is the least bit interested. He has done fourteen hours solo and so forth and it would appear he knows everybody who is worth knowing in and around London, to say nothing of the people he meets each year in St Moritz. I suppose he's bound to be accepted.

Things start to move at about 10.15. By nature I am always an impatient sort of person and as others are called before me I become agitated and apprehensive. Finally, my turn comes and I am ushered along a short passage. The commissionaire knocks at a door, opens it and stands aside for me to enter.

Three distinguished-looking men behind a large table. The one in the centre, who must be the primary member or the chairman, I suppose, is a pleasant-faced man with a steady gaze. On his right is an elderly grey-haired chap who looks harmless enough. It's the one on the left I don't like the look of all that much. Don't know why, really, but I bet he'll ask all the rotten questions, probably maths or something. My surmise turns out to be correct.

'Good morning. Your name?'

'Good morning. Wellum, sir.'

'Take a seat.' Then, before I have had a chance to settle, 'Why do you want to join the Royal Air Force?'

'I want to fly aeroplanes and the RAF is the best way of doing so and making a career in aviation that I know. Also, it won't cost me anything; money, I mean.'

'I'm inclined to agree with you. Mr Wellum, what about service to your King and Country? Say there is a war, what then?'

'I've always taken as read that one serves, sir. I've not thought about war.'

'Hmm. Oh, well. Where are you at school?'

The plunge taken, the questions come thick and fast. Which newspapers do I read? What games do I play? Do I shoot, ride? How many battleships in the Far East? (None, they're all cruisers.) How old are you? A bit young yet, then. And on and on. The nasty one puts his oar in the water. What is the tan of an angle? Sine? Cosine? (I can answer that. I thought someone would bring that up and so I checked last night. Jammy!) I feel myself being drawn out in conversation and I get the impression that things are going reasonably well. I almost begin to enjoy the experience.

'Now, this question of your age. You are still at school, of course. Can you do another term?'

'I'd like to, sir, at least until I'm old enough to join the air force. You see, I've been asked to captain the cricket XI this season.' Can't do any harm to get that one in.

'Have you, indeed? Used to play a lot myself. Well now, let's see,' and, turning to his two companions, 'We wouldn't want to interfere with that, would we? Captain, eh? Right, so if you go back to school for one more term and brush up on your maths when you are not playing cricket – and that's important – that should bring you up to the right sort of age. Well, thank you, Mr Wellum, for your time. Take this slip to the commissionaire and he will tell you where to find the doctors. Good day to you.'

'Good morning, sir.'

And that's that. The slip is blue. I hand it to the waiting attendant.

'That's only the fourth today, young sir.'

'What do you mean?'

'You see, if you get given a blue chit it means you have passed the interview. So now you go to see the doctors, and sooner you than me, sir. A pink slip and the next thing you hear is the Air Ministry regrets . . .'

He tells me what to do and where to go and by 12.45 I am about halfway through the medical. I never realized there were so many parts of the human body that required checking to see if they worked. Then everything stops for lunch and I am dismissed with a request to be back no later than 2 p.m. Finally, at 3.30, the ordeal is over and I walk out into Kingsway and a cloudy afternoon. There is no indication as to how the medical went, but I feel sure I haven't done too badly. I held my breath OK and blew up the mercury; I shall feel rather disappointed if I'm turned down.

I am not. Two days before the end of the Easter holidays comes the welcome news that I have been accepted for pilot training. I am to report to No. 7 Elementary and Reserve Flying Training School at Desford, Leicestershire, for ab initio training not later than noon on 28 July 1939.

There are instructions as to what I should take in the way of clothing (including a dinner jacket and a cap; odd mixture!), what books to read and so forth. I pay little attention. I am going to be a pilot and that is all that matters. Failure along the way doesn't occur to me and anyway, the cricket season is about to begin and I shall be fully occupied.

The summer term passes all too quickly. Days in the sun and the sound of ball on bat. Lunch taken under the large chestnut tree, the rest of the school seated round the boundary in their straw boaters watching the game and a dip in the swimming pool after close of play. I savour it all to the full, make the most of it and enjoy every minute.

Two of my closest friends at Forest School are John Howell-Jones and Henry Neil. Sometimes John, Henry and I walk round the playing fields along the edge of the forest in the twilight of fine summer evenings and discuss the future. They are both going up to Oxford. They seem to think there could well be a war and if it comes we will all be involved. I can't say that I have given much thought to it at all, yet of the three of us I shall be the first to be thrown into the deep end.

John is due to be killed leading his platoon in North Africa whilst Henry will spend four years or more chasing the Japs through the jungles of Malaya and Burma. But that summer we are young and full of confidence. We are happy. England is a peaceful place and life goes on at school as it has done for 150 years. Only vaguely are we aware that the country is rearming and preparing for war.

The last day of term arrives, and as I walk through the cloisters to the end-of-term service in the chapel I find it moving. As is routine, we monitors walk into chapel after the rest of the school, preceding the masters in their gowns, cloaks and mortarboards. 'Jerusalem' and the final hymn, 'God Be with You Till We Meet Again'. When in God's name will that be? Handshakes all round and my housemaster, dear old 'Pipes', saying, 'Cheerio, old chap; good luck and please come and see us if you get the time.'

A new boy will arrive next term and 'Pipes' will start all over again.

I walk out of the main gate for the last time, no longer a schoolboy. Another stepping stone; I am an Old Boy with immediate effect. As I get into the waiting car and move away, I don't look round or speak to Father, I just blow my nose very, very hard.

*

Before I have time to really appreciate what is happening, I find myself at Desford saying goodbye to my parents. Mother says very little except to forbid me to go too fast. It is just about a week since the end of term.

The excitement of something new about to happen is upon me and in any case I don't want to prolong farewells. I quickly say my au revoirs. For just one moment I watch their car disappear round the corner of the lane. They have gone. That's it, then, so the only thing to do now is pick up my luggage and walk through the main gate at Desford into the Royal Air Force.

The welcoming talk leaves those of us who have assembled in no doubt whatsoever as to the situation. We are not yet in the RAF and not all of us ever will be. We are, in fact, civilian 'pupil pilots' and very much on probation.

Before the service accept us for any further training, we have to pass the ab initio flying course, which will take us up to fifty hours' flying time. We are to be taught on DH 82 Tiger Moths. By the end of the course we will be able to do everything in the way of flying the aeroplane that the RAF requires: aerobatics, cross-country and suchlike. Exams will be taken and there will be a weeding-out process starting as of this moment. The air force, we are told, is fairly easy to get into these days, judging by the appearance of our course, but it is also very easy to get out of and we are to bear this fact very much in mind.

This is a rude man, not the least like my 'obedient servant'. He is, in fact, the Chief Ground Instructor and very frightening. He, together with the Chief Flying Instructor, hands out the 'Bowler Hats'.★

The Chief Flying Instructor gives flying tests to doubtful pupils and the end-of-course tests to ascertain if we have

★ RAF slang for a suspension from duty; effectively, being sacked.

attained the necessary minimum standard. What he says, goes. He has the power to pass or fail. Between them they make a right pair.

As with all courses, we are a very mixed collection from all walks of life, each, it would seem, with a false sense of his own importance. There are some South Africans, four Canadians and one each from Australia and New Zealand, all of us excited to some extent and very near to being labelled an unruly mob.

For the remainder of our first afternoon we are left to our own devices to settle in. I chum up with a chap called Peter Sears. We are to become firm friends in the months ahead.

During the course of the afternoon I go for a walk along the tarmac among the aircraft, where I savour the smell of doped canvas, petrol, oil and the general aroma of aeroplanes. I revel in the atmosphere. Tiger Moths all over the place, dozens of them. A wonderful feeling of involvement comes over me.

The next day the course starts to get into its stride. We are issued with basic flying kit, helmet and goggles, overalls, a Sidcot suit★ and a pair of gauntlets. I meet my flying instructor, a quietly spoken man who has charming manners. At the same time he's the sort of person who won't suffer fools gladly and will leave you in no doubt when you do something that displeases him. He makes it quite plain that the best is barely good enough. His name is Hayne. I'm sure I'll be able to get on with him.

The following morning I find myself standing beside a Tiger Moth with my instructor. He shows me over the aircraft, the controls and what they do, which surfaces the joystick moves (push it forward to dive, pull it back to climb), the purpose of the rudder bar, the general effect of airflow over

---

★ One-piece padded flying suit. The name derives from Sidney Cotton, the First World War RNAS pilot who developed it.

the airframe. He asks me finally if I understand and I say yes.

'OK. Then let me show you how to put on a parachute. If you ever have to jump, count three after leaving the aircraft and pull that large ring hard. Now, hop into the back cockpit and I'll show you how to strap yourself in. It would be a shame if you fell out, wouldn't it? There, how's that?'

Trussed up like a hen I'm left to make myself as comfortable as possible under these quite extraordinary circumstances. I sit totally immobile and scarcely able to breathe as I watch Hayne lower himself into the front seat.

Before I've really gathered my wits, a slow process at the best of times, the propeller has been swung and the engine started. We move quickly out on to the field, turn and, gathering speed, race across the bumpy grass with everything rattling and vibrating and sounding like a bag of nails. I just hang on to my seat like grim death and think what a damn silly expression that is to use at this particular time. I'll never be able to do this sort of thing. I've made one hell of a mistake joining this lot.

The bumping stops. We must have left the ground or something equally horrible. A quick look out as if I really don't want to believe what I'm afraid I'm going to see. We are flying.

The ground recedes and once in the air all sense of speed vanishes. The view that unfolds enthrals me; it is absolutely beautiful. A voice down the speaking tube asks 'How are you feeling? Not too bad, is it? Nice day for it.'

'Wonderful.'

'Good, then how about starting to earn your pay and getting down to a bit of work? I'm going to demonstrate the effect of controls; follow me through on the stick and rudder.'

I make a grab for what I think he said was the stick, if I'm wrong then at least it's something else to hang on to, and brace my feet firmly against the rudder bar. That's the only place there is to put them, so that part must be right. The aircraft jinks.

'For God's sake,' comes the instructor's voice. 'I said follow me through. You have got to fly this aeroplane, not castrate it. Look, like this. Relax, settle down, everything must flow smoothly.'

So a new way of life begins.

At the end of my first trip, which was mainly for acclimatization, I have actually flown the aircraft straight and level. Well, not very straight, or indeed entirely level, but after three weeks I am trying to master the knack of circuits and landings. Spinning and stalling are behind us but we have still to get this circuit business wrapped up. This is my first big stumbling block.

Most pilots have some sort of trouble mastering the art of landing an aeroplane but my personal problem, and I mean problem, is taking off. I am just totally unable to control the swing and I career all over the airfield in ever-increasing ugly great swerves. No matter how hard I try I just cannot keep the beastly aeroplane straight and, when things appear to be getting no better and I feel I am not making the progress that I should, I start to worry.

Surely I am going to master this take-off problem and become a pilot?

By now, most of us on the course have the sense to realize that we have a job on our hands. As a bunch of young men dedicated to the same cause, we are, even at this very early stage, becoming closely knit and a sense of comradeship is building up.

Yesterday, a chap called Hilton was suspended. The first Bowler Hat. For what, exactly, nobody knew or asked. He just faded away. He'd not been much of a mixer and nobody got on with him all that well. It shook us all a bit, though. After all, we've only been here for just over three weeks. It doesn't take them long to make up their minds. Certainly they mean what they say about the weeding-out process.

If only I can get over the solo hurdle. Some people never catch on to the art of flying, however much they try. I can't even keep straight on take-off. I just haven't got the knack.

I lie awake at night thinking about it. The thought of a Bowler Hat haunts me. To Peter and Hank I voice my fears. Hank Stoddard I have only just got to know and he, Peter and I often find ourselves together. We are getting to be rather a trio. They also find it's not all plain sailing and have their own individual problems, so perhaps there's hope for me yet.

Generally speaking, if you don't go solo within approximately ten hours your instructor is changed in case personalities are coming into it. If you still have not soloed by sixteen hours then the Chief Flying Instructor takes you for a progress test and, we are led to believe, very few are persevered with after that.

It is an intriguing business, learning to fly. Some days nothing goes right. The instructor tries all he knows to help but the more you try the worse things get and so it's best to pack up for the day.

After about seven and a half hours dual, I have just such an experience. My take-offs are plain dangerous and when trying to land I fly into the ground and go ballooning across the aerodrome like a kangaroo. With an 'I've got her' the instructor takes over. Try as I have never tried anything before, it's hopeless. Total depression; it's quite clear that I'm not going to make it. I shall never make a pilot. They might just as well chuck me out now and have done with it. Even Mr Hayne's vast patience is severely put to the test.

'Look, you're just getting worse instead of better. What's the matter with you, lovesick or something?'

He has been watching me in his rear mirror. I've noticed it for some time. I wonder what he's thinking. Afterwards, I hang around the crew room feeling bitter and totally destroyed. The whole thing is just too big for me.

That evening, utterly dejected, I walk alone down to the little pub in the village where we learn to drink beer, whether we want to or not. On this particular evening, however, I do want a drink and I want to be left alone.

I should be doing some work, of course. We have a lot of preparation to do. With few exceptions that's what the others are doing. Still, I won't be with them much longer, so it really doesn't matter.

I've never been into a pub on my own before, so I stride into the saloon bar as if I own the place and ask for a pint of bitter. Ethel, the landlady, produces the goods and smiles. She says nothing. She has seen people in my position before, been serving trainee pilots for a long time now.

I take a sip. The ale tastes good for once. I need this after today. It's the first pint I've ever had, it's always been halves up to now, and then, totally unexpected, the quiet voice of my instructor.

'What, may I ask, do you think you are doing here?'

I turn and look at Mr Hayne. Of all the bloody people, I have to run into him. Caught red handed. Terrific. This will earn me a Bowler Hat for certain.

'Having a glass of beer.'

'So it would appear.'

'Well, sir, it was a pretty obvious question.'

'Don't try to be clever, laddie, I want to know. Have you no work to do?'

'I'm a bit fed up to be truthful, sir, and I just felt I wanted to be on my own for a bit. This was the obvious place to come.'

'What's all this wanting-to-be-alone nonsense?'

'Many more trips like today and there will be no further need to work.'

'I quite agree, but what do you consider you know about it? Now just listen to me and don't be so stupid. Do you think you're the first to have problems? Think, don't sulk, try growing up. Don't you realize that everybody's the same, except the rest have the common sense and ability to cope with the situation? So must you if you are going to succeed.'

'It's very important to me.'

'I'm glad to hear it, that's as it should be.' He pauses. 'Wellum, would you say that I know my job?'

'Good Lord, yes, of course.'

'Well, then, if I told you that the trouble is largely a case of tenseness and of trying too hard, would you believe me?'

'Yes, sir, if you say so.'

'You have just got to learn to relax. Light on the stick. Don't grip the thing as if you're trying to catch it and you're frightened it's going to get away. It's not going anywhere. Are you getting all het up about what I call "ten-hour-itis"?'

'Yes.'

'Thought so. Well, don't. As I have said to you before, nine people out of ten go through periods of complete depression and frustration just before they are coming up for solo. It's been going on for years. Oh yes, I know the feeling all right, had it myself fifteen years ago. Nothing goes right, you've chosen the wrong job, everybody is coping better than you, you'll never make a pilot. It's nothing new. You've just got it a bit badly, that's all. Things will iron themselves out, you'll see. You're a bit highly strung and temperamental, susceptible to atmosphere; you could possibly make a fighter pilot.'

'I want to be a fighter pilot more than anything.'

'Well, you might be, if you learn to rise above things when the going gets tough. Do you understand what I'm trying to say?'

'Yes, sir, and thank you.'

'OK. Let's leave it at that, then. Snap out of it, rise above the situation, understand?'

'Understood, sir. But what happens if I have to change instructors? I don't want that.'

Hayne pauses and looks at me.

'I'll see what I can arrange but I'll doubt it'll be necessary.'

Nine hours dual and things are looking a bit better. I fly a couple of good sorties. The take-off problem is improving. Maybe I'm getting the hang of it. We taxi back to the tarmac at the end of my second sortie.

'How are you feeling?'

'Fine.'

'Well, you had better hang on a minute. Don't switch off.'

Hayne undoes his straps, eases himself out of the cockpit and without a glance jumps to the ground and walks to the office. I am left waiting for some minutes until another instructor comes out and climbs into the front seat. He has the reputation of being an absolute bastard. He doesn't say a word. I sit in the trembling Tiger Moth and a feeling of apprehension comes over me. Now what on earth is all this about? I thought I was doing better.

'Well, what are we going to do, sit this one out?'

'Sorry, sir?'

'Come on then, we haven't got all day. Taxi out and do me a circuit and landing and make it good.'

What does that mean, 'Make it good'? This can't be a Bowler Hat test, surely?

In contrast to my efforts with Mr Hayne, things don't go at all well. We swing on take-off, the circuit is ragged and the landing is a very bad arrival. The instructor looks over his shoulder at me. I can see his eyes through his goggles.

'Well, I didn't like your take-off, I didn't like your circuit and that landing was plain bloody awful. Now let's try again and for Christ's sake, steady down.'

The next attempt is little better, nor is the one after that. We don't actually break anything but I realize that I'm putting up a pretty frightful exhibition and a feeling of utter hopelessness almost overwhelms me. He is very curt; a sound of resignation comes into his voice as if he has completely lost interest.

'Taxi back to the take-off point.'

Made a pretty good balls up of this. Poor old Hayne, I've let him down badly.

'Right, that's far enough, hold it here a minute.'

I just sit in a trance as he undoes the straps of his Sutton harness and levers himself out of the cockpit. He looks at me with apparent disdain, then leans back into the cockpit and does up the straps again. Jumping to the ground, he stands at the side of the fuselage level with me. He leans closer and raises his voice above the sound of the idling engine.

'Well, we can't go on like this. Perhaps you're just having an off day, very off. You've scared the arse off me and I tell you straight, I've had enough for a bit. If you're determined to damage something, I'm buggered if it's going to be me. Try a circuit on your own. Maybe I'll see you again later, with any luck.'

He looks at me for a second longer and a large grin lights up his whole face. Never in my short experience have I seen a countenance so transformed. Is this really 'the bastard'? That grin is completely infectious. Faith and confidence flow back into me. I now realize that these instructors know the flying game from A to Z. Their judgement and summing up of each pupil is uncanny.

'Well, come on, get cracking or I'll change my bloody mind.'

'On my way, sir.'

I taxi for a few yards, check I'm pointing the aircraft dead into wind and without more ado open the throttle. Stick forward, the tail comes up and away we go. On take-off I manage to keep her as straight as a die. I get round the circuit tidily, throttle back and glide at seventy crosswind. Turn in for the final approach about now; just right. So far, so good. The hedge goes by underneath and there's a moment of concern as the ground appears to come closer very rapidly indeed. Check her, for God's sake, check her again, now stick back, wait for it, and we arrive on the ground. A small bump, but only a small one. Anyway, no matter, we are down in one piece, nothing broken.

I have flown an aeroplane on my own, no matter what happens. I have soloed.

No one can ever forget their first solo. Flying along with nobody in the front seat, the quivering bracing wires and the buffeting of the slipstream, the sensation of being suspended in the air. As the little Tiger Moth rolls to a stop I experience a feeling of sheer disbelief.

Elated, I taxi back to the apron, switch off and clamber out. With as nonchalant an air as I can manage and with my parachute slung over my shoulder I head for the crew room. My feet aren't touching the ground. They do, however, when I report to the timekeeper. He says nothing, just points out on to the airfield. I turn and there, walking back in the warm afternoon sunshine, a lonely figure humping a parachute, is the instructor. I've completely forgotten him and left him to find his own way back. That will earn me a rocket for certain. So what? I'm a pilot, I've flown on my own.

Peter goes solo later that same afternoon. He grins as I congratulate him.

'We seem to do things together, Geoff. Let's hope we can hang on.'

'We will.'

That evening Peter and I go out for a glass of beer and as we stroll down the country lane to the village pub with some of the others we are on the crest of a wave.

It is the first day of September, 1939.

Two days later we are at war with Germany. We are sitting round a radio in the ante-room hearing Neville Chamberlain break the news. There is silence at first, then someone says quietly, 'Well, that's that.'

I am not conscious of any reaction. It doesn't really register. A director of the company that runs the flying school, and whom we have never seen before, comes in and gives us a pep talk. It's something to do with attacking the Hun and having a big engine in front of us to protect us. He is pompous and the talk ineffective.

I go outside for a moment into the quiet and open country-side of rural Leicestershire, this peaceful England. Why war? It's just bloody stupid and the fact that I am going to be actively involved doesn't enter into the equation at all, yet.

Realization that something out of the ordinary way of life has occurred comes to us very quickly when we are told to taxi the aeroplanes to the far side of the aerodrome and disperse them thirty yards apart around the edge. Pickaxe handles are then issued to us and with these we are to defend the said aeroplanes to the death. Quite obviously, we trainee pilots learning to fly on our little grass airfield in the middle of Leicestershire are a cause of considerable concern to the German High Command and therefore we must, without doubt, be high on the list of priority targets to be attacked by the Luftwaffe.

We shoulder our pickaxe handles and patrol the dispersed Tiger Moths twenty-four hours a day in shifts, ready to repel the imminent attack by paratroopers of the German army. When they don't turn up, we go looking for the fifth column.

Eventually, when nothing happens for a few days, the course resumes its normal curriculum.

Divided into squads, flying in the morning and lectures in the afternoon or vice versa. People going solo; crucial moments and the pressure is on. Three of our members do not solo after sixteen hours dual instruction and silently they depart. It's done very quietly. One morning they are not at breakfast.

Air navigation, aerobatics, instrument flying, sideslipping, solo and dual . . . the days pass quickly.

The first of the RAF flying tests and mid-course examinations see two more suspended. The weeding-out process goes on and it's quite clear that, in spite of what people are now saying, war or no war, in order to succeed you must be prepared to work and take it very seriously; this is no push-over.

Generally, however, life takes on a rosy tint. We are striving to do something that comparatively few people do and indeed not everybody can. Flying is new to us, a mystery and a challenge not entirely without glamour. Some days, of course, are distinctly 'off' and morale declines, but I feel that I have had so many off days I'm beginning to brush them aside and wait and see if things get better in the morning. On other days things go extra well and I'm on top of the world. I try to accept the rough with the smooth and lift myself from the depths of despair, realizing that I have, by my own choice, undertaken an arduous and specialized career.

I suppose it's called growing up.

A few of us, about a third, are selected for a second RAF test towards the latter part of the course. Once again I worry. Am I going to get the sack? The thought haunts me. Flying has now become an obsession, it is a must, success is paramount. It is still a novelty and a challenge. The pitfalls on the way to becoming a fully fledged RAF pilot are too many to allow me to relax in any way with that feeling of well-being of the truly professional pilot.

Only the other day Julian was suspended. I liked Julian, what little I saw of him. He rather kept apart from the rest of us and gave the impression of surveying what was going on from the perimeter of the turmoil. He reminded me of how I would imagine a French aristocrat was two hundred years ago. He was turning out to be a good pilot, no problem there, but since he had gone solo the whole thing was becoming most tiresome. He liked flying – who didn't? – but only at his own convenience, not when he was told to. The course was becoming a bit of a bore, his mid-course exam was almost a farce. His attitude was wrong and he was told about it in no uncertain terms, so when he made little effort with the ground subjects and his attitude didn't change the crunch had to come and Julian and the RAF parted company. Had there been more compatibility, Julian would have become an ace, I'm sure of it.

The point that becomes immediately apparent to the rest of us is that when somebody who is turning out to be an able pilot is given the push then you really have to watch it. This threat of failure is ever with me. Am I lacking the self-confidence now that I find myself outside the sheltered, cloistered security of school, or do the others feel the same? I hope so, because this is a new way of life for me. It's a man's world and a man's undertaking. Training to be a service pilot shows me the other side of the coin: I'm on my own, it's up to me.

I hear nothing about my second RAF flying test, so presumably it must have been more or less satisfactory. The end of the ab initio course with its ground exams and final flying test looms ever nearer. If these two hurdles are successfully taken then the course goes on to an RAF Flying Training School after two weeks of indoctrination and drilling at the Royal

Air Force Depot at Uxbridge. However, there is a rumour that we may be going elsewhere because there is a war on. In the meantime, we remain civilian pupil pilots very much on probation, expendable and under the eagle eye of the Chief Instructors.

Another two were suspended last week.

The workload increases. Visits to the local pub become less frequent. Then one evening, at the drop of a hat, five of us decide to go out and give ourselves a bit of a breather and to hell with work. It is just what is needed. Dinner at a small but exclusive inn known to Hank. A table for five, Peter, Hank, Nick Bellamy, Laurie Buchanan and myself. The staff, who seem to enjoy looking after us, includes a young waitress who is very pretty. I reckon she's after Peter, with his baby-faced complexion, but Nick doesn't agree. Pints of beer at the bar whilst waiting for our meal, laughter and compatibility, each of us enjoying the spontaneous break from the pressures of the flying school and happy in each other's company.

More beer with our food, cheaper than wine and none of us knows much about wines, anyway. The conversation inevitably comes round to flying, the RAF and the war. More pints arrive and, owing to our sense of well-being, inner worries, forebodings and hitherto private thoughts are spoken of openly. An understanding and friendship is thereby cemented between us. It is something that is probably difficult to find in civilian life. We are all young, all paddling the same canoe, and as the evening progresses the certain knowledge that few, if any, of us will survive to see the end of the war binds us even closer together.

The evening out comes to an end. After our conversation the thought of the possibility of being killed is not unduly worrying or upsetting. One just ignores it. Each is convinced that it cannot possibly happen to him. We all crowd into a taxi and push off back to Desford, wined, dined and happy.

Tomorrow is another day and we are due to fly in the morning.

Thereafter, the five of us form a little clique, whenever possible meeting up in the Mess for a pre-evening-meal drink and more often than not feeding at the same table.

Three weeks to the final test and examinations. The weather is fine and we survivors settle down and work hard. Things are beginning to slot into place, make sense. There is a growing self-assurance and we begin to feel rather more confident of satisfying the examiners.

Halcyon days, warm sunshine, blue skies and light Indian-summer breezes. Flying as God meant it to be. Open cockpits, helmets and goggles, heads in the slipstream, biplanes, wood, canvas and vibration, quivering bracing wires and the eternal drumming of the engine. I am master over machine. Pride and confidence flow into me.

Wonderful flying weather; looking down on the rolling colourful countryside, English countryside, surely a green and pleasant land. Small cars on small roads passing through small villages and then a larger town with factories; nine till five, hard luck you down there.

Up here the air is pure and clean. The sheer joy of flight infiltrates the very soul and from above the earth, alone, where the mere thought in one's mind seems to transmit itself to the aeroplane, there is no longer any doubt that some omniscient force understands what life is all about. There are times when the feeling of being near to an unknown presence is strong and real and comforting. It is far beyond human comprehension. We only know that it's beautiful.

Life is so good if you know how to live it, so why war?

The last week of the course, the final crunch. Ground exams, which I at one time feared, present no problems. I even manage to read Morse. On the flying test I have the lot, everything in the book. The Chief Instructor shows me no favours. He cuts the engine to simulate a forced landing and by the luck of the gods I just about manage to make an arrival on the aerodrome. Aerobatics and I make a total mess of a slow roll. On the roll-out the nose drops away; not enough top rudder or something like that.

'Sorry, sir, I'll do another.'

'I should bloody well think so.'

I do, and it's a good one.

'Are you satisfied with that?'

'It was better than the first, sir.'

'Couldn't have been worse, really, could it?'

I agree.

'Right then, take me home. I want a cup of tea. Don't dither about. Do you know where you are?'

'Yes, sir.' (Bloody liar!)

'Right, carry on.'

He doesn't sound too upset at the moment but he jolly soon will be if I don't look sharp and find out where the hell I am. A quick search, nothing. Good God, where on earth have we got to? He's watching me in that bloody little mirror of his. He knows I'm lost. Hold on a minute, though, that smoke haze over there, with luck it could be Leicester. Take a chance.

It is Leicester. Thank God, we can get home. We land and walk back to control together.

'Have you any leanings as to what you want to do in the service?'

'I'd like to fly fighters, sir.'

'Well, there's a long way to go yet. When you think things are going well you are apt to get a bit nonchalant, you know, a "this is easy" attitude, and then you end up doing a really diabolical slow roll. You may be a little overconfident, which in its way is no bad thing, but just watch it, accidents can happen and aeroplanes cost money.'

'What about me?'

'There are plenty like you.'

Two days later a notice on the lecture-room noticeboard. The course results and all of us who managed to hang on to the bitter end have passed. My goodness, the ranks have thinned out a bit since we started. Peter and I go for a walk along the country lanes before ending up at the local to join the others. It's a great little party and the beer tastes terrific.

Next morning I seek out Mr Hayne and thank him for teaching me to fly and for being so patient.

'That's all right, Wellum.' A pause and he smiles at me. 'You know, it's really surprising what two determined men can do, isn't it? Good luck!'

2. Ad Astra

It all seems a little unreal to end up in a boarding house on the seafront at Hastings, but here I am.

A heavy drizzle blown on the wind from out at sea. Tossing disturbed waves, a dirty grey-green. Restless unfriendly crests breaking into white horses as far as the horizon. The promenade is spray lashed and deserted, no holidaymakers, no kids with spades and pails, no ice creams. It is a desolate grey picture and the first autumn of the war.

Six months ago the place must have thronged with holidaymakers and families on day trips from London. Now, seeing this resort as I do, the scene evokes in me, for the first time to any degree, an atmosphere of foreboding. The whole overture of impending world conflict makes itself felt and a sense of hopeless depression comes over me on this, our first evening. I gather I'm not the only one affected. Maybe the long train journey from Leicester has something to do with it; after all, Desford was a quiet and pleasant little spot. It's been a long day, one way or another.

We should have gone for two weeks to the RAF Depot at Uxbridge, there to undergo the transition from being civilians into potential officers in the Royal Air Force. Instead, reason unclear, the powers that be in their wisdom ordained that the fearsome world of service discipline, arms drill, marching, shouted words of command and the swinging of arms up to the level of the waist is to descend upon us with all its military grandeur at Hastings.

We join forces with another ab initio course from Ansty, a

similar crowd to ourselves, noisy, young and full of the joys of living.

The next day we start our drilling and marching. I am once again back in the OTC at school. We march to the far end of the promenade and then turn and march back again. Oddly enough it's all rather friendly, not too much stamping or banging about, no guardsman stuff and if the morning is fine I rather enjoy our little 'walks' up and down the front. Presumably it's all in the cause of progress.

Our uniforms arrive from the tailors in London, are fitted, taken away and then fitted again until they are just so and pass the close inspection of the Adjutant.

I don't feel as I thought I would when I first go out into the street wearing the RAF blue. The uniform tunic looks bare and uninteresting without those coveted pilot's wings and the one very thin stripe looks unimportant and insignificant.

A visit to the doctor for inoculations, all of which are inflicted on us in one go. I react badly to them. Never can I recall feeling so ill. Two days later I emerge feeling very secondhand but, being pronounced better and fully fit, I form up with the others and start again where I left off, marching to the end of the promenade and back again.

There are a few lectures on the history of the Royal Air Force, all twenty-one years of it, and then comes the day when we hear that our course is destined to go on to Flying Training School at Little Rissington, a modern station in the Cotswolds. The FTS is equipped with Avro Ansons for twin-engined training and the North American Harvard Mark I for single-engined training.

Sounds pleasant!

The other news that pleases me is that Peter and I are among those who have been selected for 'C' Flight, which is responsible for the training of pilots for single-engined aeroplanes and that, of course, could mean fighters. Only five of us from Desford are going on to Harvards, which isn't very many. The rest of the course are on Ansons. Can't say I envy them, but they seem happy enough and so am I. Anyway, things seem to be going more or less according to plan as far as I am concerned and I have that contented feeling that all is well.

There is an air of excitement and anticipation. Peter and I sit together and chat continually, mainly of course about the future.

Both of us realize that the real task is only just beginning. Life so far has been relatively easy. Little Rissington is going to be something else entirely. Compared with initial training at Desford the pressure is going to be very much greater. We are still only civilians in RAF uniform and on probation. The going will be tough, no doubt about that; after all, the task of an FTS is to transform such people as us into proficient pilots and, at the same time, instil a sense of responsibility and discipline to enable an individual to do the job of a general duties officer in the Royal Air Force. This transition is to be accomplished in approximately seven months. I am quite certain, therefore, that the workload I can now expect will be considerable indeed.

The eventual arrival is not inspiring. A tremendous anti-climax. For a start, it is cold and raining and this does little to help matters. It always seems to be the same when we arrive somewhere new. As the transport deposits us at the main gate, Little Rissington gives the impression of an austere, out in the sticks, enormous and unfriendly place.

No one at the main gate to meet us or tell us where to go or what to do. In fact, nobody knows anything about us. The corporal in the guardroom hasn't been told, and obviously doesn't give a damn anyway. We just stand around in our shiny new uniforms, self-conscious and utterly lost. It is a matter of five minutes or so before a fearsome individual, who I think must be a warrant officer or some such, forms us into threes and marches us to a cold, large red-brick building. We go inside and find ourselves in a lecture room of some sort in possibly the ground training block. The fearsome ugly man tells us to sit down and wait. After twenty minutes, we are still waiting. Some of us get fidgety.

A car draws up outside. The banging of doors and into the room strides a figure who has the look of authority.

'Attention, stand up when the Station Commander comes into the room,' a voice bellows.

It's that bloody frightening ugly looking warrant officer man again. The Station Commander also frightens me. So far we have only met two people and they both scare me stiff. God help us all!

The Station Commander is elderly. Iron-grey hair and a row of First World War ribbons. He has a slight stoop, which makes him look smaller than he really is.

He starts talking and harangues us with an eloquence of long practice. We are left in no doubt as to his personal opinion about his new arrivals. By standing about outside the main gate of the camp in a disorderly mob where everybody can see us we have already created an extremely unfavourable impression. Having got all that off his chest he then explains what is expected of us whilst under his command. Once his personal vendetta is over, what he says makes sense. He goes into detail concerning what they hope to achieve during our stay at Little Rissington and his sincerity begins to impress me.

Nevertheless, we feel that at least half of his talk was overdone and not really necessary and we are a pretty miserable bunch when we are dismissed some forty minutes later.

We are then marched to the Officers' Mess.

'Let's have a bit of discipline!'

It's a cold walk, rain is in the wind and, to crown it all,

when we arrive tea is over and I for one could murder a cup. Altogether, not a good start.

Later, after a bath, a meal and a few drinks, things look a little better. The Mess is modern, large, warm and comfortable but everything is strange and I feel strung up, tense and lonely. I spend a sleepless night.

A chap called Clive Winston-Smith and I share a room. Didn't see too much of him at Desford, he was in another clique, but he's a decent sort and is going through the twin-engined course on Ansons. Peter is two rooms away, so at least we are in the same wing of the building.

When things start to move next day apprehensions are forgotten. A visit to stores, where I draw my flying kit. A new helmet with a face mask and a microphone in it, leather gloves and inners made of pure silk, overalls and a Sidcot suit and flying boots. Down to the parachute section and then to the ground training block.

'Take that pile of books and sign here.' Some pile it is, too. The whole set-up reeks of hard work. My feet haven't touched the ground so far. It's been chase, chase, chase the whole damn time. It's going to be like school again with evening preparation, examinations, the lot.

That same afternoon I report with Peter, Nick and Laurie to 'C' Flight in No. 2 Hangar.

The Flight Commander is a tall, slim, good-looking bloke who gives us yet another introductory talk. He also is rather terse and very much to the point but he gives the impression of being a fair man who will help all he can. Thank God we've found somebody! After the previous day there is something almost comforting about him. I take my parachute and flying gear and find myself a locker in the crew room and then it happens. A quiet voice behind me, a voice that I'll come to know so well.

'Good afternoon, sir, my name is Lewis. I am to be your

instructor and we will be flying together during your stay in "C" Flight.'

'Good afternoon, sir.'

'You don't call me "sir", sir. I'm Flight Sergeant. I call you sir, you call me Flight Sergeant.'

'I'm sorry, Flight Sergeant, I'm very pleased to meet you.'

A small slight figure stands before me. Steady blue-grey eyes, surely the blue-greyest ever? Lined at the corners, those eyes are fixed on my face, eyes I guess which have scanned the sky and earth from many different cockpits all over the world during his years of service. Thinning, short, slightly sandy hair, a thin hollow-cheeked face and a small neat moustache. His uniform is pressed and immaculate.

Immediately, in those first few seconds, this slight, tidy man has won my complete respect. His eyes never seem to leave my face. I feel myself drawn to this personality and so I just stare back at him and wonder. I can't think of anything else to do.

I feel a peculiar sense of humility. After all, here is a man who has worked his way up, over many years, to become an NCO pilot in the peacetime Royal Air Force; no mean feat in itself. Feeling the impact of the moment and at the same time a little uncomfortable, I smile, but his expression does not change. However, I detect humour in those eyes and I realize and accept that he is sizing me up.

In return, I sum him up as representing all that is best in the Royal Air Force, one chosen from many applicants from the rank and file to become a sergeant pilot and, eventually, an instructor in a service that demands the very highest qualities and nothing less. Flight Sergeant Lewis is just such a person and here I am standing in front of him being called sir, an eighteen-year-old boy dressed up in his new shiny blue uniform with its very thin stripe.

Acting Pilot Officer Geoffrey Wellum on probation, sir!

His job is to make not only a pilot of me but, also, a man capable of doing a man's job in a man's life.

He speaks quietly and clearly.

'This afternoon, sir, we'll have a look at the Harvard aircraft and then tomorrow morning you will be on flying and we can then really get down to it. Now the Harvard, as you know, is an American training aeroplane and, in comparison with Harts, Audax and the like, is a very modern and advanced aeroplane indeed. It has retractable undercarriage and flaps and a constant-speed airscrew.' What on earth is a constant-speed airscrew? 'There is no aeroplane in service today more advanced. Treat it with respect and you will find it a very pleasant and safe aircraft to fly, but it is a low-wing monoplane with a fairly high wing loading and I must stress yet again that it must be treated with respect, especially at low speed. Pull it about like a Tiger Moth or a Hart, abuse it, then it will turn round and bite you; understand?'

'Yes, Flight Sergeant.'

'Good, right then, let's go and look one over to give you an idea.'

We stroll together into the huge hangar, which is full of Harvards, purposeful stubby aircraft with a pugnacious appearance not without attraction. He asks me about myself, how I got on at Desford, and so our acquaintance begins.

'How do you see yourself in the service, what are your ambitions?'

'I would like to go on to fighters.'

'Well, we'll have to see.'

As we walk through the hangar, somebody passing calls him Eddy. So that's it, Eddy Lewis.

We reach a Harvard at the back of the hangar where it is quiet and out of the way. Eddy Lewis tells me to get into the front seat and shows me how. It's a lot bigger than the little Tiger Moth, of course, and I am conscious of this as I climb up on to the wing and lower myself into a fairly spacious cockpit.

I can understand that by previous standards it is complicated to say the least. I find myself surrounded by so many dials, levers, switches, warning lights, taps and knobs that I just sit aghast: good grief!

'Gosh, Flight, I'll never learn this lot.'

For the first time he smiles and it is a sort of 'I know how you feel' smile.

'I bet you do, sir.'

A more than loaded reply.

For the best part of an hour and a half I am shown that aircraft inside and out. By the time we have finished I feel saturated with facts and figures and absolutely punch drunk. But at least I am beginning to understand a little about it.

I know that the Harvard has a rather bad name throughout the RAF, having killed several experienced pilots, but this only goes to make the challenge greater. One thing is very obvious: such combinations as Eddy Lewis and the Harvard aeroplane are what the Royal Air Force uses to sort out the men from the boys. Only total application is good enough and an all-out effort is essential if one is to make good. Eddy leaves me some typed notes on the fuel systems, hydraulics, data concerning the engine, the correct revs and manifold pressure (whatever that is) to fly for climb and cruise, take-off and landing procedures and drills and goodness knows what else. He leaves me with a quiet summing up:

'Well, there we are, Mr Wellum. Look through these notes tonight and we'll have a go in the morning and you can at least get the feel of the aeroplane. You must memorize these notes and procedures and learn your cockpit and emergency drills off pat. You must be able to do them automatically. Only total and complete understanding is adequate. You must be able to find your way about the cockpit layout blindfolded.'

There is much food for thought. I want to be alone for a moment. Around me I see self-confident and assured men. The whole place exudes an atmosphere engendered by a way of life associated with man's calling. Is the whole thing going to be too big for me? I feel alone and unsure. This Flying Training School at the moment is a remote and unfriendly place and I find the atmosphere depressing.

That night after dinner Peter, Nick and I have a little get together over a drink in the ante-room. All we seem to discuss is the Harvard and the excitement of the challenge. Helped on by our enthusiasm, we converse over our half tankards of ale until the bar closes, by which time I feel rather more settled!

The next day we start in earnest. Parade is at 8 a.m. and the course is divided into two flights. On alternate days we fly in the morning and have ground work in the afternoon and vice versa. On this particular morning, our first flying day at FTS, I find myself in the crew room dressed and ready to go with time in hand, restless and excited.

Harvards are lined up on the aerodrome being warmed up by the ground crews. They create an impressive sight. Looking at them I try to imagine myself careering about the sky in this modern tubby little aircraft. However, imagination is brought to a halt by Lewis, who comes into the crew room dressed in a Sidcot at least one size too large.

'All OK, sir?'

'I think so, Flight.'

'Well, let's make a start then. The wind is a bit gusty near the ground so I will do most of the flying for this trip.'

I follow him out to the flight line and the waiting aeroplanes. He leads me round our Harvard and shows me what to look for on the external checks. He talks quietly and slowly, totally calm and composed, instilling immediately my confidence in him. Everything is satisfactory and within a short space of time we are airborne. This is a very different set of answers from the little Tiger Moth. It seems a more adult situation and Eddy Lewis's voice sounds calm and completely relaxed. Yes, I like him.

Over the next two weeks, alternately coaxed and harangued by my instructor, I become slowly acquainted with this advanced trainer. Certainly it requires handling with respect and care. The first stall terrifies me. It is very vicious indeed. I have heard it referred to by trainees of the senior course as a 'whip stall'.

Eddy's voice comes from the rear seat: 'Now, just watch while I demonstrate the stall. Throttle back, get the nose up, just follow through on the controls, easy on the stick, I've got her on this one. Notice the speed, it's dropping off very rapidly, it's getting quiet and the controls are getting sloppy, the nose is well up and here we go.'

There is a strong buffeting; now where on earth are we, what the hell goes on? The whole aeroplane gives a quick shudder, the starboard wing flicks down with breathtaking speed and it appears to me that we are almost on our back, although I can't be sure! I look ahead over the short nose and there is the ground. I'm sure it shouldn't be there. If it's there, then . . . To hell with this, we're pointing vertically downwards! That calm voice from the back again.

'Ease on the stick, not too fast or this happens.'

The stick is pulled back with a positive quick movement and the next thing I know is that we have stalled again in exactly the same manner.

'By easing out of the resultant dive too fast the wing loading is increased to an abnormal degree and you get a repetition of the stall, as I have just demonstrated.'

So now we know. Without my really being aware of it, the aircraft has resumed normal straight and level flight. We cruise gently around.

'This is where people have got into difficulties,' Eddy goes on. That's one way of putting it.

'Now you have a go and we'll do some spins, nothing to worry about.'

I experience my first spin in what I now consider to be a very vicious aircraft indeed. At 7,000 feet, Eddy Lewis takes over to demonstrate. It at once occurs to me that if an experienced pilot like my instructor takes 7,000 feet before he starts a spin then in future, if indeed there is a future, I will do the same.

'Are you strapped in tightly?'

That's ominous.

'Yes, thanks.' I pull down on the harness tighteners. I'm going to make bloody sure about this.

'OK, then let's do a spin. Sky clear all round? Check below as well. Take a careful look and always take your time checking. Now follow me through again, especially on the recovery. This is most important and the only way that the Harvard will respond. To recover, the stick must be eased right forward on to the dashboard and at the same time firm opposite rudder applied. Just watch while I talk this through. Throttle back, raise the nose and just before the stall apply full rudder. We'll do one to the right.'

The wretched aeroplane immediately executes a terrifying leaping lurch to starboard and starts to spin down in vicious flicks, losing height at an alarming rate. The sheer speed of the spin is unnerving and I don't really have the faintest idea what goes on, but we recover easily.

'All right, now it's your turn. Have a go!'

I do. Once again that frightening leap and flick to starboard followed by a rapid vicious spin.

'Right, now recover; rudder, stick right forward – now come on, right forward, not too harshly.'

I do as I am told but leave the stick forward on the dashboard too long before easing back and we dive out far beyond the vertical. Reassurance from the back seat again.

'That's OK. Not bad. Don't worry about that. Now, ease out of the dive, here we come, not too quickly, nicely; don't forget the throttle. Come on, don't leave it looking at you, open the thing. That's the idea. Now resume normal flight. Piece of cake, isn't it? It is? Good, then we'll go and do another one.'

'Jesus Christ!'

'I beg your pardon?'

'Sorry, Flight, I said Jesus Christ.'

'What's He got to do with it?'

'I don't know, Flight, but I hope to God He's here!'

A quiet chuckle over the intercom. All is well. We do three more spins and by the time the sortie is finished I almost enjoy spinning a Harvard, even if I am feeling a bit sick.

Progress. I get the feeling that I'm beginning to understand a little about aeroplanes and there is no doubt in my mind that I'm liking the Royal Air Force. The walk down Kingsway when going for my interview and the sight of the hurrying businessmen worrying their way to their various offices seems a long time ago. There is no question about my having made the correct decision.

My feeling of contentment and general well-being is enhanced the next morning as we march down to flights. It is a beautiful day. Ground frost and a nip in the air. A pale blue cloudless sky and a slight haze as the sun rises. The Cotswolds look glorious and, as our marching feet ring out on the concrete road, I can tell by their bearing that the others are experiencing the same elation. Nick is on my left and I catch his eye. We grin at each other and, as if alerted by a sixth sense, Peter, who is immediately in front of us, looks over his shoulder at both Nick and me and winks. I recognize that moments like these will stick in one's memory.

Down in the locker room I am getting my flying kit organized when Eddy Lewis comes breezily into the crew room and beckons me to him.

'Go and get 5784 started and ready to go. I want you to do the odd circuit with Flying Officer Hall this morning. Here you are, sign the Form 700 and look lively.'

I check the fuel state and the signatures and sign.

'Any particular reason for this, Flight?'

'Just do as you're told. I've a job to do here and I won't be around for a while. Now off you go.'

Grabbing my helmet and parachute, I stroll out into the morning sunlight towards the line of waiting Harvards. At the far end of the line Peter is strapping himself into one of them. He gives me a cheery wave and I wave back. Finding 5784, I settle myself in comfortably and start up. I sit waiting as Peter and his instructor taxi away from the flight line out on to the aerodrome, the Harvard waddling like an old goose over the rough grass. Well that's fine, but what do I do? Just wait around, I guess. Being a little put out by the change in routine, I impatiently look towards the crew room and see Eddy Lewis and this Flying Officer Hall bloke talking together. Don't know too much about Hall. He seems a quiet sort; bit of an arty type. He hurries towards me. I sit waiting in my aircraft, closing the throttle in order to lessen the slipstream as he climbs into the rear cockpit. A quiet but distinct voice comes over the intercom.

'Right, Wellum, let's go and do a few circuits. Taxi out in your own time and just carry on. I want to say as little as possible; any questions?'

'No, sir.' How could there be? He'd been clear enough.

'OK, then, she's all yours and let's see if we can have a nice quiet ride. Carry on.'

We do a couple of fairly tidy circuits, not perfect but passable. The air is still, there is no turbulence. I'm beginning to like Hall's method of instruction. Can go on like this for ever!

'Right, take me back to the flight line.'

Blimey, that's quick. We've only been about twenty minutes.

'This will do here. I'm going to leave you to yourself. Spend the rest of the hour doing circuits and landings and then come in. See if you can do at least three. OK?' Before I can answer he disconnects the intercom and is out of the back seat. Slinging his parachute to the ground he leans into the rear cockpit and secures the Sutton harness. Satisfied, he slams shut the hood, walks up the wing, thumps me on the shoulder, gives a thumbs-up sign and without a backward glance jumps to the ground. Picking up his discarded parachute he walks away in the direction of the crew room. As I watch him go, hardly daring to believe what is happening, I notice Eddy Lewis come out of the crew room dressed in his flying kit. He pauses and looks towards Hall, who waves him away. Lewis turns and disappears into the crew room again.

Well I'm damned, it couldn't have been much of a job he had to do! The whole thing smacks of a frame up to me, crafty old devil! Can't help grinning to myself. All right then, Mr Lewis Flight Sergeant Royal Air Force, I'm going to enjoy myself as well if I can only get rid of this bloody great lump in my throat. First solo in a real service aircraft. I don't think anybody else has done one yet and what a lovely day for it.

No problems, the trip goes well. I feel the same old elation and have difficulty in believing that it is really happening. As if to reassure myself, I turn round and look towards the rear seat, just to make sure it's empty. The long canopy gives a beautiful view of the Cotswold countryside. I'm up here alone; this is the life!

Nick and Peter go solo on the following afternoon and to celebrate we retire to the local inn for the evening. A cheery trio sharing a common undertaking; after all, it's not everybody who can fly an aeroplane! Good company and great content. I feel sort of warm inside and at peace with the world. Consequently, I have half a pint too much and feel rather sick going back to camp in the taxi. That'll teach me, but I'll be fine in the morning so what the hell?

Life proceeds according to schedule. Flying, lectures, evening work in our rooms, a full day in fact and this is only the beginning. As expected, the workload slowly but relentlessly increases, though somehow it doesn't seem to worry us unduly. Thinking about it I fancy we are taking things rather for granted, a little too easily, and I say so to Nick and Peter. They don't seem at all interested in my opinions. Nick is too busy being happy and Peter is a brainy bloke anyway. Peter always does well in his written work and is very helpful to Nick and me into the bargain. Neither of us is in his league and at times I feel just a little uneasy. I think it's conscience; it's no good kidding myself, I'm not exactly overdoing the ground work at the moment.

My apprehensions must have been born of a sixth sense. One member of the Anson Flight has been told that his services are no longer required and one of the people from the Ansty lot has been informed that his progress in pilot training is not up to the required standard and offered a transfer to the Equipment Branch. This shakes us all to no mean degree. No doubt this has all happened before but, somehow, we had all talked ourselves into believing that having got so far the air force would persevere with us.

It would appear that the invitation to transfer to the Equipment Branch was not taken up. As I go into the Mess for tea, I see a solitary lonely figure in civilian clothes complete with bag and baggage, getting into a taxi waiting at the Mess entrance. The expression on his face and the way in which he carries himself is, to me, frightening. The sight affects me more than somewhat as I imagine him taking off the blue uniform for the last time and returning empty handed to civilian life.

Somehow, I had put the thoughts of Bowler Hats and suspension out of my mind. The prospect of it happening to me was too disturbing, yet here it all was again. Suspension, the weeding-out process rearing its ugly head. Things won't let up until the day we leave this bloody place. I don't know about the others but memories and doubts during ab initio come flooding back to me. I feel very much on probation and I vow to myself to try much harder and be less irresponsible.

It would seem I am too late in my resolve. It's shattering when I, together with four or five others, including old Nick, am called before the Chief Ground Instructor. I know what it's about, of course; among other things I didn't do at all well in a recent intermediate navigation examination as well as other things connected with Ground School.

The Chief Ground Instructor is a squadron leader; a peacetime permanently commissioned officer. He is a member of the old school.

We are to be seen singly and I am to be seen first.

I don't like this one little bit and never in my life have I felt quite so wretched. The headmaster's study has nothing on this. I enter his office, salute and stand to attention in front of his desk; best uniform, gloves and peaked cap. My right knee is trembling and I can't stop it. He stares at me for what seems a lifetime. I detect no expression of anything in his eyes. This is going to be nasty.

'Do you know why I have sent for you, Mr Wellum?'

The 'Mister' part is horrible. Impossible thoughts; I've got the sack, am being drummed out. My God! What will Dad and Mother say? I've just chucked away the chance of a lifetime. Thoughts of Peter, clear of all this down at flights. He's possibly in the air at this very moment. Oh Lord! Let the

office floor open and swallow me up. Perhaps it's just a bloody
awful dream and I shall wake up in a moment at school.

'Well, I'm waiting.' Christ, don't flannel him, Geoff.

'Yes, sir.'

'I should damn well hope so. At least it shows that there is
some glimmer of intelligence. I have you here to inform you
that your progress during the time that you have been at Little
Rissington is not only unsatisfactory but quite unacceptable
to the Royal Air Force. You have failed to maintain your
earlier standards, and God knows they were low enough.
Your ground work is not merely below average, it's frightful.'
He refers to what is obviously my personal file.

'I'm sorry, sir, I have recently realized this and am resolved
to try very hard to make amends.' He looks at me with
complete disdain and almost explodes.

'Be quiet. I do not recall giving you permission to speak,
Mr Wellum.'

It must be at least five minutes that I have been standing
here listening as his tirade continues without a moment's
pause. After a bit, I don't really hear him. Get it over with
one way or another. Standing there ramrod stiff I have to
concentrate on keeping calm and not getting to the stage
when I shall lose my composure and say something that I shall
regret. I know I'm in danger of letting things get the better of
me and I fight the urge like hell. All the time he speaks he
watches me. Just when I feel that I fully understand what he
has to say and there is no point in carrying the conversation
further and, in spite of my efforts, I'm really in danger of
ignoring all discretion, he pauses and his line alters. His shoulders seem to relax and he stares out of his office window.
There is a silence that seems to be indefinite.

'Now, listen to me most carefully.' His voice is no longer
raised as it was a moment ago. 'I am going to do no more than
tell you that your progress on the ground and in the air and

also your general behaviour is being watched over the next few weeks very closely indeed; very closely. Do I make myself perfectly clear?'

'Yes, sir.'

'You must start to think about growing up, Wellum. The RAF wants men, not boys. Men of the calibre required by the service must have the intelligence and plain common sense to appreciate their responsibilities. The Royal Air Force is not a club, it's a fighting service and it has no time or room for people such as you are at the moment. Frankly, I'm not certain that you are going to make the grade anyway. If you don't improve, make a vast improvement within the next few weeks and show you are capable of growing up and becoming a man, then you are just not good enough and you will be on your way before you know what's hit you. I must make it quite plain that even if your flying was above average, which in your case it most certainly is not, should you not measure up on the ground subjects and your examinations, then you will be out. At the moment, Wellum, we haven't much time for you. You are existing here on a knife edge. Now go away and think about what I have said. Get down to it and do a little hard work for a change or else . . . or else. If you have the sense to try we might even yet make an RAF officer of you. That's all. Now go.'

Salute, about turn and out of the door quicker than that. I don't look at the others who are waiting to follow me. All I want is a breath of fresh air. Once outside I take my time and walk quietly down to the flights. I ponder deeply over the last ten minutes. What he said was, of course, perfectly true. I've had a let off, that's what it boils down to. I now know just where I stand and I'm quite determined to profit from this experience. In fact, I'm so determined, I no longer worry about it. I know exactly what I have to do and after all he did say that I could possibly make an RAF officer.

The course proceeds. Clive, like Peter, has a bit of a brain and he and I work late into the evenings in our room. He is a patient chap and when I fail to understand something, which is quite often, he always seems to have the answer. Sometimes Peter comes in with Nick and we sit and talk with a smattering of work into the small hours. I suddenly become aware of how much I enjoy these evenings. Peter, Nick and Clive are beginning to mean a lot to me. I think we all find that the friendship of our quartet is important to each of us in our own way. Life has assumed a distinct pattern.

Flying enthrals me. I find it easier to try hard and things start to go well, slot into place. I'm having a good patch. I've got over my ticking off and I feel a new confidence is growing. Eddy Lewis coaxes me along. At aerobatics he perseveres until I can do a perfect slow roll or whatever the manoeuvre might be and then I am sent solo to practise by myself. As time passes I really begin to get to know and like the Harvard. The stories concerning its bad reputation are, I feel, somewhat exaggerated. I look forward to each sortie and, when that one is over, the next. It's a wonderful way to earn a living.

Nick Bellamy is dead.

I go back in my own mind over the events of the last few days. I am writing this on Monday. Nick was killed last Friday.

It was the first weekend of the course that we were to be allowed a forty-eight hour leave. Flying was due to finish at midday on the Friday. At 08.30 hours Nick and I were each detailed to take an aeroplane and complete a height test. All this entailed was to take-off, climb to 15,000 feet and stay there for half an hour. It was then just a question of finding the airfield and landing. Oxygen? What's oxygen?

I finally got airborne at 10.00 hours. As I started to taxi out I saw Nick come out of the crew room and walk towards the flight line. The weather was perfect with only a covering of very high cloud way up at 20,000 feet or so.

Nick was not back by the time I landed. Peter had just finished an aerobatic detail. We taxied in to the flight line together, switched off, clambered out of our aeroplanes and sauntered back to the hangar to sign the authorization book DCO.

'Good trip?'

'Yes, Pete, and you?'

'Fine. Where's Nick?'

'Don't know, he took off a little after me. Should be back at any time now, probably hogging it a bit.'

'Either that, or the silly ass has got himself lost. Probably find he'll phone in from Croydon airport or some damn place.'

'Serves him right if he does. Should be more careful on the morning of a weekend off. What train do you reckon we can catch to London?'

'There's one at about two o'clock from Kingham, Geoff. Shall we try for that?'

'Sure, let's get on up to the Mess for a wash and brush up and then get the hell out of here. It'll be nice to get away for a break.'

We caught the train by the skin of our teeth and sat watching the countryside roll by, relaxed and content with that wonderful feeling of having fully earned a few hours' respite. A thought came to me through my contentment.

'By the way, Peter, did you see Nick before we left?'

'That's funny, I was thinking along the same lines. No, I didn't. But if he lost himself for even a short while he probably wouldn't have got back before we left.'

'Suppose not; we got away pretty smartish, didn't we?'

I left Peter at Paddington and went home. It was good to see my parents again, good just to be with them at home, to sleep in my own room, which was just as I had left it, everything in its place, my cricket bat still in the corner by the dressing table. As I got into bed that night I pondered on the months that had passed since I was last there. There is something hopelessly unrealistic about the whole situation. What a transformation in my life, and no doubt in Mum and Dad's. It can't have been easy for them. Dad of course wanted to know all about everything but Mum didn't. She just wanted to fuss. My favourite meals were provided, my uniform brushed and hung away for a few hours at least.

'Food is getting a little difficult, you know, dear, but I expect you feed well enough in your Mess or whatever it's called.'

I just lounged around in a pair of old flannels and an open-necked shirt and the weekend passed all too quickly. On one or two occasions I caught Mother looking at me when she didn't think I'd notice. She is a very brave person; after all, I am her only son, only child for that matter. As the time for departure neared I realized with quite a guilty conscience how eager I was to get back and start flying again.

My goodbyes were not prolonged and, as I turned into the main street at the end of our road, I looked back through the evening gloom to see two figures standing at the garden gate, both waving. God bless Mum and Dad.

I was due to meet Peter in the Paddington Hotel bar in time to catch the 19.02. He was there as arranged, in great form, grinning all over his face and not a care in the world. We had a quick drink, then hurried down to the train to be sure of getting a seat. Comfortably settled, we chatted about the weekend before lapsing into silence as the train got moving.

'I wonder how Nick got on, Peter,' I said eventually.

'OK, I expect. He'll be bloody angry if he had to miss his weekend leave.'

I dozed until the train pulled into Kingham station. Back again. That weekend went quickly!

Peter dashed off to rustle up a taxi. Good luck to him, I thought. I didn't feel like rushing about myself.

There was a winter feeling in the air when we arrived back at the Mess and it was good to get into the warm entrance hall and sign in. Waiting my turn behind Peter I sensed a presence and a shadow fell over the table. It was Clive; there was a strange, calm look on his face.

'Geoff, I'm afraid Nick is dead. He was killed on Friday. Sorry, you two, but I thought I'd better tell you as soon as you came in.'

I just couldn't believe what I was hearing. At first it hardly registered at all – Peter didn't say a word – and then the realization. Christ! How ghastly. How did it happen? Nobody knew for sure. I couldn't accept that I'd never see Nick again.

'Thanks for telling us, Clive,' I said. 'Let's go and have a drink. I think we all need one.'

This situation is something new to us. It was bound to happen sometime, of course. OK, people are suspended and get Bowler Hats, that is one thing, but death, that's another thing entirely. I suppose the fact that we might be killed hadn't really occurred to most of us, or was it that we just didn't allow our thoughts to dwell on such matters? Certainly, I hadn't considered the prospect to any great extent. I knew that accidents happened, of course, but that's about as far as I had allowed things to go.

The circumstances of Nick's death were explained to us. It appears that at about 3 p.m. on Friday, as Peter and I were safely on our way to London, the burnt-out wreckage of a Harvard was found in a field bordering a large wood about seventy miles north of the FTS. In the wreckage was the body of its pilot, Nick.

Presumably he was lost, possibly low on fuel and trying to

make a forced landing. Undercarriage and flaps were selected 'down'. He must have been distracted and allowed the speed to drop too low. It would appear obvious that he stalled; that quick unforgiving stall. You can't do that sort of thing in a Harvard with no height to spare and get away with it.

Eventually, I suppose we will get used to this sort of thing happening. Just learn to accept it. Quite obviously, if you let your imagination run riot in this flying game then you might as well pack up. So we mourn Nick in our own way, the way it is done in the Royal Air Force, the only way. How close to each other we feel. As for those civilians who decry us as being socially not quite the thing and can't or don't want to understand us, to hell with them. I bet they don't have comradeship like this.

We stayed in the ante-room for the remainder of the evening having a quiet glass of beer together. Slowly the numbers swelled as people returned from their weekends. Lively conversation, laughter and an enjoyment of each other's company. I shan't tell my parents.

The long-suffering mess stewards are on hand to answer our request: 'Same again, please.'

I raised my glass to Nick: 'Cheers, old mate!'

Peter and I are drawn even closer together in the days to follow. Our training proceeds apace and it takes all our time and effort; well, certainly mine!

Cross-country flights are the next hurdle. We are about to start when, for the first time, the weather really turns against us. It is appalling and the aerodrome rapidly turns into a sea of mud. Many are the days that we wait in vain for the rain to stop and the clouds to lift. When an opportunity does arrive we fly like mad things, with the consequence that the flying field becomes more and more churned up. The mud gets deeper and deeper until eventually conditions become so bad that all flying has to stop. The days are now spent entirely in the lecture room, morning and afternoon. This makes everybody thoroughly fed up, none more than me, but thank goodness I have the sense to remember my warning at the hands of the Chief Ground Instructor and work hard. We are now, of course, well up with our ground work and so on two or three evenings a week a crowd of us repair to the local pub. They are cheery little parties. Peter standing firmly, legs straddled and clasping his tankard of ale as if he was in dread of losing it to somebody. The smoke, the noise level of conversation and laughter. It all goes to imprint itself on one's memory.

Some local young ladies to talk to; perfume and jewellery. A pretty girl called Lesley attracts me and obviously I her. Peter smiles approvingly with a 'bless you children' sort of look. Then one day Lesley is not around any more. Enquiries reveal that she and her family have moved to Leeds, of all places. What a truly bloody silly thing to do!

Following the rain, the month of December turns bitterly cold. Severe frosts and snow turn the mud on the airfield hard as rock. In our spare time we skate on the tennis courts and here the Canadian members of the course excel. So up to date are we in ground work that we are sent on two weeks' leave for Christmas. Not having flown for so long I get restless. There is a feeling of unreality. Things are beginning to fade into the past. It even feels strange at home. Mother does war work in an office of a small factory, keeping the books so she says, and Dad is running the local Air Defence Cadet Corps squadron. Nothing is quite the same any more. I am glad to get back to the security of the air force again. The weather improves in January, but it is still terribly cold.

Things start to look up when the aeroplanes are ferried over to Kidlington, an aerodrome near Oxford. Wooden-hutted and tented it is rather primitive, to say the least, but at least we will be able to fly again. We are told that Little Rissington will not be operational except for ferrying purposes until midsummer at the earliest. Daily we get up early and travel by coach from Rissington to Kidlington, returning each evening in time for a bath and a late dinner. All in all it is a long day.

Nevertheless, it's good to be back in the air again and generally in the atmosphere of the aeroplanes. The smell, the noise, the chug of the petrol bowsers and an oily tarmac, we like our newfound flying field; it's a friendly little place.

Somehow, though, things don't seem to be going quite so smoothly now that flying has started in earnest. I feel that I have gone off the boil, as it were. Naturally we are behind in the course flying programme and, therefore, under considerable pressure. There is no doubt in my mind that, as far as I am concerned, the long break has had an effect. I do a few circuits and landings with Eddy followed by a solo flight in which I am allowed freedom to do what I like just to get the feel of things again. I have no problems and enjoy every second of it. There is nobody in the back seat making me do things I don't want to do. We have now started to do cross-country flights and air navigation, but I have trouble in settling to the task. I can steer a course all right – who can't? – but my map reading is bad. For some reason I have no idea of distance gone. Time and time again I get hopelessly lost until Eddy Lewis gets really cross. He reckons it's pure lack of concentration and effort and says so in no uncertain terms. On one triangular cross-country lasting about one and a half hours he really has a go. I feel I am beginning to get the hang of it but, in the end, the more he goes on at me the worse things become and I begin to get desperate and cross with myself. We abandon the exercise and return to Kidlington. When I see the airfield I can't wait to get on the deck and away from this bloody aeroplane. I thump it down

on the first clear strip I see. The only problem is that I've
landed on the half of the aerodrome normally used for taking
off.

'I've got her.'

The stick is snatched out of my hand, the brakes are harshly
applied and we taxi quickly out of the way of those waiting
to take-off. Now I'm for it!

'You're just the sort of bloke that makes everybody bloody
annoyed. What the hell do you think you're up to?' His tirade
continues as we taxi back to the flight line and by the time we
get out of the aircraft I am feeling thoroughly destroyed and
completely off balance. I make no effort to prevent myself
showing him that I am fed up and angry. I am probably going
to be put up for suspension anyway. He says nothing but
just stares at me with those steady blue eyes of his, face
expressionless. I wonder what he's up to. Never before has he
been a verbal bully, either in the air or on the ground. One
thing, he's certainly not bluffing. At last he speaks.

'Well, sir, the whole thing was just plainly frightful; total
failure. Failure what's more in every respect. Not only your
navigation but your general airmanship. You don't appear to
be learning a thing. Either you can't learn or you don't want
to learn.'

He must know that I'm stretched like a piece of elastic, yet
he keeps the pressure on. Is he trying to make me lose control
of myself and shoot my mouth off? I'm feeling total dejection
and strangely near to tears. Rightly or wrongly, I don't respond
to bullying of any kind, never have done, but obviously I've
got to make some response.

'Flight, I'm sorry, really I am, but I was sure I was just
beginning to get the feeling, to get the hang of things. I know
what the problem is. If you would only stop shouting at me
for a trip or two and allow me a chance to concentrate instead
of wanting to opt out, I'd get you round any cross-country

you or anybody else could set me. If things go on like this I might just as well pack up and take a Bowler Hat.'

'Mr Wellum, I will overlook your tone this once and this once only. Do I make myself clear, Mr Wellum?'

'Yes, Flight Sergeant.'

'It is not you, by any stretch of the imagination, who are in a position to talk about opting out. You don't opt out of anything; you are sacked. I would ask you to bear in mind who I am and what I am as far as it concerns you and your training.'

'As I have said, Flight, I'm sorry and I apologize, but what I said I believe to be the truth.'

'Maybe. Right then, we'll do as you suggest and put you to the test. Take-off tomorrow at 10.00 hours and I require you to do the same exercise that you failed to complete today because that sortie was totally unacceptable. It wasn't even below average, it was a nonentity. Anyhow, it's happened and that's all there is to it, so I will review the whole situation tomorrow. Today's disaster must not, repeat not, happen again. OK, now you are on your own; what happens between now and tomorrow lunchtime when we will be due back at Kidlington is up to you.'

So saying, he walks away towards the instructors' tent. It's the end of flying for the day and I am left standing, drained, nonplussed and destroyed.

That evening in my room I get down to preparing in detail for the next day's ordeal. I find concentrating difficult. I'm a failure. Must put today behind me and get down to work. I have managed to scrounge a new and unmarked map and I carefully lay out and measure the tracks, studying and memorizing the landmarks as I expect to see them. Some I remember from today and I go over the whole course once again.

I spend a sleepless night worrying about this wretched cross-country and my review. Suspension stares me in the face. If this sort of thing keeps me awake what will it be like when I am on operations? If I ever get that far, that is.

The next morning, as soon as we arrive at Kidlington, I go straight to the Met Office and get the winds at 3,000 to 5,000 feet. Then I go to work on the computer. By 9.15 I am all set and waiting impatiently in the flight tent. Now that the trip is imminent I just want to get on with it. As soon as I see Eddy Lewis I tell him that I am ready to go whenever he is. He looks at me steadily. I detect a smile in his eyes for just a second or so before it vanishes.

My instructor goes over to the authorization book and the Forms 700, which are laid out on a trestle table. Without turning he says, 'Off you go, then. Start up 5788 and I will be out in a moment. Have you done all the preparation?'

'Yes, Flight Sergeant.'

In the aeroplane I settle down and start up. Now that I'm in the aircraft I feel far more relaxed than I thought I would. Right, Geoff, show that little man if it's the last thing you do!

Eddy turns up three or four minutes later, climbs into the back seat and then quietly says over the intercom in a confidence-giving voice, 'OK then, sir, let's have a nice quiet ride together. Just carry on in your own time.'

Without hurrying I take-off, climb up and set course bang over the centre of the airfield. All goes well, particularly when I am fortunate enough to pick up a pinpoint that shows me, as I estimate it, as much as four miles south of track. So much for Met winds! I make doubly sure of my position on the map, work out a correction and then alter course for my first turning point. Over the intercom I hear Eddy Lewis humming quietly to himself. Probably pleased that I picked up that error pretty quickly. I relax a bit and begin to enjoy this experience. What a contrast to yesterday! I'll win this bloody battle yet.

The rest of the detail is completed with no trouble at all. Landmarks come up when expected and we end up slap bang over Kidlington an hour and a half later. I rejoin the circuit and make a good landing on the correct side of the airfield. As I taxi back to the flight line, two words come from the rear cockpit: 'That's good.'

Maybe it was, but it's a pity he had to bully it out of me. Why couldn't I have done a passable cross-country for him in the first place? If I'm to make it I've got to try even harder.

Back in the flight tent Lewis comes up to me. 'That will be all for today, Mr Wellum. This afternoon I want you to take 5820 together with Mr Sears and do a compass swing; it's overdue. Tomorrow you can do your first solo cross-country with the same aeroplane. It's quite a simple one; piece of cake, in fact. You go from here direct to Grantham, where you are to land and report to the Duty Pilot. You will then fly back to Kidlington. I will talk to you further in the morning but, in the meantime, you can get on with the initial preparation this evening. Questions?'

'None, Flight, that's fine, thank you very much.'

It's good being entrusted to take an aircraft away on a cross-country on your own for the first time. I get a feeling that the pugnacious little Harvard is my own private property, a feeling of partnership in a new adventure. A bit dramatic perhaps but, nevertheless, pleasant; I like the thought of landing at a strange aerodrome.

As I take-off and circle Kidlington prior to setting course for Grantham, I feel totally part and parcel of my aircraft. The cockpit seems a friendly place as I settle down and climb to 4,000 feet. The dials on the instrument panel show me that all is as it should be, the needles quivering slightly as if to attract my attention to the fact that they are normal.

It has been snowing during the night and it's a beautiful sight from up here. The countryside looks glorious, crisp and clean with its light covering of white. Below, I can see someone taking off from the airfield, a small aeroplane followed by a wispy feathered trace of powdered snow driven by the slipstream.

I circle, gaining height. Hold the aircraft steady, straight and level whilst I set the directional gyro to coincide with the heading shown on the compass, when it decides to settle down that is. There now, our heading is 305 degrees. Cage the gyro, set 305, uncage and we are synchronized. So far, so good. Now start the turn so as to set course for Grantham over the centre of Kidlington. Round we come, nearly there, turn three or four degrees to port, a little more, that's it, bang on. We're on our way. Now just hold things nice and steady and settle down. I get out the map and tick off the landmarks as they appear.

A quick check around the cockpit. Manifold pressure OK, revs where they should be, oil temperature and pressure look good and the cylinder head temp nicely within limits. How's the fuel? Flying on the port tank, which shows three-quarters full, starboard tank full. Bags of juice and in any case I can always top up at Grantham if I'm in any doubt. Shouldn't be necessary, though.

Apart from one small alteration of course things go easily and according to plan. Dead on ETA a town comes up and that must surely be Grantham. It's where Grantham should be, unless someone's moved it. I check the map carefully. Yes, that's it all right. The Great North Road and to the east, on top of the hill, the aerodrome. OK, Geoff, let's go on in and land like the man said.

I look down on the large area of snow-covered airfield. There is nothing in the circuit, in fact there appears to be no flying going on at all, so I pick the longest run and make my approach. Cross the hedge and a good soft landing, the snow obviously acting as a cushion. Taxi in and switch off, parking brake on and I clamber out and jump to the ground with as much of a nonchalant, nothing-to-it sort of air as I can manage. I feel decidedly pleased with myself. The Duty Pilot makes a note of my arrival. I tell him I require no fuel and will be returning to Kidlington in about twenty minutes. Think I'll take a stroll in the fresh air for ten minutes or so.

I take-off for the return journey to Kidlington. Check the fuel and turn over to the starboard tank. It helps to balance the contents of the wing tanks. At height and on course the landmarks that I passed on the outward trip appear reassuringly. The only change is that the base of the high cloud seems to have lowered somewhat.

It continues to do so as I proceed on course. I am flying about 300 feet below a level layer. The visibility is not as good as it was, either, not by a long way. I think the answer is to get down to 2,000 feet. Yes, that's better. It's much more comfortable down here. Another pinpoint, I remember that railway running along the side of the funny little wood with the hole in the middle. Checking the map constantly it would appear that we are nicely on course. All goes well. It is turning out to be one of those nice friendly trips and when the time is due, the spires and towers of Oxford appear. It's getting somewhat murky out to the west. I don't reckon on this weather for much longer. Never mind, we're home. I put away my map, carry out my cockpit checks and let down into the circuit. Rich mixture, fine pitch, cockpit hood open and wheels down. Cheery green lights show, undercarriage safely locked down. Turn in for the final approach and flaps down. As I slide towards the ground, something white is flashing by the cockpit. It is snowing. Don't think I'm seeing things. I even timed the weather right! Why can't all trips be like this one?

Even with the hood open it is warm and snug in the cockpit. The ground races up to meet me, check her, there goes the road, the hedge, back again, throttle right back, stick back and we land lightly on three points. Fair enough, that one. It was bound to happen some time; law of averages.

Snowing considerably harder now. No matter, I'm on the deck. Cockpit check done, taxi in and switch off. Into the flight tent and sign the authorization book as having completed and then into the dining hut for the late lunch that I had ordered; I can do with it.

Five days later Eddy details me for the final cross-country test, which is over a longer and more difficult triangular course. He calls me to him at the end of a day's flying.

'Right, sir, how about another cross-country tomorrow, solo?'

'Fine, Flight.'

'Good, here's the form. First I want you airborne at 08.00 hours sharp, actually as soon as you can after arriving here, in fact. If I give you the route now you can work on it this evening and get your planning tied up for a quick getaway. OK?'

'Yes, Flight.'

'Right then, let's have a look at the map.' He lays a new map out on the trestle table. 'Here we are, then. From here you are to fly to Debden, then down here to Netheravon, where you are to land and refuel. From Netheravon you are to return back here to Kidlington. I've already checked on the weather and it looks good so there should be no difficulties. Take this fresh map. Any questions?'

'What height do you want me to fly at?'

'The usual, 4,000. Just watch it though when you arrive at Debden and the surrounding area. It's a pretty busy place these days. There are a couple of Hurricane squadrons there so, as I say, keep a good look out. The same at Netheravon, it's an FTS but the navy have it, so anything can happen; just watch out for sailors in aircraft. You should have a good day and make a good job of it. I think you may finally be catching on.'

It's the first time that I've known Flight Sergeant Eddy Lewis to be flippant. He strides away in the jaunty way he has. What a truly great man he is.

I look down and set course for Netheravon nicely over the centre of Debden. The first leg from Kidlington was fine, although I was a little late in getting away. No matter, there is plenty of time. I change over fuel tanks to balance things up a bit and start the long run to Salisbury Plain and my destination. The engine purrs away smoothly and with the sun now behind me the spinning airscrew is like a shimmering disc. Once again I find it difficult to accept that things are so. I wonder if any of the others get these feelings of unreality. I gaze around at the countryside stretching away all around me and then at the short stubby little wings on either side that support me in the air. Peering behind I am able to see the fin and rudder and tailplane. This aeroplane is all mine. Nobody in the rear cockpit. I search the pale blue sky above, the ground below and over the short nose through the disc of the turning propeller and I revel in the situation. I love this flying!

Slowly I eventually come out of my daydreams to realize that I am unable to see quite as far ahead as I could a few moments ago. Ahead I can see what appears to be a belt of fog stretching away in front and right across my path. With the sun shining on it, it looks remarkably solid. We are approaching the north-western edge of London and this muck must be smoke; that's it, smoke haze. Horrible dirty yellow curry-coloured smoggy smoke. Fancy having to be down there breathing that stuff! The further I fly the less I can see and in next to no time I am in the thick of it. Never flown in visibility as bad as this before. This is a new experience. Only directly downwards can I see the ground. I can always turn 180 degrees and go back to Debden of course, if I really get into trouble, but that would be defeat so let's carry on for a bit. Map reading is out of the question so the drill is to stick to the compass and then start to look around on ETA Netheravon. Hopefully, by that time the visibility will have picked up a little. Reset the DI, hold steady on course and we drone on. I could always try and get above the haze, of course, but for the moment things are fairly comfortable so let's stick it out.

The sun is hot through the canopy. There is no horizon, nothing at all, and it occurs to me that over the past ten minutes or so I have been relying on my instruments more than I've ever done before. I enjoy this slight challenge and I'm rather surprised that I feel so relaxed. Perhaps Eddy Lewis is right and, at last, I'm beginning to learn something.

Thoughts of Nick; this is what I'm being trained for, to meet these situations and cope with things when they don't go quite as planned. Accepting the reality, I adjust my thoughts to concentrating on the flight.

Five minutes to ETA and there is little change in visibility. Perhaps it's a shade better but not all that much. Holding course, I start to take a careful look around. There is little to see but the ground directly below me. Peering down over the leading edge of the wing I see only a rather large building that appears to be isolated. It has a jagged, saw-edged roof and, with a certain amount of surprise, I arrive at the conclusion that it could possibly be an aircraft hangar. Throttling back and letting down slowly to 1,500 feet, I make a 360-degree turn in order to inspect this phenomenon rather more closely.

There is no doubt that this is an airfield of some sort. Surely my luck cannot be that this is Netheravon? That would be too jammy to be true; nobody would ever believe me! The visibility is a little better down at 1,500 feet so I circle round twice more to try and identify what is obviously a rather deserted aerodrome. I should think that if it isn't Netheravon –

and the odds are that it's not – then it certainly cannot be very far away.

Checking the fuel state I note that, although things are fairly comfortable, both tanks are below half full. I reckon I'll have one more go to try to identify the place and, if I'm unable to do so, then I'll go in and land and ask. If necessary, I can also take on a little fuel. With no more ado I make a couple more circuits and inspect the airfield closely. At 1,200 feet the visibility is quite good. The place seems deserted and I don't know where I bloody well am! A check on the windsock, choose a good long landing run and go on in. It's a ghost town, not a movement anywhere. I taxi up to what is obviously the Watch Office, switch off and make my way to a door marked Duty Pilot. Through the window I can see a face looking at me in mild surprise. I knock and a voice calls out, 'Yes?'

Opening the door I am confronted by a disinterested look-ing flying officer who is sitting at a table with a cup of tea and an Edgar Wallace novel. My eye is attracted by the tea. Gosh, I could do with one of those! He says nothing but just looks at me, so I feel that it is up to me to open the conversation.

'Excuse me, but is this Netheravon?'

'No.'

'Where am I, then?'

'Upavon.'

'That seems very close; where's Netheravon?'

'Over there.'

'Where?'

'Where I am pointing.'

'What, those sort of shed-type buildings on that ridge?'

'Yep.'

'Well, that's where I am supposed to be.'

'What are you doing here, then?'

'There was a lot of smoke haze between Debden and here

and I saw this aerodrome on my ETA and landed. Not bad, actually; I'm only a couple of miles out.'

'Maybe, but somehow it makes all the difference, doesn't it?'

'Yes, I suppose it does. Can I push off then, please?'

'You had better and be bloody quick about it. Do you want me to report you as having landed at Upavon?'

'No. Thanks.'

'I didn't think you would. Cheerio.'

I beat a hasty retreat from my flying officer friend and in next to no time am airborne and circling Netheravon. The circuit seems full of aeroplanes. It's a pity I didn't take longer searching when I first hit upon Upavon. Never mind, it's easy to be wise now. In fact, being so near and having had no landmarks to check from, I don't reckon I handled the situation too badly. I'll know in future. Anyway, nobody else could have done much better, only two miles better in fact. Five minutes later I switch off outside the Watch Office at Netheravon and nonchalantly say to a corporal 'Top her up, please. No immediate hurry, I shall be leaving in about half an hour.'

'Right, sir, straight away.'

As I report my arrival there is great satisfaction in seeing the petrol bowser at 'my' aircraft. All we have to do now is to fly the last leg back to Kidlington and home, but I'll have a bit of a breather first and I'll find or scrounge a cup of tea if it kills me.

Later, back at Kidlington, I report to Eddy Lewis. I have a grin on my face, apparently.

'You are obiously very pleased with yourself. What time did you land at Upavon?'

'How did you know that I landed at Upavon?'

'I didn't, but I do now. It's a fifty–fifty bet. At the very least half of you end up at Upavon. Always been the way of things.'

That's taken the wind out of my sails completely.

'Does that mean that you want me to do the sortie all over again?'

'No, I'll let you get away with it this time. Anyway, it's probably as good as you'll ever do. Not your strong point, navigation, is it?'

'Suppose not.'

'Well, good show, anyway. At least you didn't make any excuses about the visibility. Wasn't all that good, was it?'

'No, not very.'

'Right, so much for that then. By the way, we're starting night flying next week. That should be fun for everybody.'

'Delighted you think so, Flight.'

Night flying; don't know if I'm looking forward to it or not. After all, it was described by somebody with the phrase 'Only birds and fools fly by day and only owls and bloody fools fly by night.'

We'll just have to wait and see.

I stand outside the flight tent waiting for Eddy Lewis. Inside, two hurricane lamps give a sickly yellow light as they stand on the trestle table. Dusk is falling and night rapidly approaching. I am tensed up and fidgety. Forcing myself to try to relax I nevertheless shiver in the cool late-evening air in spite of my Sidcot suit. I look up at the ever-darkening sky. How strange to be starting work at this time of the day. High cirrus cloud stretches in an unbroken sheet as far as the eye can see. There is no moon and, with the cloud cover, not even starlight. It's going to be as black as Toby's arse.

Away over the airfield I can see the flares shining in the near darkness. Eddy calls me into the tent. Resigned to my fate I turn, pull back the flap and enter. My instructor is in his most relaxed and quiet mood.

'Now, there is nothing super magic about this night flying.

We'll go off and I will do a circuit first to give you an idea of what it's like. Remember, it's far more difficult from the back seat than it is from the front so, if I can do it from there, you should have no trouble from where you are. Now, there is one thing I am going to stress and it is most important. The moment you leave the ground and are off the flare path do not, repeat do not, no matter how tempted, try to look outside the cockpit . . . it will be very black and you will have no horizon or any means of orientation whatsoever and so we will have to rely entirely on our instruments. This is the whole secret of night flying. We climb straight ahead to 600 feet and then start a 180-degree rate-1 climbing turn to port. We keep the climb going all the time until we find ourselves on the downwind leg at 1,500 feet. We then Morse our identification letter on the downward ident light and, when we get an answering green from the flare path, we continue and carry out our normal landing procedures and that's all there is to it. OK then, there can't be any questions so let's go and do some night flying.'

Ten minutes later Eddy opens the throttle and we go tearing down the line of flares. I watch fascinated as they go flashing past the port wing. We leave the ground just before the last flare and plunge into a black void. I can see nothing. It is absolutely pitch black and I have no idea as to the position of the aircraft relative to anything, let alone the ground. I hear Eddy Lewis talking quietly to me over the intercom.

'Straight on to instruments, keeping the rate of climb going and concentrating on the artificial horizon. Don't hurry anything, undercarriage up, throttle back to climbing power and revs and all the time the little aeroplane on the artificial horizon is level and showing a gentle rate of climb. My eyes never stop scanning the instruments. Artificial horizon, rate of climb, air speed indicator, directional gyro and so on.'

He makes it sound so easy. The voice from the rear cockpit continues.

'Here we are at 600 feet and we start a rate 1 climbing turn to port. Now, if you look over your left shoulder, you will see the flare path coming into view; here we are downwind at 1,500 feet or very close to it. Now I am Morsing our identification letter and there, as you can see, is the answering green on the Aldis.'

We turn crosswind, undercarriage down, fine pitch, flaps and, turning on to final approach, we line up on the flare path. The line of flares seem to advance slowly and then, as we get closer, with rapidly increasing speed. As I follow Eddy through on the controls I feel him check the rate of descent and then check again. As we touch the ground the throttle is closed. There is no movement on the stick, our wheels touch again and then the tail wheel. The aircraft settles on the rough ground and trundles to a halt. Turn off the flare path and taxi clear.

'Got the idea? OK then, now you have a go.'

After an hour's dual during which I find myself concentrating harder than I have ever done before, Eddy seems satisfied for a first try.

'Right, that'll do for a bit. How did you like it, piece of cake, isn't it?'

'I don't know about a piece of cake, Flight, but it's not too bad and certainly it's something different.'

'Well, you did very well indeed for a start. We'll have a rest and do another trip later.'

To satisfy Eddy Lewis is something out of the ordinary but, for the life of me, I cannot see how I shall ever be safe enough to do this little caper solo. We fly another detail, just three circuits and landings, which I feel should be more accurately termed arrivals. I am not sorry when we pack up for the night as after the second detail I suddenly realize that I am more tired than I can ever remember having been before.

There is no doubt that it is a great mental strain the first time one goes night flying. Add to that the intense concentration required and it is not altogether surprising that at the end of it all you begin to feel a little whacked. Anyway, it's over for the time being. It will be good to get to bed. I bet I sleep like a log, then it will be up in time for lunch and back to the aerodrome in the afternoon. We are at it again tomorrow night.

It is pitch black as I taxi out to take-off on my first night solo. I am aware of this next step in the training of a service pilot; it is towards the end of the course syllabus.

Arrived this evening at the flights to find that I was down to fly with the new Flight Commander. He is a large pleasant-looking man in his early thirties, sandy haired with a kind open face. I have liked him from the moment he took over the Flight, although I haven't seen too much of him. He greets me as I enter the tent to check the authorization book.

'Good evening, Wellum. Let's see if we can get you off solo tonight, shall we? You will be the first tested so far. Don't worry about anything, I just want you to carry on in your own time; OK, any questions?'

'No, sir.' What else can I say?

A pause and he looks at me for a second. 'OK, old lad, let's go, shall we?'

I like the way he keeps saying 'shall we?'. One gets the feeling of friendliness from a man who is only out to be helpful. He chats away as we walk to our waiting aircraft in the blackness. I wonder if I am underconfident. Hope he can't tell what's going through my mind but I wouldn't put it past him. He's a wise man, I feel. We have a short chat about sea fishing, in which he has an interest, and I tell him about Cornwall, but all too soon it's down to business.

We do a couple of circuits and landings without anything too dramatic happening. As we taxi back for the third time he says, 'OK, Wellum, that will do nicely. Stop here and drop me off.'

He makes the rear cockpit straps secure, climbs up the wing and leans over my cockpit, raising his voice against the noise of the engine.

'Feel OK about it?'

'Yes thank you, sir.'

'Good man. Now see if you can get three circuits and landings on your own just like you've done for me. They were pretty good. Take your time about it and when you have done three come in and that will have finished your night flying for a while. Three solo landings is all that is required, so make a good job of it.'

He pushes back his helmet and I can see his face in the glow of the cockpit lights. He grins, pats me on the shoulder and then jumps back off the wing. He gives a wave as he strides away into the blackness, parachute slung over his shoulder.

It feels a bit lonely sitting out here in the pitch darkness in this bloody great aeroplane. What a stupid place to be.

I open the throttle and taxi slowly towards the flare path. Blimey, it's black. Stop here and do the checks. Cockpit lights a little on the bright side, or are they? I dim them slightly; that's better. Make sure the gyros are uncaged, trim, pitch, fuel, rich mixture, straps, everything set? That's about it. Morse my identification letter and the answering green from the night-flying crew. Taxi on to the flare path and line up on the flares standing out clear and bright just as they did before. Reset the directional gyro and check again that the artificial horizon is uncaged. Trims set? OK, Geoff, let's go. One more check around the cockpit, a quick glance. I feel a bit of a clot for checking everything three times but all is OK. The cockpit lights give a cosy warm feeling. I feel settled and composed.

I open the throttle steadily and we accelerate off down the

line of flares. Correct a little bit of swing, keep her straight and we are off the ground. Once again as we roar over the last flare the blackness hits me in the face. Straight on to the artificial horizon and I glue my eyes to the instruments. I am conscious of being on my own and find myself concentrating harder than ever on the blind flying panel. Life depends on it.

Wings level, the little aeroplane on the instrument just above the horizon bar, that's right, keep the rate of climb going, undercarriage up, there is a glow of the red lights, don't worry about them, just concentrate on the instruments. Throttle back to continuous climbing revs and settle down; relax and concentrate. That's nice, Geoff.

Height coming up to 600 feet. Start the climbing turn, don't hurry it. Keep the climb going and don't be in too much of a hurry to look for the flare path, not just yet awhile. Fly on those instruments, nothing else matters. Right, have a quick look out now. Yes, dear old lights. There they are, coming into view, twinkling away. How friendly they look and how welcome. Up here in the darkness a feeling of loneliness comes over me. I am detached from my fellow man. Those lights are the only friends I have at the moment. All I can really count on to get me down on to the ground again. Downwind and I have to will myself to relax. OK, Geoff, Morse the ident letter and see if anyone is down there. A reassuring green light flashes in reply. You're not alone, Geoff old chap, there is somebody down there who wants to help. The same old drill, undercarriage, pitch, flaps, by now automatic. My eyes keep moving between the flare path and the instrument panel. Turn 90 degrees to port crosswind and throttle back a goodish lump. Positioned about right and now another 90-degree turn on to the final approach. Line up on the flares and slide gently down through the night sky to meet them. They seem so slow in their approach and I have to pay particular attention to keeping the correct glide path. I experience a most pleasant feeling of tranquillity as we drop down through the still night air. Not a bump or eddy or downdraught in the sky. The feeling of peace is totally opposed to the job in hand. There's something about this night flying.

The lights are coming towards me with ever-increasing speed. I don't appear to be moving, it's those lights. A quick glance at the airspeed, eighty, fair enough, five miles an hour extra, gives me a little to play with. The first flare is racing to meet me. Check her! The red light on top of the Chance Light* sweeps by, another check, quickly. Right, hold it there, hold it! Number one flare goes by. Christ where's the ground? Then we touch; cut the throttle, come on Geoff, right off, a little bounce, we touch again and then the tail drops and there is the comforting rumble from the tail wheel over the rough ground. Now, don't relax, keep her straight you twit, it's not quite over yet. That's better, it is now though. Strewth!

Turn quickly off the flare path, taxi clear, stop, parking brake on and now do your cockpit checks. I look out of the cockpit. I can see the navigation lights of somebody else on the final approach as I start to taxi slowly back to the take-off point again. Right, now let's go and do it all over again.

It's a bit bloody chilly out here. I pour a cup of coffee from my thermos and take a bite from a huge corned-beef sandwich.

Officer in charge of night flying, if you please.

You just cannot rely on anything in the air force, that is anything that is at all reasonable, or even logical, for that matter.

Bad leadership, the top, that's where the trouble is. War or

---

* Floodlight manufactured by Chance Bros to provide runway illumination. Normally, two Chance Lights were allocated to a runway, one at either end, positioned at the left-hand side as seen from the approach and aligned axially.

no war, the service wants a sort out and quick if sense is to prevail, let alone win the war.

It's a pity about this evening. I think it not unreasonable to expect a night off when one has completed one's night flying. I was the only one to finish last night and it would have been nice to have been able to enjoy a well-earned night off when the others were flying, but not a bit of it.

'Wellum,' the man said. 'Wellum, you will be on the flare path tomorrow night. It'll be good experience for you. Can't have you doing nothing.'

How did he know I was doing nothing? In fact, I had arranged to go into Cheltenham with Peter to have a civilized meal and see a film. Well, Peter didn't complete last night; doesn't bloody well matter – I could have gone with somebody else, anybody, on my own if need be. No, there's no getting away from it, the Flight Commander made a wrong decision there, no thought. After all, we have been pushed around by all and sundry ever since we arrived, especially that warrant-officer bloke or whatever they call him, the one who takes us for drill. Bloody sadist; rude as well.

This sandwich tastes good; coffee's not bad either. What time is it? There are two airmen assistants with me. Oh yes – I've not only got one assistant, I've got two.

'Flash the torch on my watch, please.'

Thirty minutes past midnight and only another two hours to go.

'Have you lads had some grub?'

'Yes, sir.'

'Either of you still hungry?'

'I am a bit, sir.'

'Here you are then, there are a couple of wads in here, help yourselves.'

A Harvard engine starts up on the other side of the airfield. The whine of the inertia starter and the engagement of the clutch followed by the noise of the engine as it fires comes clearly on the still night air. The second detail is about to begin.

For the umpteenth time I cross to the small table and check the Aldis lamps to see if they are still working. Right, then let's start to pay attention to what's going on.

The first Harvard of the second detail taxis towards me and stops. He seems to be there for ages. Making sure of his checks, I suppose. The pilot, whoever it is, flashes his letter on the ident lights. A couple of quick flashes on the green Aldis in reply and I watch as he edges slowly on to the flare path, turns and rolls forward a few yards, lining up before stopping again. His navigation lights gleam brightly in the darkness and the white downward identification light reflects back off the ground on to the bottom of the fuselage. The engine is idling and the smell of its exhaust gases wafts towards me.

There is no wind to speak of and the night, as last night and the night before, is very dark.

The dim glow of the cockpit lights reflects on the masked helmeted figure of the pilot. He finally looks up and turns, peering in my direction. I think I recognize him as Laurie Buchanan; I'm sure, dear old Scottish Laurie. An awfully kind person; very quiet though; keeps himself to himself. Haven't seen too much of him, come to think of it, since our night out in Leicester. Nick Bellamy was with us then, of course.

I'm glad Laurie is going solo. I fancy he was having quite a bit of trouble with this night-flying caper. I give him a wave and a thumbs up. He lifts his arm out of the cockpit and waves back. Picking up the Aldis I flash a quick green.

'Go it, Laurie old son, show us all how it's done.'

He gives another wave, lifts his head to peer over the engine cowling at the line of flares stretching away before him and slowly opens the throttle, feeding on the power steadily. Brakes off and, as the Harvard starts to roll, I even notice the slipstream plucking at the shoulder of his Sidcot suit as the aircraft, its engine note deep and rich filling the night air with sound, accelerates quickly down the flare path.

It's a fascinating spectacle. I watch his lights going farther away until they start to lift off from the earth, safely airborne. I continue to watch as he rises into the blackness. I don't know if it's my imagination but he seems to be climbing a bit steeply and possibly drifting off to starboard also. It's not my imagination you know, he's quite definitely off to the right and going up like a lift.

Oh, good grief!

Now watch it, Laurie old mate. Come on, laddie, ease it a bit and watch that swing, you're way off. As if in answer to my entreaties the rate of climb lessens, but if anything he is swinging further off to the right, judging by his tail light. Come on, Laurie, you can do better than this. Turn to the left you clot and now watch the height. Don't go to the other extreme, don't overdo it, you're running out of climb.

The lights continue to swing to the right and now he's quite definitely losing altitude, and I don't mean maybe.

I know what is going to happen. My stomach turns itself into a knot and suddenly I feel very sick. Something is radically wrong up there. What on earth can I do? I'm bloody helpless. Things are now happening so quickly it's frightening.

Oh, God, don't let him lose it, please.

The engine note rises, filling the night with the noise of a thousand banshees, lifting itself to a tortured pitch, obviously on full throttle.

The lights continue their curved downward path. I hold my hands to my ears in fright and horror. There's not much time to go. Come on, Laurie, let's have you, do something, correct, pull up. *Come on, mate.*

'God, now listen to me: If you are around, please help Laurie. I realize that you're a difficult person to find and perhaps I don't try all that hard, but I'm trying now, so please hear me.'

The lights of the Harvard plunge earthwards and disappear from view. There is a dull thud. The noise of the banshees is cut as if someone has switched off a radio. The silence is deafening. Another dull thud, shattering and ghastly, and a red glow lights the night skyline behind those trees on the hill over there.

> But remember please, the law by which we live,
> We are not built to comprehend a lie,
> We can neither love, nor pity, nor forgive,
> If you make a slip in handling us you die.

Rudyard Kipling, 'Secret of the Machines'

Lectures during the afternoon of the next day. In spite of the fact that the wings examinations are now dangerously close I am not able to concentrate. I hear little of what is going on. Nick and now Laurie both gone. From the night out in Leicester, three of us remain.

Got to get used to this kind of thing happening if ever I'm to be of any use in the service. The others seem to be taking it better than I, but then they didn't see it all happen, did they?

Down at the flights the following morning. Really, Kidlington is a pretty little place. It is fine and clear with a touch of frost. I regard the lined-up Harvards with hostility. They are still at it. Blokes are still getting killed and yet they look friendly enough. Peter and I are walking alone to the flight tent not saying very much to each other when we are approached by an instructor, 'The Flight Commander wants all pilots in the dining hut right away. The others are already on their way, so jump to it.'

We hurry along, find a seat and, needless to say, settle down to wait. Five minutes and we get to our feet as the big man stalks into the room.

'Sit down.'

He picks up a piece of chalk and walks over to a large blackboard that has been imported and which I hadn't noticed. Without saying a word and amidst a silence you could cut with a knife he writes two words in very large letters:

COCKPIT DRILL

He underlines them with two heavy lines. Pointing at the words he turns and seems to look at each and every one of us, instructors and pupils in turn. It feels like an age before he talks. He then speaks in a slow, clear voice.

'Bad cockpit drill killed Acting Pilot Officer Buchanan two nights ago. How? He took off with both his directional gyro and his artificial horizon caged. I repeat, DI and horizon caged. A complete waste of a young life and a future pilot for the Royal Air Force, not to mention the destruction and loss of a valuable aircraft.'

He goes on, but I don't hear. I've heard enough. That explains everything. Poor dear old Laurie. It's not really the fault of the aeroplane at all. You just cannot afford to make mistakes like that. Take liberties with modern aircraft and they will turn round and bite you. I wonder, would he have got away with it in a stable old biplane like a Hart?

Everybody's getting up. The Flight Commander must have finished. Chairs scrape, conversation starts and Eddy Lewis crosses the room to me.

'Let's go and fly an aeroplane. I want to run through a typical wings test and this is what we will concentrate on daily from here on. It's a nice morning for it; should be ideal for our purpose.'

So starts a period of the hardest flying I have yet done. Dual for the first trip of the day and then solo practice to iron out my many faults, with another dual check late in the afternoon. I have so many bad habits and faults that I get annoyed with myself as the days pass. Possibly I'm getting a bit het up and tired. Add the intense flying lectures and evening work and you've got yourself maximum pressure and a very busy time. No trips out to the local pub. The chips are down.

My instructor keeps up the pressure and I have the good sense to hang on and accept it. I figure that other instructors are doing the same. Nothing slips by Eddy Lewis. He is meticulous. He knows what he wants from a pupil and he is going to get it if the pupil has it in him to give, no matter how hard he has to bully to extract it, and so the tempo is sustained. Even at this late stage two Anson blokes are transferred, one to become a navigator and the other to the Equipment Branch. Poor sods! The rest of us, about half of all those who started out, soldier on.

'A little more top rudder coming out of that roll; you're not straight in coming out of your rolls off the top, you're getting the stick back too quickly in your loops, now come on, Mr Wellum, this just is not good enough, no good at all. You can do a lot better. You won't have me in this bloody seat holding your bloody hand every bloody day, do another one; now that's a lot better. Why couldn't you have done one like that in the first place? Why? Because you're bloody lazy, just plain bloody lazy, nothing more, nothing less. Good God, man! There you go again; that was terrible.'

Oh, shut up, you noisy bastard!

Another fine morning. I report to the flight tent but I can't see my instructor anywhere. Now where the hell has he got to? Peter goes off on a dual trip, doubtless practice for the wings test soon to come, but what about me? I'm left waiting alone. This is wrong, not to say inconsiderate. Judging by yesterday's rehearsal with Eddy, I'm in need of more help and practice than most and yet here I am left to my own devices, dolled up in flying kit but doing sweet damn all. There is only one thing to do and that is to be patient and look obvious.

As it turns out, I don't have to look obvious for long. The Flight Commander comes striding out of the tent and beckons me to him.

'Sorry to keep you hanging about, Wellum, but Lewis won't be here yet awhile. For this morning, I want you to ferry 5784 back to Rissington. It's due for inspection. You'll be brought back by an Anson, which will wait for you at the Watch Office. Report to the CO Flying when you land. He's been told you are coming and is expecting you.'

'Understand, sir; right away.'

'Yes, get away as soon as possible and get back here. Oh, by the way, you'll be taking your wings test this afternoon. Lewis says you're as ready now as you'll ever be and the CFI will be taking you probably at about 15.00 hours; get that hurdle behind you, OK?'

'Yes, sir.' What else can I possibly say?

'Right then, get cracking.'

I sign the authorization book and, grabbing my helmet and parachute, find 5784. Once in the air for Little Rissington I muse over the conversation I've just had. 'Oh, by the way,' he said, purely as a rather tedious afterthought. 'Oh, by the way, you'll be flying your wings test this afternoon.' Just in passing, dear old chap. That gives me the remainder of the morning and afternoon to get myself worked up into a rare old stew; concentrates the mind wonderfully. Very considerate, that; good thinking. Get a bloke all tensed up and then he makes a balls up of the test and becomes an equipment officer. Short of equipment officers, they are. Well, I hope I make CFI whatever-his-name bloody air sick. Probably will, too, through sheer bad flying.

★

It's a pleasant afternoon with no cloud to speak of and a wintry sun sinking slowly down the sky in the last quarter of another day.

My examiner is strapping himself into the rear cockpit. I look at my watch. It is just 15.10 hours, not much more than an hour of reasonable daylight left. I have been waiting with the engine running for a good five minutes and ready to go. Gave myself plenty of time to settle down and become comfortable. This is the hour. The whole future depends on it, my future; it's important.

Since this morning I have been concentrating on condition-ing myself to accept this challenge and now I feel eager to take on whatever test the RAF cares to sling at me. There is absolutely no reason why I shouldn't show this bloke what I can do. After all, I have done everything that I'm going to be asked to do with Eddy Lewis at one time or another and what is more I have done everything pretty well. It's just a question of stringing it all together and doing everything well at the same time in one sortie.

'OK, Wellum, all set?'

His voice coming through the intercom shakes me out of my reverie. 'Yes thank you, sir.' Try a little politeness on him, can't do any harm.

'Right then, taxi out, take-off and climb on due west to 8,000 feet. Carry on in your own time.'

Straightforward instructions, better do what the man asks.

Obeying all the rules that God ever made for aviators I take-off and turning on to due west start to climb up to 8,000 feet. Now that I can feel the aeroplane through my hands and feet I find myself relaxing enough to revel in the joy of flight. Once again all sense of speed goes and slowly the countryside unfolds itself as we climb higher. The visibility is pretty good. Only in the far distance does the horizon become blurred in a reddish brown haze which reflects the late afternoon sun.

Down below, a cluster of cottages; smoke from their chimneys rising vertically into the still air. Not much wind about; might be useful to remember that point. Anyway, this is a wings test, no time for musing, got to keep my mind on the job in hand.

Passing 5,000 feet the aerodrome must still be dead astern if the illustrious CFI wants to know. We are almost at the top of the climb when my next instructions come over the intercom.

'When you get to 8,000 feet, level off and do a spin to the right; I'll tell you when to recover.'

'Right, sir.'

'Yes, that's what I said, to the right.'

'Certainly, sir.' Stupid bastard.

Level off at 8,000 and I take my time and steady myself down. A good look around, all is clear. I throttle back and raise the nose.

'Here we go, sir.'

'When you're ready.'

That little shudder, a vicious flick as I apply full rudder and with the stick back in my tummy we are spinning. My examiner allows the spin to really wind up and we are fairly flashing around. I hold on. Any minute now, I hope.

'OK, recover.'

Take off the rudder with firm pressure, ease the stick right forward, the spin stops, thank God, and I ease out of the resultant dive, open the throttle and resume normal flight. Allah be praised!

'Yes, that's the idea, now climb back up to 6,000 feet and we'll do some aerobatics.'

The workouts that Eddy Lewis has put me through and his constant badgering for perfection hold me in good stead. I settle to the task of waging war on the wings test and the bloke in the back in particular. Everything he asks of me I find I can do without much trouble and he throws the book at me. He shows me no favours. I know that so far I'm giving him a pretty fair ride. I feel within myself that things are going reasonably well. The roll off the top of a loop is a good one. I'm lucky in timing the opening of the throttle with the backward pressure of the stick. As we come up to the top of the loop I crane my head back as I see the horizon appear, stick over, a little top rudder and we roll over as straight as a die.

'Very good indeed, very good. Was it a fluke?'

'No, sir.'

'OK, do me another one then.'

I do and it's another beauty. Pick the bones out of that.

'OK, now a steep turn to port and hold it until I say.'

I start the turn. The nose travels around the horizon. I get the stick well back with plenty of power on and a really steep turn.

'Right, now straight away a steep turn to starboard and hold it.'

It seems to go on for ever. I'm beginning to feel somewhat warm. There's no doubt this chap goes through the whole routine.

'Right, straight and level.'

I come out of the turn and try to pick up my bearings but, before I have half a chance, the throttle is suddenly closed. Instinctively, I try to open it again but it won't move.

'I'm afraid you've had an engine failure and you will have to make a forced landing.'

Oh, brilliant, that's bloody clever, that is, very smart. What a charming chap. This, of course, is an old dodge. They cut the throttle on you and tell you to force land after you've been hurtling all over the sky doing steep turns, aerobatics and Christ knows what else and have no idea of your position. It's a 'don't just sit there, do something like land' situation and, of course, you have no option when some clot is sitting in the back holding the throttle closed. Of course, the big question is, my dear sir, where?

The altimeter reads 5,200 feet. Now come on, Geoff, take it quietly, settle the aircraft down into a comfortable glide. You've got a bit of height in your favour. That's the idea! Now then, where on earth are we exactly? Should have remembered this ruse of course but I was getting just a bit too cocky; now he's cut me down to size, down to earth in fact. But what is my position? Should pick up something. Bloody got to. Search around initially to no avail. For a second or so a sense of despair bordering on panic overtakes me. I realize that I'm in danger of making a mess out of what was, ten seconds ago, proving to be a good test.

There seems to be nothing on the port side and so I search to the starboard. Dammit, I should be able to pick up something. I have been flying around this area for months and should know it well. Down below the trailing edge of the starboard wing and just coming into view there is a largish field. I reckon that will have to do. I've got to make up my mind sometime and this would appear to be it. As I turn the nose of the Harvard to get a better view I recognize my 'field' as Witney aerodrome, a smallish airfield used by De Havillands for something or other. Well, that's put it beyond all doubt, this is the answer. Lucky I saw it, but I bet the bloke in the back knew it was there.

I feel much better now that I am able to see my target, as it were, and have made a decision. Automatically I start to position myself for the best possible approach. I am just able to pick out the windsock, which shows only the lightest of breezes, virtually nothing in fact, so I must be very careful not to overshoot.

'What are you going to do?'

'I'm going to land with my wheels down on Witney aerodrome.'

'I see.'

Keeping an eye on my speed, I watch Witney like a hawk. This has got to be right first time. It's easy to make errors from 5,000 feet. All part of the test and done on purpose, of course, so concentration is required. The altimeter slowly unwinds and when I finally approach across wind it is apparent that, perhaps, I have just a fraction too much height. Not a bad thing to have a little height in hand, so no matter. Anyway, hold on to it for a moment. You can always slip it off as you turn in for your final approach. Slide back the hood, the cool air is refreshing. Things are beginning to look not too bad. I could turn in almost any time now really. Right, select wheels down and fine pitch, come on bloody wheels, let's have you. There they are, green lights. Check rich mixture, come on quickly, OK, now flaps, there we go, OK, turn in on to finals now. You're high, Geoff, slip off a bit in this turn, not too much you idiot, blast that's too much, no perhaps not but you're not going to miss the near hedge by all that much. Don't want to really, do I? Little wind, small airfield.

He's gone deathly quiet in the back. So would I if I were in your seat right now, mate; little do you know.

Bit too fast, check her, over the main Burford road, a short distance on and just over the hedge, that extra speed seems to have gone somewhere, stick back, nicely, a little more, here we go and we sink to the ground on three points. Praise be to Allah yet again. A bit firm that one but not a bounce and utterly safe.

Pretty well ideal for a forced landing in fact, now I come to think of it. Braking gently, we roll to a stop comfortably in the middle of the aerodrome. I feel very hot and lean out into the slipstream.

'Not bad at all. Warm work, isn't it?'

'It certainly is, sir.'

'What do you make the time, my watch seems to have gone U/S?'

'Within a minute or so 4.15.'

'Right, taxi round, take-off and get me back to Kidlington via the low-flying area. Let's see what you can do and be sensible about it. We're going to lose the light very soon, so let's go.'

Never a dull moment. Twenty minutes later, having done the low flying and cleared the low-flying area, I pull up to 1,500 feet and soon the friendly shape of Kidlington is just below the nose. The airfield looks homely in the early dusk, peaceful and quiet. Suppose everyone is packing up for the day. Wouldn't mind being with them.

'We've arrived, sir.'

'Thank you, do me a normal circuit and landing powered approach.'

Delighted, my dear squadron leader, I assure you. Ease down into the circuit, it's nearly over. What an afternoon!

Still obeying all the rules I approach, land, brake easily and allow the aircraft to come quietly to a stop. The engine is ticking over, taking a well-earned rest, and for the life of me I am unable to prevent myself slumping back in my seat. I rest my arms on the side of the cockpit rim and notice the slip-stream plucking at the sleeves of my Sidcot. My examiner sounds very matter of fact.

'That will do very nicely for you, Wellum. Taxi back to the flight line and we'll call it a day.'

Thank God for that.

I feel reasonably satisfied. The trip turned out quite well in the end and I reckon he certainly couldn't have failed me completely on that performance. At least I would be surprised if he did. I'd hate to fly that detail again.

Later I walk down to the hut where we keep our flying kit to put mine away. The Flight Commander and the instructors have offices there, too. As I enter, the boss has his door open and is sitting at his desk. He calls me in. He is smiling.

'I understand you have done a good test, Wellum. Well done. Now I want you to take your parachute and helmet back with you in the transport to Rissington and then, tomorrow afternoon, fly a Harvard back here.'

'Right, sir.'

'I don't know the number of the aeroplane you'll be bringing back but it will be, or should be, waiting at the Watch Office from 13.00 hours onwards. In any case, wait until it is ready if there is a hold up. I want that aeroplane back here tomorrow afternoon, understand?'

'Yes, sir, understood.'

'Then you had better cut along or you will miss the transport. Good show about the test.'

From then on the pressure on the flying side seems to decline – the flying test is over – but now the ordeal of the written examinations preys on my mind. For the past few days I have been working away at the ground subjects rather harder than the others, I fancy. Either I am less intelligent than most or I have been encouraged by the flying test; possibly a little of both. It's been pleasant seeing the others going through the wings test routine knowing that I have done mine and so I work hard in the evenings, sometimes with Clive but mostly on my own. Generally, I see a lot of Peter during the day, of course, and he also has the flying test safely behind him. Possibly he is working also but as we feel the imminence of the written exam we don't see so much of each other during the evenings.

The thought of failure is still too awful to contemplate and my uniform looks naked and ashamed without those most elusive RAF pilot's wings. Is there any badge anywhere in the world more coveted?

The two great days arrive. It is all very official. Separate

1. School first XI cricket team in 1937. I am second on the right in the back row and wearing second XI colours. I was awarded first XI colours at the end of the season and took over the captaincy in 1939 before I joined the RAF.

2. My father and I at Buckhurst Park, Sussex, in July/August 1941, towards the end of my stay with 92 Squadron. I had been invited down for a dining-in guest night.

3. The Harvard I: an advanced trainer from the USA.

4. Tony Bartley, Allan Wright and Brian Kingcombe. They survived the war. This picture was taken, if memory serves, just after they had been given their DFCs. The car was Tony's Lincoln V12; the date: December 1940, a very trying time for us all. I did a second tour as Tony's senior flight commander with 65 Squadron in 1942. Allan was a lovely chap: kind, quiet and introverted. Brian was brilliant, the best leader I ever flew with. Tony was fun-loving and adored by the women, a typical fighter pilot.

5. Allan Wright getting out of his plane. I find this picture difficult to understand – it may have been posed for the press as the aircraft is up on trestles (see inside the undercarriage). I do, however, recall him returning to Duxford after a sortie over Dunkirk well shot up, by which time the squadron letters were QJ.

6. Repairing the plane. Without men like these, working in all weathers to keep our Spitfires flying, the Battle of Britain could not have been won. They were the salt of the earth.

7. Pembrey aerodrome in 1940, showing one of the dispersal tents. There was another on the opposite side of the airfield.

8. Boarding a plane at first light. This is a picture taken later in the war of a Spitfire Mark IX prior to a fighter sweep.

9. First light. This is a wonderful picture and very apt. I find it moving.

10. This Messerschmitt 109 being inspected by police and soldiers crashed in a Sussex wheatfield, 12 August 1940.

Sailor Malan, Mike Robinson

Jamie Rankin

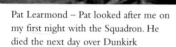

Pat Learmond – Pat looked after me on
my first night with the Squadron. He
died the next day over Dunkirk

Sebastian Maitland–Thompson

Gaskell, Lund, Wade, Mottram, Kingcombe

Tony Bartley

F/Sgt Payne, John Bryson,
Sgt Eyles

Tommy Lund, Sgt Allison

Geoff Wellum

Roy Mottram, Brian Kingcombe, Sammy Saunders

12. Being debriefed after action against Me 109s in about November 1940. Discussing whether we had shot down one or two planes! Action took place off North Foreland over the sea. Myself, Don Kingaby, Ronnie Fokes, Bastian Thompson and Tom Wiesse, our intelligence officer.

13. I am by the swimming pool at a home requisitioned for the staff of the Ops Room. Pilots used to go there for a swim and cool off between sweeps/escorts in 1941. Taken between the morning sweep and the afternoon show.

desks, we sit miles apart from each other; well, just far enough to stop you having a gander at what the next bloke's putting down. Pity that, because the person next to me is Pete and he knows his stuff.

This is worse than School Cert. and to say that I view the whole thing and my chances with trepidation is the understatement of all time. However, like all bad things, the examination comes to an end. I feel reasonably satisfied. At least I've had a real go.

A large crowd all chattering away around the notice board in the ground training block. The exam results have been posted. I've passed. One of the Anson chaps has failed. Now what? Hard luck, mate.

Another notice: 'The following Acting Pilot Officers are entitled to wear the Flying Badge with effect from the date of this notice.' That's enough of that. Look down the list. Yes, there it is . . . APO G. H. A. Wellum. That's me. With a nonchalant 'no more than I expected' attitude I stroll casually away and, when I am far enough down the passage, hurry to my room to get my batman to sew those wings on right away.

I'm behaving like a kid at Christmas time but for me this is a great day. I call for my batman but no reply. Blast, trust him to be out the one time I really need him. Turning, I head for the room and there is Clive leaning against our door waiting and laughing at me.

'OK, Clive, what's so funny?'

'You've just done what I've just done and every other bugger's just doing. Anyway, come in and look at this.'

Hanging on the outside of our wardrobes are our best uniforms, the pilot's wings sewn on. They dominate the room. Good old batman (his name is Milman, with one 'l'). This is nothing new to him but how did he get to know before we did?

Clive must be as excited as I am. It's all we can do not to put on our best blues right away for lunch but there is a dining-in night this evening and we decide to wait until then.

Later, properly groomed for the evening's revelries and attired, of course, in my best blue, I look at myself in the wall mirror. Vanity? Certainly, but I don't give a tinker's. Frankly, I admit to myself that never before have I known such a feeling of pure self-satisfaction as I do at this moment. I can see nothing but those wings. A real pilot and a badge on my tunic to prove it. There must be thousands of young men who would give everything to swap places with me. I am a very fortunate chap. No one will ever take that badge away. Wouldn't Nick and Laurie have revelled in this moment?

A final day with 'C' Flight before a spot of leave. I go and seek out Eddy Lewis. We have done our last trip together. Know where to find him, of course: in the flight tent. In fact, as I approach, I can see him standing outside. He sees me coming and walks a few steps to meet me. He has that half smile sort of expression on his face that I know so well.

'Don't know quite how to say this, Flight, but I just want to thank you for all you've done to help me.'

'That's all right. We've had our moments, of course, but we got there in the end. Are you happy with your assessment?'

'More than that, I'm on top of the world. The only thing that worries me is that I just don't believe it. I'm not above average or anything like it, I know it and you know it.'

'That's as maybe, but you did a very good wings test and you impressed the Flight Commander on that night solo check he did with you, so, what they said went. I was doubtful because you're bloody lazy unless there is something special on or you are bullied and get angry. You're not consistent; anyway, sir, well done.'

'Thanks once again, Flight, your next pupil is a very lucky chap.'

'Let's hope he thinks so. Just one thing, Mr Wellum, before you dash off on leave, remember you still have an awful lot to learn and a long way to go. The going is still liable to be tough, so may I just wish you the very best of luck in the future.'

Two weeks' leave, which I feel has been earned by all. I am utterly content with my lot but, after a week, I am like a fish out of water. I can't wait to get back to the air force and our advanced training.

Advanced Training Squadron and the Flight Commander appears a reasonable person with a decent bunch of instructors to keep an eye on things. Spring is not far away. The weather is improving and the skies are clearing. What will 1940 bring? Where will we all be at the end of the year?

We pupils now fly, more often than not, in pairs as partners sharing an aeroplane, one as pilot and one as the observer. Peter and I team up. Long-range recce, formation flying and formation take-offs and landings, camera-gun work, low-level bombing and more night flying, which passes off with no major problems. Our self-confidence grows.

Some days when Pete and I each have an aircraft on a solo flight we rendezvous in the low-flying area and go careering over the Cotswold countryside at nought feet chasing each other and thoroughly enjoying ourselves. Afterwards, we frolic our way back to Kidlington, looping and rolling our Harvards all over the sky, normally ending up with a spot of formation flying. Looking across at Peter in his Harvard keeping station just off my starboard wingtip, no more than three or four feet away and swaying gently as he maintains position. He has his face mask unhooked and I can see him laughing at me across the narrow distance separating our two aircraft as I lead him home. It is infectious; I laugh back. The sheer joy of it all.

Days pass into weeks and one is occasionally aware that the end of our training is in sight. 'Occasionally aware' finally becomes reality.

The last thing in the syllabus is two weeks at practice camp on the south coast at Warmwell carrying out air-to-air and air-to-ground firing with live ammunition. After Warmwell we can expect our postings, we all hope direct to squadrons. That should keep us all on tenterhooks.

Peter and I fly down to Warmwell together, he as pilot and me as navigator/observer. The whole flight flies in formation. I enjoy the ride, watching Peter do all the work and listening to his quiet voice from time to time over the intercom.

It proves to be an absorbing pastime, firing hundreds of rounds at various targets, trying desperately to hit them and then not believing anybody when they tell you you haven't.

I cannot imagine the weeks and months ahead after I have finished training. Will I in fact go on to a squadron? It's by no means certain. One day, I grant you, it's more than likely but, so soon after leaving FTS? Who's to say? There is talk of operational training units being opened where a new pilot will go to convert to the operational type of aircraft he is to fly. So many things can happen as far as fighters are concerned. What about Lysanders and army co-op or even a battle squadron in France? God forbid! They have suffered terrible casualties. Generally, my private thoughts leave me unworried. After all, worrying now can't possibly have any effect whatsoever on the future. I'll just have to wait and see.

I'm not too certain about old Peter, though. Future prospects, I think, concern him. There have been times recently when he lapses into long silences, when he seems to have retired into a shell where even I cannot get to him and, therefore, nobody else can. He goes for walks around the airfield on his own. We always used to go together. Behind his calm exterior there lurks, I feel, an extremely sensitive young man. We still get on well together, of course, and there is no denying the closeness of our friendship. I suppose this deepened after Nick's death. That seems a long time ago.

I'm more than a little concerned about my friend Pete. I know for sure that he is fighting an inner battle with himself and I can't help; nobody can. It's something private, but win his battle he most certainly will.

A week has passed since I jotted down my thoughts concerning Peter. Poor weather has enforced our stay at Warmwell for a few more days at least and even now it's raining steadily outside; just flyable but useless for air firing. Tea over, we all sit chatting round the mess fire, an RAF ritual it seems.

I enjoy this hour of the day. Soon it will be time to bathe and change before the evening meal. Peter is sitting just across the way reading a copy of *Country Life*. He is his old self again; he's won. Pleasant thoughts and great content, a bath and a couple of drinks before dinner.

'Sears, Wellum; here a minute.'

The Flight Commander's voice; nothing worse than authority breaking in on one's reverie. I find myself crossing the room and Peter is beside me. The boss comes straight to the point, no messing about.

'I'm afraid you won't be finishing your practice camp, either of you; you've both been posted.'

'Good Lord! That's a bit quick, any idea where, sir?'

'I don't know. I'm led to believe it's direct to a squadron. They have the posting notices at Rissington. It's all very urgent. Things are looking bad in France; in fact, it looks like a real bloody disaster. Now the drill is that you will both be going back to Rissington in the morning in a Harvard that is due for inspection. Wellum, you can fly it. Both get packed up tonight and an Anson will be coming to collect your kit. Be ready to leave about 09.00 in the morning. The panic can't be helped. There's obviously good reason for all this.'

It's been too quick and rushed for any great degree of emotion. The train clickety-clacks over the rails on its way to London. I am sitting opposite Peter in the restaurant car having lunch. We talk quietly, both wondering what on earth has hit us in the last twenty-four hours.

This time yesterday we were with our course at Warmwell. I've very nearly got the same feeling as I had when they put me in charge of night flying that dreadful night at Kidlington. My goodness, when was that? Two months? Three months? Time means nothing. It only seems a few weeks or so ago that I walked out of the school gates for the last time, but it can't have been a matter of weeks because I'm dressed up in a blue suit with a pair of wings on it. It's got a very thin stripe on the sleeve as well, just to finish things off.

The situation may be termed as being confused. Confused because I somehow feel that I should be excited but I'm not, not in the least. There is an awareness of the importance of the occasion but I am thoughtful and withdrawn; not at all like the reaction I had led myself to expect on the day that I had achieved an ambition, *the* ambition.

My posting is to a squadron based, I'm told, at Kenley. Its number is 92. It is an operational fighter squadron.

The general war situation gives me food for thought. In France our army and the French are being defeated. It seems nothing can stop these Germans from driving us into the sea. We are falling back on Dunkirk apparently. Our Battle and Blenheim squadrons have taken tremendous casualties and our few precious fighter squadrons have been overwhelmed by numbers, although they have given good account. I suppose the survivors can fly back to England, but what of the army and our ground crews? Can any of them be saved? Even if the navy get some troops away, what will be the loss in equipment? So many imponderables.

This then is yet another milestone in my life. I realize that, like leaving school, training days in the peaceful Cotswolds are over and I'm aware that Peter and I are going to be faced with total war in the air because presumably Churchill will fight on, and this Teutonic monster will hurl the might of his Luftwaffe on to this island with a view to invading. That's where Peter and I will come in, trying to stop him.

I shall never forget May and June 1940. If I survive, that is.

3. Fighter Squadron

'We shall fight in France, we shall fight in the seas and oceans, we shall fight with growing confidence and growing strength in the air; we shall defend our island whatever the cost may be. We shall fight on the beaches, we shall fight on the landing grounds, we shall fight in the fields and in the streets, we shall fight in the hills; we shall never surrender.'

Winston Churchill, 4 June 1940

Another train to another destination and yet again, no doubt, a new way of life. I am on my own and feeling a lot better than I did on the journey up to London with Peter. I should be at Kenley in about ten minutes.

Saying goodbye was not easy and coming as it did on top of hurried au revoirs to the mates at Warmwell and Little Rissington it helped, I'm sure, to engender my withdrawn mood of the morning. Those of us who had survived the system and become RAF pilots had gone through a great deal together during training. A hell of a lot fell by the wayside.

The parting with Peter was quick. We both had the same feeling and that was not to prolong the agony.

'God bless, Geoff. Take great care of yourself and write when you have a second. You know the address, 145 Squadron, Tangmere. We'll meet one day in London if all goes well, won't we?'

'Nothing will stop us. Watch yourself, old mate.'

'We both made it, didn't we?'

'Yes, Pete, we made it all right.'

A very quick handshake, pick up our luggage and go our separate ways, he to Sussex, I to Kent. I shall miss that chap. I hate goodbyes, I really do. Peter had a strange composed look about him, which I don't want to think about too much.

After a day of rushing about and travelling by air and rail, my arrival at Kenley is, to say the least, an anticlimax. The Station Adjutant looks at me with a mixture of amazement and pity.

'Number 92 Squadron, old lad? Well they're certainly not here, never have been. Sounds as if there has been a bit of a balls up somewhere or other, doesn't it?'

He turns to his assistant.

'Have you heard of 92 Squadron or of their whereabouts, Rupert?'

'No.'

'We'll find out something right away.'

The worthy Rupert looks flustered and rather persecuted.

'I've got a secret file somewhere that I've probably lost, knowing my luck. So much bumf around these days, just because there's a war a-waging, that one has to burrow in the stuff to find anything.'

'I'm positive that you are right, but do you think we could possibly ascertain where approximately fifteen aeroplanes and let's say a hundred personnel designated number 92 Squadron are located?'

Poor old Rupert raises his eyes to heaven. 'I think this is the file that we want. No it ain't, this one refers to Bren guns. Ah! Here it is.'

Rupert liberates a pink folder marked 'SECRET' and thumbs through some papers.

'Yes, this is it. Here we are, number 92 Squadron, they are at Northolt; just moved there from Croydon, it seems, and, if you are interested, they have Spits.'

'Well that appears to be the answer,' said the Adjutant. 'We'd better fix you up with a railway warrant and you can be on your way. Sorry about it and all that but it's the best we can do, the Mess here is full to overflowing.'

Half an hour later yet another train, returning to London. By this time, I'm more than a little fed up with all this mucking about. I'm damned if I'm going to traipse with all my belongings out to Northolt tonight. I'll ring up Mother when I get to London and go home for the night. I can then report to Northolt in the morning.

What with one thing and another, I don't get to Northolt until 1.30 p.m. and, having looked in at station headquarters, I make my way quickly to the hangar where I'm told I will find 92 Squadron's offices. I knock on the door marked 'Adjutant 92F Squadron'. A quietly spoken voice bids me enter.

Sitting behind the desk in front of me is a pleasant looking elderly man with a moustache. He wears the 1914–18 war ribbons and a pair of wings with RFC in the middle. I throw him up my very best salute.

'Good afternoon, sir, my name is Wellum and I have been posted to 92 Squadron.'

'Really, well I never. What a wonderful world this is, full of surprises. Anyway, nice to meet you.'

'How do you do, sir.'

'We weren't expecting you, of course. However, take a seat. Another young man called Wade, Trevor Wade, arrived yesterday evening. We weren't expecting him, either. I should think your posting notices will arrive sometime within the next six months.'

Looking at me for a few moments he asks, 'Are you straight from training?'

'Yes, and I didn't quite finish that.'

'Oh, Lord! God help us all. Wade is in the same boat. I suppose that means that there's no hope that you've flown a Spitfire?'

'No, I'm afraid I haven't. Actually, I've never been allowed to look over one.'

'Splendid, that will please the CO I don't think. Anyway, I'll see if I can get you in to see him as soon as he gets back from lunch, which should be at any moment. His name is Bushell, Roger Bushell. He was an auxiliary of long standing and in private life is a barrister. He's quite a bloke to serve under. Don't be put off by his manner. To him his squadron and his pilots are everything. Once you are accepted into his squadron you will never find yourself alone. He'll bollock you from arsehole to breakfast time but he'll support you up to the hilt if necessary and you won't know a thing about it. By the way, how old are you exactly?'

'I'm nearly nineteen.'

'I said, how old are you exactly?'

'Eighteen years and nine months.'

'That's what I asked you and remember that when you see the boss. How many hours have you flown?'

Oh, Christ! I don't like all these questions. 'One hundred and sixty-eight.'

'And how much of that was solo?'

'Ninety-five.'

'Jesus H!' The Adjutant looks at me for a few seconds.

'Well, that will have to do I suppose, but it's totally bloody stupid. What a way to try and win a war! Let me have your log book. Did you get anything in the way of assessments?'

'Above the average.'

'Good, that's at least something. What's your Christian name?'

'Geoffrey.'

'Good.'

'I'm called Geoff.'

'Are you, indeed?'

He smiles at me. I probably remind him of the first day he joined the squadron. 'I'm called Mac. My name is MacGowan and I'm a doddering old sod left over from the last war, SE5 and 5A, Western Front 1918. We shared an aerodrome with 92 for a short time. It's a good squadron, always has been.'

I'm beginning to warm to this character when a noise from the adjoining office attracts his attention.

'The high priest has duly arrived back from lunch. They must have run out of port in the Mess or something horrible. I'll go and see if he'll have a word with you now. Wait here.'

He takes my log book and is gone for some minutes. I hear muffled conversation. Only once do I hear a voice raised and it isn't the Adjutant's. Something about 'not another one' and the word 'training' comes into it. Finally, Mac reappears grinning.

'He'll ring when he's ready. Don't look so apprehensive.'

'Well, I only hope I come out grinning like you are.'

The man at the desk has a tremendous personality. He's a pretty hefty chap and is just plain ugly in a pleasant sort of way. He stares at me for some seconds. If this is an example of a typical barrister then God forbid that I should ever end up in a court of law. He has my log book open in front of him. It cuts no ice.

'Not very bright, is it? Where were you trained?'

'No. 6 FTS Little Rissington, sir.'

'What did you fly?'

'Harvards.'

'So at least you've flown something that folds up, under-carriage, flaps and that sort of thing?'

'Yes, sir.'

'Well, that's about the only thing in your favour, but even so you are of not much use to the squadron. I pay little attention to an assessment made after a hundred-odd hours' flying.'

'I appreciate that, sir.'

'I'm bloody sure you don't. Half-trained youngsters who think they know all the answers are just a pain in the neck in an operational squadron in time of war. You've never even seen a Spitfire, I gather, let alone flown one.'

'I'd try very hard, sir.'

'There's no other option in this squadron, Wellum; if you stay with us, that is. Apart from the time involved, which we haven't got, I just can't be bothered with taking untrained people if I'm unsure whether they are going to measure up. It's not fair to them or to the rest of the pilots and if anybody doesn't attain the standards that I set myself and the rest of the squadron then they are out so bloody quickly that they don't even know what's hit them.'

His face is devoid of expression.

'How old are you?'

Shades of the Adjutant, who I bet has told the CO.

'Eighteen years and nine months.'

There is a pause.

'Well, I haven't got the time to train you and that's flat. This squadron was re-formed a few months ago and what's more it's going to be a damn good squadron. None is going to be better. We were declared operational yesterday and we are waiting for our first action, which, if I'm not very much mistaken, will be any hour now at Dunkirk. We have the best aeroplane in the service, or in the world for that matter, and if you break one there will be merry hell to pay. Again, I just cannot afford to have untrained pilots like yourself thrust upon me at this particular time. There are operational training units starting up to do that very job, do you see my point?'

'Well, if you do send me away to a training unit, sir, I would ask to be allowed to return to 92 Squadron.'

'Why 92 particularly? There are many others still working up.'

'It's my squadron, sir; Air Ministry have just posted me to it.'

I am back with Mac. The CO's interview is over. I gather I'm a frightful prospect for any Commanding Officer to have to consider. Mac laughs at me.

'All right?'

'Do you ever get the impression that you are just not wanted?'

He laughs openly. 'Sit down and have a cup of tea.'

'I'd love one.'

'Millie, a cup of tea for this officer, please, and one for me.'

'Sugar, sir?' A trim and very pretty little WAAF smiles down at me.

'Yes please, three lumps if possible, I'm suffering from shock.'

Mac's face creases with laughter, which is infectious and I join in. He seems to be staring at me, though. Behind the well-met exterior I feel he is assessing me; I can sense it. A bellow from the next room: 'Mac!'

'Coming, sir,' and Mac wastes no time. I sit quietly and sip my tea. A few minutes later he is back, obviously amused.

'I gather that you told the big white chief that 92 was your squadron as well as anybody else's because Air Ministry said so.'

'Yes, something like that.'

'Good for you. The CO referred to you as "that cheeky young cocky little bugger", but I can tell he likes the cut of your jib. I don't somehow think you'll be going to an OTU for the moment. See how you face up. Anyway, we'll just have to wait and see. Here's your log book back.'

That evening in the Mess all is new to me and exciting. I am with a fighter squadron as one of its pilots, if only for a short time. I have got where I have striven to be, yet I am still not totally involved. I am on the sidelines.

An atmosphere of impending drama. There is a gaiety which I'm sure is a little forced. I am surrounded by fighter pilots, self-assured in one respect but conscious of the fact that they have yet to prove themselves worthy of that title. Their chance is very near and they are aware of it.

In my boyhood and up to a few days ago they were my idols, virtually out of reach. Now I am near to being one of them. I eat at the same table, the stewards who wait on them with drinks also hurry at my bidding but, as yet, that is where it all ends. I feel unimportant and out of things but that is only to be expected. I am a new boy, a bit of an outsider. They are a team that formed the squadron and worked up together and who are now being drawn closer together by the imminence of their first action. They are as one and I rather an intruder. Little notice is taken of me.

Mac introduces me to Pat Learmond, 'the best aerobatic pilot in the squadron and ex-Cranwell', and Pat in turn introduces me to the others, one of whom is a quietly spoken, wavy haired young man. His name is Allan and I'm told later his surname is Wright. He seems quieter than the rest and appears to be totally in control of himself and the situation. He stays talking for quite a while before he excuses himself. He is also ex-Cranwell and I feel that Allan is going to be a helpful friend to have around. The rest are polite, but that is about all. I can't yet remember all their names but if that's the way things are to be at the moment then so be it. Trevor Wade, the other new man, feels the same. Pat stays talking to the pair of us and occasionally Mac turns up.

'How's it going, all right?'

Pat gets caught up in the general suppressed atmosphere that prevails throughout the ante-room. I understand. These chaps are waiting for the word to go. I shall be one of them one day, God willing.

A large blond man comes up to Trevor and me. He is a flight lieutenant and says he is to be our Flight Commander. He introduces himself as Paddy Green and in his fist he holds a half-pint tankard of brandy.

'When did you arrive, Wellum?'

'Just after lunch, sir; I gather I'm staying on the squadron, then?'

'Possibly, if I say so. And you don't have to call me sir. I'm only a rather humble flight lieutenant at the moment.'

Maybe, but he looks big enough to me.

'We'll have a talk in the morning, both of you. Don't know what time so be on tap.'

He wanders off to talk to the CO. They laugh over something and look right together. They are obviously great friends. 'Old Olympic ski mates, my dear chap. Known each other for a long time. Jobs for the boys and all that.'

I try to learn the names of the rest of the squadron from listening to the conversations. There's Allan Wright, of course, Butch Bryson, Bill Williams, Tony Bartley, Bob Holland and Gus Edwards, a Canadian, and the other Flight Commander, Robert Stanford Tuck, known to all it would seem as Bob Tuck. Two others come over and introduce themselves as Sam Saunders and Howard Hill, a New Zealander, but they don't stay and talk. Also a charming chap called Roy Mottram, who stays chatting a little longer.

Finding myself alone with Trevor Wade we engage in polite conversation. He is small and rather rotund. At first he doesn't impress me as he puts on a supercilious air and seems to delight in making cynical remarks at other people's expense.

However, as the evening progresses and we talk together over our drinks I realize that behind his exterior lurks an extremely likeable chap who has a great sense of humour and can talk with a wit and intelligence that makes his company an ever-increasing pleasure. There is an impishness about him which, on knowing him better, becomes infectious and on occasions his eyes twinkle with a mischievous humour that seems to carry one along with his mood. He tells me he is called Wimpey; Wimpey Wade, very apt. We both agree on the position in which we find ourselves in the squadron and we decide to play it quietly and do as we are told until it is felt they have time to take more notice of us.

At that moment excitement, almost like a wave, ripples across the room. They have just heard, the squadron is alerted. They are on standby. Ops are on, tomorrow, first light.

Mac comes up to us and tells us that we are to be his assistants for the next few days as the squadron may have to move from Northolt.

I am almost caught up in the general atmosphere and elation but, somehow, I still feel strange and out of it. I quietly push off to my room. Didn't see what happened to Wimpey. I am restless and can't get to sleep at first. After all, it's been pretty hectic for the past day or so. I expect my class are still mucking about down at Warmwell. I wonder how Peter is getting on. Dear old Pete. Thoughts tumbling through my mind but, eventually, I doze off and finally fall into a long dreamless sleep.

The Officers' Mess at Duxford is a good one. It has a friendly atmosphere and as I sit writing a letter to Peter I can hardly believe the events of the week that has passed since I joined 92 Squadron. I have a new Flight Commander, Brian Kingcombe. The big blond one failed to return. Brian has just told me that I will be doing my first trip in a Spitfire tomorrow morning. I did a dual check in the Master this afternoon; first time airborne since leaving Little Rissington. Must have gone all right, I gather. Anyway, it's a week since I last put pen to paper, so, to recap:

The first day after Wimpey Wade and I arrived, the squadron went to war; Dunkirk. At the end of that memorable day four of our pilots had been lost. We had shot down sixteen and the price had been paid. There have been two moves, one to Hornchurch and a few days later to Duxford, where we now are.

Never shall I forget the sight of those pilots as they came into the Mess that first evening at Hornchurch after two days of hard fighting. The CO, my big blond Flight Commander Paddy Green and Pat Learmond were not among them. Pat Learmond was seen to go down in flames and Paddy badly wounded. Nothing has been heard of the others as yet. It gave me my first intimation of what war is all about. These pilots were no longer young men with little care in the world, they were older mature men. On that day alone, most of them had been over Dunkirk three times and it was a day of the very fiercest fighting. No quarter asked and certainly none given. They now know fear. They also know what it takes to conquer fear because they have done it, not once but three times.

Thinking about it all, it becomes so clear to me. These chaps have won their private battles and these are battles that they will have to go on winning, for there is another day tomorrow. As of now, however, they have proved themselves men. I wonder how long one can go on doing this sort of thing if this pace is maintained? In addition to bodily fatigue – a good night's rest will fix that – there surely must be a tremendous mental strain that builds up day by day and from which it takes far longer to recover, if in fact one ever does completely recover. In order to have the chance, of course, you must first of all survive.

I am terribly conscious of the fact that this test is still to come as far as I am concerned. Exactly when, I don't know. I shall no doubt have time to dwell on this matter and I must confess that it worries me. Will I have what it takes to prove myself as the rest of them have done or shall I be a coward? Having been through the mill as these chaps have been and having conquered fear, that most common of all human emotions, can anybody ever be quite the same again?

My God, I'm getting serious, but it makes you think.

'The battle of France is over. I expect that the Battle of Britain is about to begin. Upon this battle depends the survival of Christian civilization. Let us therefore brace ourselves to our duties and so bear ourselves that if the British Empire and its Commonwealth last for a thousand years, men will say: "this was their finest hour".'

Winston Churchill, 18 June 1940

Spitfire K for King stands waiting. The narrow legs of its undercarriage give it an almost delicate appearance. It has the air of a thoroughbred horse watching the approach of a new and unknown rider and wondering just how far to try it on and generally be bloody minded.

I sense this as I walk steadily towards her and whilst doing so I am quite unable to analyse my feelings. How strange; after all, this should be the biggest day so far in my short flying career. It is the day I've been waiting for, the day I have worked for and the day for which Mr Hayne and Eddy Lewis exercised so much patience and understanding when transforming me from a schoolboy into an RAF pilot and, possibly, a man; will have to wait and see on that score.

To fly a Spitfire, the latest step to becoming a fighter pilot. Think of the hundreds of pilots all over the service who would give their right arms to have this opportunity; to be a Spitfire pilot.

There it stands, getting nearer the whole time. Only 170 hours, or just less, and here I am confronted by this lithe creature. No mistakes in this aircraft. There is only one seat for a kick-off and no room for your Eddy Lewises. Just got to get it right first time, Geoff old boy, and that's all there is to it.

My parachute feels heavy slung over my shoulder and my helmet is tight across my forehead. The as yet unsecured oxygen mask flaps annoyingly in rhythm with my steps. Standing beside their Spitfire, the two ground crew watch my approach. I imagine their conversation with each other:

'Another bleedin' sprog. We always seem to get them on our kite just because she's a bit old; wonder if we'll get her back in one piece? 'Bout time some other crew 'ad a basinful. Ah well, two six.'*

I arrive on the scene and put on my parachute. Without a word the two airmen help to strap me into the cockpit. The small door is shut and I am left to my own devices, no getting away from it, totally on my own.

Take my time doing the cockpit checks and try to remember what I've been told. This aircraft has an undercarriage that has to be pumped up and down manually. Carrying on through the engine-starting procedures, I find myself not a little surprised for some odd reason when the Merlin roars into life at the first touch of the button, sending back clouds of smoke and a stab of flame from the exhausts as it does so. The whole cockpit area is enveloped but, as the engine settles down to run evenly, it clears quickly. All a bit intimidating.

The aircraft has become alive with feeling. It is transformed and seems to have a certain impatience to get on with the job and get into the air, its natural element.

---

* Military slang for 'all together now', sometimes followed by '*heave*'; for example, ground crew might use the expression when pushing an aeroplane in unison.

As I start to taxi, I remember snippets of advice: view is bad on the ground so when taxiing swing the nose from side to side so you can see what's ahead; don't take too long taxiing as these things overheat if you run them too long on the ground; use the brakes very carefully, if you don't they'll tip up on to their nose as soon as look at you; they are bloody nose-heavy on the ground. Then of course, there was the warning, the CO's parting shot, the one and only time I spoke to him: 'If you break one there will be merry hell to pay.'

We reach the far end of the aerodrome and stop crosswind. For the third time I do my checks. My God, this is an incredible piece of machinery to be in charge of. The glycol temperature is up to 105 degrees and that is just a shade on the high side. I'd better get cracking. There's no excuse for waiting around here any longer.

With the narrow undercarriage in mind, I make sure I am exactly into wind and, almost with a feeling of resignation, I let off the brakes and slowly open the throttle. The power comes on in a huge surge, deep and smooth. There is a rich throaty growl from the Merlin as I open up still further, purely out of habit. The acceleration is something I have never experienced before and the port wing has dipped down with the terrific torque. Direction is held quite easily on the rudder and with a touch of aileron. We seem to be charging over the ground and I am still opening the throttle when the Spitfire hurls itself into the air, dragging me along with it. I feel I am hanging on to the stick and throttle in order not to be left behind. In truth, I don't know where the hell I am and there is no doubt whatsoever that the aircraft is flying me and not the other way round.

It seems to be behaving pretty well though, all things considered. Height is gained very rapidly and gathering my wits I decide it would be a splendid thing if I could do something about raising the undercarriage. Change hands on the stick. As soon as I take my hand off the throttle it starts to close all by itself. I make a frantic grab back again. I haven't tightened the friction nut enough, sod it! It was OK for a Harvard but not one of these things.

Bloody hell, this is becoming ridiculous. This wretched aircraft seems to be laughing at me as if it's having me on a right old goose chase. Can't have that, it's about time I took charge! For a start, continue to climb and don't be in too much of a hurry to raise the wheels. These elevators are light, very light in fact. We are racing up into the sky. Now, Geoff, throttle back a bit and coarsen the pitch, no constant speed as in the Harvard, which is a bit backward. Things quieten down. That's better. I begin to feel I'm just beginning to catch up with this aeroplane. I change hands on the stick again and start to pump the wheels up. Another snag! As my right hand pumps, so does my left, which is on the stick, in sympathy. The outcome of all this is that we end up careering into the wide blue yonder giving a splendid imitation of a kangaroo. This damn aeroplane is still laughing at me. Well, mate, it will be my turn soon. Levelling off, we settle down and things begin to sort themselves out. Possibly I'm just beginning to get the feel of this beast. It's about time we turned back towards the vicinity of the airfield and almost before I realize it my thoughts have been transmitted to my hands and feet and we are turning, a slow easy turn, the long nose appearing to sweep round the horizon in front of me.

The Spit is beginning to feel a friendly aeroplane. The cockpit is snug and has a homely feeling. There is a sensation of being part and parcel of the aircraft, as one. This is turning out to be a magnificent machine.

Elation! We sweep effortlessly about the sky, upwards between two towering masses of cumulus cloud and through a hole like the mouth of a cave beyond which lies a valley leading into clear sky. We climb up to the very tops of the clouds which stretch away on all sides and I revel in the sheer beauty of the scene around me. Indeed, the very shape of the Spitfire wing is a thing of grace and form. I marvel at its ability to keep the machine in the air. Curved leading and trailing edges, not a straight line anywhere, it's beautiful.

Looking out of the tiny cockpit as we flow about the cloud-dappled sky I experience an exhilaration that I cannot recall ever having felt before. It's like one of those wonderful dreams, a *Peter Pan* sort of dream. The whole thing feels unreal and I just can't believe this is really happening. I must be getting light headed! What a pity, in a way, that an aeroplane that can impart such a glorious feeling of sheer joy and beauty has got to be used to fight somebody. Maybe that somebody even now is doing some practice flying in his Junkers or whatever, over on his side of the Channel.

I am brought to my senses by spotting Cambridge some considerable distance away. Must think about getting back. You go a long way in a short time in this aeroplane. Have to think about getting this thing back on the ground, Geoff my lad. As I turn in the direction of base I let the nose drop to get rid of surplus height. The speed builds up so quickly it is unbelievable. A glance at the airspeed indicator shows the needle at almost 400 mph and I wasn't even aware of trying. This is an incredible aircraft and a terrific experience, now to think about the question of landing. A very important part of the sortie, this bit.

To begin with, things go fairly well. After the Harvard the Spit seems to take a long time to lose speed. I find myself tense with concentration and I try to relax a little; after all, what is so special about landing a single-seater fighter? Make believe Eddy Lewis is there in the back somewhere or other.

Throttle back a fair chunk and fine pitch. Speed reduces to just below 180 mph, select wheels down and pump. A bright green light shows up clearly on the instrument panel with the

word 'Down'. Wheels down and locked. Checking on my
position I notice that I am possibly rather a long way downwind. Never mind, don't suppose that will matter too much,
anyway. Turn in now on to the final approach: 140 mph and
flaps down. Yes, I'm undershooting, a bit more power needed.
The nose comes up as I apply throttle. We are moving very
fast, or what seems to be very fast, in a tail down attitude.
Can't see ahead, this bloody great nose is in the way. That's
the hedge underneath, at least I think and hope it is, speed just
over 80 mph, shade fast, maybe?

'If you break one there will be merry hell to pay.'

Lots of grass flashing by underneath and getting closer every
second. The aircraft sinking steadily towards the ground that
I sincerely hope is the airfield. If only I could see ahead.
Aircraft still sinking but absolutely stable. Christ, stick back a
bit, cut the throttle for Pete's sake! It's all happening very
quickly indeed. The nose seems awfully high. I suppose I'm
in charge of this bloody thing. Hold it and we arrive firmly
on the ground, firm but not the sign of a bounce. Throttle
right off, keep her straight, now easy on the brakes, remember
what you were told. We bump across the uneven turf and
finally roll to a stop. I find myself looking out of the cockpit
down past the trailing edge at the ground. Yes, I've arrived,
no doubt about it, a Spitfire has landed at Duxford with me
inside it.

Didn't know an awful lot about that one and I feel that
perhaps the aeroplane had the last laugh. She was flying me
during that landing almost as much as during the take-off.
However, I mastered her in the air so perhaps honours are
about even and, in any case, I shall win in the end.

Looking at my watch I am astonished to find that I have
been out for over an hour, longer in fact than the period for
which I was authorized. I'd better taxi in and pack up. Take
stock of the lessons learned. One or two things need ironing

out, but not too bad for a start. At least I didn't break the thing.

Flaps up, radiator shutter open and I taxi slowly in to the waiting ground crew. Don't know their names yet but they are smiling. I've brought their precious aeroplane back in one piece.

'All OK, sir?'

'Yes thanks, absolutely wonderful.'

The ice having been broken, I find myself kept very busy during the next few days and totally happy. Never would I have believed that a man-made machine, in this case the Vickers Supermarine Spitfire, could have such an effect on any human being. I find myself thinking of little else. In the Mess I ask questions and this is frowned upon. My fellow pilots, now battle experienced except for Trevor, do not talk shop when off duty in the Mess. I retain, therefore, this feeling that I am not really accepted at the moment. It must be that I am young and, as yet, still immature. This is a plain fact that I have to accept and live with for the present. It's only a question of time. Let them get on with it if that's the way they want it.

I devote myself to flying whenever I can scrounge a Spitfire. My new Flight Commander, Brian Kingcombe, is helpful and I think finds me rather amusing. He has a personality that attracts me, is tall and his face is ugly; a very pleasant type of ugliness, however. Women adore him. A dry sense of humour and a prodigious capacity for pints of beer. He is a product of Cranwell and, therefore, the holder of a permanent commission. Always cool and confident, he never seems to get excited or in any sort of flap. As a fighter pilot he is first class. A lot older than myself, I find that I tend to copy him and always go to him with my many problems rather than anybody else.

I fly all I can to learn quickly. At least two trips a day, general practice flying, battle climbs, practice dogfights (about which I have a hell of a lot to learn), cross-country, aerobatics and endless formation flights. Slowly I become more proficient and I get to love the Spit as my flying hours mount and I come to know the feel of this truly superb aeroplane.

The new CO, Sandy Sanders, finally arrives and there is a danger that Wimpey and I are to be posted to another squadron that is just forming and, therefore, non-operational. I get more than a little brassed off after my endeavours so I talk to Brian about it. He, it would appear, talks to the CO. The CO in turn talks to Group and I don't know what happens after that and I don't care all that much. Wimpey and I stay with 92 Squadron. We hear no more of the threat of the sack.

Things move quickly. From Duxford the squadron is moved to Pembrey in South Wales. The flight down is exciting, a new experience. It is the first time that I have been part of a squadron formation. Twelve aircraft all thundering along as if locked together over the fresh green countryside of an English spring. What a sight! The colour, the different shades of green of fields and woods, the bright roundels on the Spitfires; this is something very close to my idea of beauty. No doubt I would incur the derision of the self-styled intellectuals and pacifists, but I bet they have never felt as totally happy and wonderful as I do at this moment. This is what being a fighter pilot is all about.

The airfield at Pembrey is a mile or so from the sea and a long deserted beach. It is magnificent with the sand hard and firm. We take our cars on to it and use them as changing rooms and swim in the calm green water. The weather is glorious day after day. The sun is hot and, except for the fact that one flight or the other has to be on readiness from dawn till dusk, you just wouldn't really know there's a war on.

Those first few weeks here have left lasting impressions. I

see our marquee at dispersal. Those who are at readiness at first light spend the night there. Visions of grey dawns and dewy grass. Sleepy tousle-headed pilots carting their parachutes to the waiting aircraft and the dark brooding hills of Wales in the not too far distance, the tops possibly tipped with light from the early rising sun. I hear the staccato crackle of Merlins being warmed up and tested in the half light and then comes the waiting. Waiting, so much time is spent just sitting around. At first I find it exhilarating, the anticipation of a possible scramble and interception, but that very soon wears off and I become resigned to just waiting, hearing the telephone orderly's report to Ops, '"A" Flight now at readiness', with little emotion.

Summer advances and daily sections are sent off to chase isolated plots★ which appear off the south-west coast but they are invariably at great altitude and we don't get up to them in time. Sometimes a success. Tony Bartley, Gussie Edwards and Sergeant Fokes shoot down a Heinkel 111 near Bristol and one evening the CO and I chase what we are told is a Junkers 88 as far as Weymouth but there is low stratus over the sea. We see an aircraft skimming along the top of the cloud and we give chase. He sees us in good time and drops down into the clouds and that's the last we manage to see of him. Each day far and wide do we chase after the odd Hun but a great deal of effort is required for little success.

The squadron is to start night flying. The idea is to protect Bristol and to catch the Hun on his way to and from places such as Liverpool and the West Midlands. I have not flown a Spit at night, of course, and neither has Wimpey. We both must become night operational as soon as possible.

Dusk landings are the first order of the day. Blinkers are

★ The movements of enemy aircraft were plotted on a large board or table in the Operations Room. Such aircraft were referred to as 'plots'.

fitted to the Spitfires, strips of metal fixed to the cowlings just forward of the cockpit to blank out the very bright flames that come from the exhausts and which will be virtually blinding in the dark. The big snag is that blinkers considerably restrict the already limited view from the Spitfire cockpit when landing. It's very noticeable in daylight as I come to find out during dusk landings, so in the dark one will have to be on the top line.

The dusk landings go pretty well, all things considered, and indeed my final landing was in almost total darkness. That was last night, tonight is the real test. I'm due to take off at 21.00 hours for one and a half hours during which I must do at least three landings.

At teatime I check up on the weather prospects as there seems to be rather a lot of cloud with visibility no more than fair. The Met bloke says that the weather is expected to remain very much as at present but that the visibility may pick up a little when it gets dark. There is no moon so that means it's going to be pitch black.

Later, taxiing out to the take-off point I am not as relaxed as I was last night. It is Kidlington all over again, no wind and total darkness; the Met man was right. For some reason I feel tired and generally lethargic but I expect it will pass off once I am in the air. Opposite the Chance Light I line up carefully with the line of glim lamps.* The green on the Aldis and without wasting any more time open the throttle and away down the flare path into the night sky.

Immediately, shades of Kidlington. A black void, no horizon and so straight on to the instruments and a steady climb ahead up to 1,500 feet. Levelling off and turning to port I am just able to pick out the glim lamps showing me where my

---

* Portable lamps marking the flare path, dimmed so as to be invisible above 1,500 feet.

friends are and the aerodrome is located. Yes it's dark all right, think I'd better have a quiet fly around for a little while. Still feel on edge about something. Probably just plain scared. I'm not finding things easy for some reason so a few minutes of local flying may help to settle things down a bit. Throttle well back, reduce the revs and trim her out to assume a comfortable cruise. The glow from the exhausts, helped by blinkers, is acceptable at these engine settings.

After ten minutes or so things feel a little better. Except for the flare path there is nothing else I can see. A line of glims is not very bright in the best of circumstances and there is not the faintest suggestion of a horizon, no use worrying about it, there's nothing I or anybody else can do about it so perhaps I'd better try a landing.

My first effort is a wretched exhibition. On the final approach I completely lose sight of the line of flares. There is a moment of bewilderment. Those bloody lights were there a few moments ago, so better open up and go round again. Come on Geoff, look lively, don't waste any more time or you'll be into the deck. I open the throttle wide, wheels up, flaps up, not too much of a hurry and away up to 1,500 feet again.

Well, what on earth happened there? Surely they wouldn't switch those lights off? I suppose they might have done it if there was a Hun about but, even then, not with a chap on the last stages of his final approach. Impossible anyway, glim lamps have individual switches. They are not connected to any main switch as far as I'm aware. In any case, there are the lights off to port now so let's have another go and take it easily and quietly.

Exactly the same thing happens again and as I overshoot and climb away for the second time I realize that I'm doing something radically wrong. That time on the overshoot I caught a quick glimpse of the flares and I seemed to be crossing them at a good 30 degrees to the line. No Eddy Lewis to assist this time. My night flying during training was good and it was OK last night, so why not tonight? For goodness' sake, think.

For the life of me I can't work it out, can't seem to apply my mind to the problem. The urge to just sit here and make believe the whole thing is not really happening and to quietly run out of petrol and crash is overwhelming. When I force myself to snap out of it I merely get the sensation of having my hands very full of aeroplane. It's a horrible feeling.

A bloody fine pilot you are, I don't think.

Well, I can't stay up here all night so let's try again. Help me God, please don't let me do a Laurie. I'm a bit frightened and lonely up here in the dark. I start my third attempt to land. As I turn crosswind, keeping my eyes on the flare path, the blackness seems to close in around me. I know in my own mind that I haven't solved the problem. I'm not certain what it is exactly that I'm doing wrong. However, turning in on to finals I manage to line up nicely on the line of flares. This one looks better altogether, much better. A quick glance at the instruments to check my speed. I'm a shade too slow and perhaps a little short of height, nothing much but just a fraction. Correct, Geoff laddie, a touch of throttle and keep your line on those flares for Christ's sake.

Look out of the cockpit for the final effort and the friendly line of flares has vanished. Oh, God, no; please! This is bloody impossible.

There is absolutely nothing to see but a jet black void, and I mean black. Sod it! It just cannot be. Those bloody lights were there a couple of seconds ago. Think, Geoff, quickly for God's sake. I feel a sweat break out and experience fear, stark unblemished fear. I am incapable of movement or thought, things must take their course. A voice of reason in my mind; for God's sake, Geoff, for God's sake, there's going to be a crash. You are about to die. So this is what it's like. One is composed and reconciled. I picture what will happen when I hit the ground. A blinding flash and a noise of tearing and tortured metal. Glare, a white light, very bright and a mass of sparks from the exhaust. Never seen so many before. Perhaps I've throttled back or, more likely, I'm on fire and going to burn. Oh, Dad! What a waste of money on my education. Poor Mum, she will be heartbroken. What a fool of a son they've got. I just don't understand anything any more, just don't know what is happening except that I'm in the process of crashing and dying. Come on then, God, get it over with or I'll go over to the other side, you see if I don't. Ask the Devil. What was it the man said, 'If you break one there will be merry hell to pay'?

Presumably instinctive reactions. Opposite rudder and stick back into my tummy. I sit waiting for it. No longer frightened strangely enough; just totally resigned. I'm amazed it hasn't happened yet. It's terribly dark, only a sort of rushing sound, almost soothing and I close my eyes. A heavy thud; something's touched. I wonder what? Come on, why delay it any longer?

Listen, God, you're not only difficult to find but you're also a hard task master. All is now so quiet, it's peaceful. Another fearful thump followed by a bump and a strange sensation of what appears to be the rumble of wheels over rough ground. I just do not understand it, or is it that I'm dead? That probably is the answer. Yes, that's it because we seem to be stationary and it's so quiet. We've stopped, I'm sure we have. Am I alive or is this death? I think I'm alive and that's all that matters, but it's very very still and quiet. Perhaps I've bought it after all; then again, perhaps not. It's all so confusing. The red cockpit lights still glow and the cockpit itself is almost cosy. Induces a drowsy feeling, but why is it so quiet? I don't think the engine is running, which is odd. Of course it's not odd, you stupid bastard, if you've crashed. But if we are sitting on the ground in a more or less normal attitude, then surely it should be running? It all happened so quickly, whatever is going on.

It would appear that the ignition switches are off. That would be the reason for the engine being stopped and the stillness. I must have switched the magneto switches off somewhere along the line but I don't remember doing it. Must have acted pretty quickly. I just sit strapped to my seat. It's quite comfortable and peaceful. I wonder what has happened. What really occurred?

Well, I suppose I'd better make a move and see if I can get out of this thing and then that would prove once and for all if I really am alive or not. I can't open the door. I must be dead. Someone is standing on the wing beside the cockpit. The red cockpit lights reflect on his face. He's ghostly; ah! that's it, the Holy Ghost or a ghost of some sort. Or is it Brian? The figure looks at me for a few seconds.

'What the bloody hell do you think you're up to? What are you doing? Come on. Don't just sit there.'

'I don't know and please don't rush me.'

'Look, Geoffrey, come on. Get out of this aeroplane. Come on. Make a move, we can't stay out here all night. Here, I'll give you a hand.'

'OK.'

'What the blazes went wrong with you? You hit the Chance Light one hell of a crack.'

'Oh, is that what I did?'

'I'll say and, furthermore, you've not only written off the Chance Light but at least a quarter of your port wing is stuck on what was the top of it. By God, Wellum, you were lucky. I've never seen a prang like it, how bloody lucky can you get? You should have been killed.'

'Yes, I must have been very lucky indeed.'

'Let's go and see the CO. He's very very cross indeed, Geoffrey, to put it mildly, and so am I. I made the mistake in assuming you were at last getting some idea of how to fly a Spitfire. The CO tells me I'm wrong and I bloody well agree with him; he's dead right.'

'It seems that I've let everybody down. Sorry, Brian, really sorry. What was I doing wrong?'

'Not now, we can talk some other time if you're around and, believe me, there will be plenty of time.'

I've been grounded for an indefinite period. The CO gave me one hell of a dressing down; everybody knows it.

If only I could fade away and die quietly somewhere. It appears I am quite useless to him, my Flight Commander and the whole squadron in general. How can they rely on me and trust me when we're in action? I am not up to the standard of any sort of RAF pilot and least of all a fighter pilot. Certainly I'm not fit to be a member of 92 Squadron. People rely on each other in a fighter squadron; how can I be relied upon to do anything?

I accept it all. I have to. He's probably right but he overdoes it somewhat. Repetition, lots of it, and when he cools down I hope he will realize it. One thing, I'm quite determined to profit by this accident if ever I get another chance. One doesn't get away with that kind of accident twice.

I have a long talk with Brian who has some things of his own he wants to say, but at least he listens. Together we go into the whole affair. A more curved approach for night flying is the answer. I was too long, low and flat, the nose was coming up so that I couldn't see and the end product was that I was ending up at an angle to the flare path and eventually, of course, the Chance Light got in the way. Now that I know the reason and the answer I go quietly away and think long and hard about the problem. I work out in my own mind just how I will go about things next time. I am sure I will be able to fly at night as well as anyone else in spite of what the boss said. Brian was right. I was very lucky indeed. One thing I know for certain, no matter which outfit I fly with or where I fly, I shall never make the same mistake again.

The days pass. I feel horrible disgrace in being grounded. Nothing is said by the rest of the squadron and Wimpey is far too nonchalant. Actually, I don't see too much of them or him. Permanent Orderly Officer, which incidentally is against King's regulations, and OC night flying when there is any. I wonder what the ground crews are saying? Everybody must know. Life becomes utterly miserable.

One day hostile plots appear all over the board and the squadron is busy and constantly on the go from first light onwards. I am not asked to help out. By about teatime everybody is exhausted but elated. They have shot down four between them during the course of the day and still more hostiles appear. I decide to take the bull by the horns and plead with the CO to let me fly. Would he revoke my grounding, in view of the circumstances, for just one scramble? After all, it will be dark in an hour or so.

He turns me down flat. No discussions, no arguments. He's busy and I'm just not worth worrying about. Feeling hopelessly lost and in a very low state generally, I walk across the airfield towards the hangar where my crashed Spitfire is being repaired. Sod the bloody lot at dispersal and sod the whole bloody air force in general. I'll resign my commission in the morning.

Inside the hangar my aeroplane looks out of place up on its trestles. It is totally out of its element. The remains of the old wing are propped against the wall and the new one, as yet still in its primer, is waiting to be fitted. What a mess I made of that little lot! The place is deserted but as I turn to leave a middle-aged grey-haired flight sergeant comes into the hangar. A typical flight sergeant of the old school, backbone of the service, salt of the earth, utterly reliable.

'I'm sorry about this lot, Flight. It seems I've caused everybody a great deal of bother.'

'Oh, I wouldn't say that, sir, I've had worse in my time, much worse. With any luck we could have her out in a couple of days if we don't come up against any snags.'

He smiles at me, a deep sincere smile.

'I've sent the lads to tea. We'll get another two hours or so on her tonight.' He laughs. 'You didn't half clout that light, you know; can't wonder at the damage, really. Anyway, it makes a change, the lads are quite enjoying it.'

'Glad to hear it. I wish I was.'

We both laugh but mine is not really genuine and this wise old bird knows it.

'Don't you go worrying too much, sir. I've seen this sort of thing happen to young pilots time and time again. Stiff upper lip as they say, sir, at least you're still here to become an old pilot!'

'Yes, that would be nice.'

It is ten days since I was grounded.

I taxi the aeroplane that I broke to the far side of the airfield, turn her into the wind, check that all is well in the cockpit and open the throttle. Once again that exciting surge and the Spit accelerates over the ground with an urgency as if it can't wait to get back into the air and its natural element again after its enforced stay in the hangar. In next to no time we are off the ground and climbing away into the late-afternoon sky.

Just to feel the aeroplane under me and experience again the instant response to my very thoughts acts as a tonic. Hope this means that I'm being given another chance. Flight sergeant seemed to think so and he should know. Grinning all over his face he was.

'There we are, sir, all ready for you. I hope you find we've done a good job on her.'

'I'm sure you have, Flight.'

They have indeed. She's flying a little right-wing heavy but nothing to worry about and certainly nothing to make me land back yet awhile.

It's been an altogether better day for me. Brian came up to me at lunchtime; 'Your prang is out of the hangar sometime this afternoon so, as soon as she is ready, you can give her an air test. I don't know what time exactly, you'll just have to hang around.'

'Right, Brian, thank you.' But he was already on his way to catch the transport, he was on readiness.

Airborne again and, what's more, I'm going to make the most of it. At 10,000 feet I level off and turn due west. St Govan's Head and Milford Haven are just off to starboard, the sun is lowering in the sky and there is a little haze which gives a copper colour to the sea which, from this height, looks like molten metal. We fly on towards the west with nothing but the sea and the setting sun ahead. Isolated and alone with this little aeroplane. It is just glorious. If only one could fly on like this for ever. With something like reluctance I turn through 180 degrees back on to east and head in the direction of base.

Over Pembrey again with the Gower Peninsula looking beautiful as it stretches away to the right, I feel aloof and comfortable. I am detached from my fellow man. I don't want to land where all those nasty rude people are, I want to be up here alone for a little longer.

Dropping down to 4,000 feet it seems to me a good idea to do a few aerobatics just to round things off and prove to myself that I haven't lost anything by being on the ground for so long. To hell with all COs. Didn't they ever have a prang? A slow roll to start with. It's a good one, a very good one in fact, so I do two more, one straight after the other. They aren't too bad, either. Well, they said they wanted an air test, didn't they? Right then, an air test they'll get and a jolly thorough one at that. Let's do a roll off the top. The Spitfire responds as only a Spit can. I'm enjoying this. What about trying two upward rolls, one straight after the other? All you want is plenty of speed. I have a go and they work out just fine. You lot down there can get knotted.

Suppose I should think about getting back on the ground. It's getting rather late and I shall be in trouble again. Come what may, that was a good half an hour or so, over three-quarters actually. That's a reprimand, so what? I really enjoyed that trip. Close the throttle, roll over on to my back and pull through into a half roll. Slow down and rejoin the circuit. Right Geoff, now put your thoughts into practice. Do a night circuit and prove to yourself exactly where you went wrong. A trickle of motor and a steady curved approach, slip off a fraction of excess height now across the hedge, throttle fully closed, check her, stick back and a rumble of the main wheels and tail wheel tells of a good and safe three-point landing.

I taxi in feeling a lot better. That was a good and thoroughly beneficial sortie. As I switch off, the flight sergeant is waiting for me together with Davy and Bevington, the normal ground crew. It looks as if I'll be flying their aeroplane more and more, even if I do break it for them now and again. Suits me, nice people and they know their job.

'All OK, sir?'

'Fine, Flight. She's just a shade right-wing low but apart from that, first class. A nice aeroplane.'

'Right, lads, let's button it up then and we'll fix the trim in the morning. OK, sir, the Flight Commander is waiting for you over by the tent and says would you nip along, like?'

'Sure.' Now what the hell have I done? Well, I honestly don't know and I don't care all that much. He can get rid of me if he wants to. Some squadron somewhere will make use of me. I now know, even if the CO doesn't, that I'm capable of flying a Spitfire and when I get more experience like some of the others, better than a lot of them. Confidence in myself is restored.

Brian is standing by the CO's little service Hillman car. The CO is with him and it is he who speaks.

'You're late down, Wellum. You were only supposed to do an air test and that shouldn't take you almost an hour. What kept you?'

'Nothing kept me, sir, it's merely that I didn't want to come down once I was airborne. I just didn't realize the time.'

I look at him steadily. He can do what he bloody well likes. In any case, no pilot worth his salt would wish to continue with any squadron, no matter how good it was, under these present circumstances. There is a distinct pause.

'Fair enough. Well, we've been released and it so happens that the squadron has been invited to the Golf Club's annual dinner-dance. They appear to be concerned because they have too many popsies and not enough blokes; menfolk away at the war or something.'

'Let's hope the ladies are grateful when you get there, sir.'

'Shut up. By taking your time and being late down you have not only kept your Flight Commander and Commanding Officer waiting but, unless we are very careful, valuable drinking time will be lost. And finally, whilst we're together, Geoffrey, don't be a bloody fool all your life. I want no repetition of what happened the other night, so don't you ever do anything like that again, not ever. People get hurt flying into Chance Lights and it's just not allowed, so no more accidents. Understand?'

'Understood, sir.'

'Those aerobatics were pretty good, by the way.'

'I feel a lot better now, sir.'

'Yes, I'm sure you do. Now, let's get off to this party.'

'I'm sure the spare popsies will be grateful.'

'For what?'

'Presumably, anything, sir, no matter how small.'

He grins. A feeling of such relief and peace comes over me. I feel as if I'm once again back with the squadron. I've learned a lesson and a half, by God I have. Anyway, it's now behind me. I open the door of the car and scramble in. As I do so, the flight sergeant hurries past, as much as he could ever hurry that is, quietly humming.

Night flying again and, as I climb up into the blackness after my first landing, I feel totally in control of the situation. My first approach and landing was at least safe and the approach itself was just right. The second was even better. I am just thinking of levelling out for the third circuit when my earphones crackle and a voice says: 'Bamber Blue 2, this is Peanut, are you receiving me?'

There is no reply, and then the voice again. 'Bamber Blue 2, this is Peanut, do you receive?'

Why doesn't the stupid fellow answer? Who on earth is Blue 2? I didn't think anybody else was airborne at the moment. Blue 2? Hold on for Pete's sake, Blue 2, blimey, that's my call sign, that's me. Come on, Geoff, get your finger out and answer the man.

'Peanut, Bamber Blue 2 loud and clear.'

'OK, Blue 2, we have bandits over Ashley Sector, vector 120 and increase to angels twenty.'

'Peanut, Bamber Blue 2 received and understood.'

Let's see, Ashley, that's the code name for Bristol. I turn on to 120 degrees and continue the climb. All thoughts of circuits and landings are behind me. This is operational.

A thin layer of cloud. We are through it in about 500 feet and now with a sense of urgency I keep the Spitfire climbing hard. I find myself concentrating on the instruments yet at the same time I feel relaxed. That shouldn't be so strange. That's how it is supposed to be.

'Blue 2, this is Peanut, angels please?'

'Blue 2, passing through ten.'

'Blue 2, continue, there are friendly aircraft in the area.'

'Blue 2, understood.'

I can't see an awful lot as we climb higher. Above the clouds the stars stand out clear and their light allows just the faintest of horizons. Anything, no matter how faint, is an asset. The glow from the exhausts of a Merlin on full song makes seeing difficult, to say the least. I regulate the oxygen to 25,000 feet. There are a few searchlights ahead and slightly off to starboard. That must be Bristol. Almost there and 20,000 feet is just coming up on the altimeter.

'Peanut, this is Bamber Blue 2 levelling off at angels twenty.'

'Thank you, Blue 2, well done. Some bandits proceeding north and a customer for you. Vector 020 and buster.'

'Blue 2, received and understood.'

'Blue 2, your bandit two miles ahead of you, slightly above and closing from the starboard.'

Instructions keep coming from the controller. I do my level best to fly accurately the course he passes to me. I know that inwardly I'm a little keyed up and excited. All this is new. I'm not quite certain what to expect next. The thought that the chances of seeing my quarry on a dark night from an aircraft like a Spitfire are not very good just doesn't come into my reckoning. Somewhere out there in that black void are Germans in a black-crossed aeroplane, the controller says so, and I peer outside into the blackness trying to get a visual with something approaching desperation. The Hun turns back towards Bristol from the north. The controller directs me and I follow. He tells me that my bandit is only just ahead of me and he asks if I have any contact and I have to say not at the moment. If only I could catch a glimpse of his exhaust flame.

Ahead, pinpoints of light flash momentarily in the darkness and then are gone; ack-ack. In fact I now wake up to the fact that the flashes are all round me. Either they are firing at me or I must be bloody close to that Hun. In the middle of some of the bursts I can see an angry redness. They must be a mite close. A couple of searchlights seem to wave rather aimlessly about the sky and the barrage becomes quite intensive, at least, intensive enough for me.

Looking down I can see a fire of some sort, obviously made by bombs. Even as I watch, a line of flashes shows up on the ground. More bombs, the bastards. I feel so helpless, I'm trying but there's nothing I can do about it except find the sod and I can't see enough to do that. I bet those bombs came from the Hun that I'm chasing, must be very close to him. Keep looking, Geoff, he's not all that far away, but, search as I might, I can't pick him up. I'm just suspended in space. The noise of the Merlin and glow of the exhausts from behind the blinkers are the only things that seem real. If anything, it seems to be getting blacker outside and I find myself having to refer to the instruments more frequently. Perhaps I'm getting a little tired.

I check my watch. Is this a sign that subconsciously I have given up the unequal task of finding my Hun? I have been out now for over an hour and a fuel check shows that things are getting a trifle on the low side. Those circuits and landings at the start must have used a fair bit. Mustn't forget to keep an eye on that.

Bristol is by now quite a way astern and the war seems to be a lot quieter. Excitement and tension start to wear off and in their place a sense of futility in wandering aimlessly around in this black arena of a night sky at 20,000 feet looking for a needle in a haystack, and a needle that's the same colour as the bloody hay what's more. Let's give Peanut a call, it's getting lonely up here on my tod. Think of the bar in the Mess with people having their half tankards of ale. Seems a decent sort of place right now. Not far off closing time, though.

'Peanut, this is Bamber Blue 2, are you receiving me?'

'Blue 2, faint but clear. I have been calling you.'

Christ, I hadn't heard him. Must have been far too pre-occupied. That's not very good, really. Will have to think about that one. He's very faint indeed. Probably why I didn't hear. He sounds anxious. Must be at extreme range.

'Peanut, this is Blue 2, have you any instructions? I think I am well to the south of Ashley.'

'No, Blue 2. The bandits are well to the south of you and going off home. Vector 300 for base.'

'Understood, Peanut, turning on to 300.'

'OK, Blue 2, hold on to your height for the present. You are almost off the board at extreme range. What is your fuel state?'

This chap is concerned, I can tell by his voice. Check on the gauge. Hell, we're down to no more than twenty-five gallons at the very most.

'Peanut, this is Blue 2. I'm down to about twenty-five gallons maximum.'

'Blue 2, this is Peanut, understood, maintain present heading and height. You are coming in nicely.'

His signals are beginning to get stronger again. However, there is no doubt he's concerned and I feel a little anxious myself. During the next few minutes he keeps calling and passing me courses to steer all within a couple of degrees or so. I seem to be plodding on almost indefinitely. This might get dodgy and I apply boost and rev settings to fly for range.

'Blue 2, this is Peanut. You're coming along well. Reduce to angels five.'

Great, this will save a bit. I acknowledge, throttle back and allow the nose to drop and quietly almost sink down into the blackness towards home. The feeling of loneliness is now very real. The sky is so big and my aeroplane is so small. There is solid ground and some fairly high hills somewhere around as well. I shan't be sorry to get back on the deck again. The cloud appears to have broken a little. We pass through a thin broken layer. It is very dark indeed and I think I'm in the clear below it. The instruments stare back at me. Feel a tiredness suddenly descend over me. Not long to go now, Geoff. Take it easy, son, don't hurry anything and make a balls up like killing yourself. Not done too badly for a start; better than a couple of weeks ago, anyway.

'Blue 2, fifteen miles to go.'

The visibility must have picked up a bit for, on looking up from the instruments, I can just make out a flashing beacon. Let's hope it's base because the fuel situation is getting serious. There won't be much to spare. Must try and read what the beacon is flashing. They must have put it on especially. As we close the distance things become easier. It's flashing 'PB', I'm sure it is. There it is again, distinctly 'PB'. By all that's holy, how wonderful, good old Pembrey. What a jolly good controller. It's a great relief to see base again, even if it is as yet no more than a flashing light on the ground. I call up and tell the controller who, with almost as much relief as I now feel, thanks me and bids me goodnight.

At 1,500 feet I cross the airfield and can just make out the six glim lights. I let gently down into the circuit. Now take it nice and quietly, Geoff, remember you have not got all that amount of fuel left if you make a mess of it and have to go round again.

A thousand feet downwind and the glims stand out clear and friendly. Wheels down, green light, that helps, trim her out and turn for the curved approach, flaps, trim again and ... what about fine pitch, Geoff, you bloody stupid idiot? More concentration, now come on, mate. Not much longer to go now. Just a little bit extra and then it will all be over. A green Aldis, clear to land. Stick around God, there's a good chap.

Not too bad, this approach is OK. Keep it going, round we come, now don't overcook it, that's pretty good, straighten out, nearly there. The red light on top of the new Chance Light flashes past. Missed it! Throttle back, hold her off, easy docs it and the first flare goes by. Must have been a shade fast. The aircraft's light, of course, feel for the bloody ground, it must be there somewhere. We touch, a little bounce, steady on the stick, we touch again, the tail drops and we rumble and bump down the line of remaining flares. Roll to a stop. Blimey, that feels good.

Turn and taxi back to dispersal. Pick out the two torches held aloft and waved by Davy for me to follow, guiding me in. Finally he holds them steady. That's it, then, park here. That will do for one night; switch off.

You can cut the silence with a knife. The night air is damp and heavy with dew. The smell is fantastic; it's good to be down. I shall sleep well tonight.

I am sitting outside the dispersal tent on the far side of the airfield writing these notes. It is mid-afternoon and the sun is hot. Only a slight breeze from time to time blows the hair into my eyes. I can hear some bees in a patch of clover not far away. On either side around the edge of the aerodrome the Spitfires wait and brood. It's all very quiet and peaceful.

Brian, Wimpey, Butch, Tony Bartley and Gussie are stretched out in their armchairs, some reading and two playing a game of chess. Wimpey Wade is asleep as is usual. We are at readiness and as always waiting. This is all we seem to do these days. The other flight is at fifteen minutes available for the moment at least.

August 1940 and there is talk of the squadron being transferred up to the London area to replace one of the hard-pressed and tired squadrons who have been facing the might of the Luftwaffe and bearing the brunt of the action right in the front line. I have a strange indefinable inner feeling. Apart from chasing isolated German aircraft all over the South West, I haven't yet been in a big action. The prospect of a move to a part of the country where things are pretty hot from all accounts gives me cause for thought. I've still to prove myself really and I remember the others on my first night with the squadron.

My impressions of the last two months or so revolve around dawns. Pink dawns, grey dawns, misty, rainy and windy dawns, but always dawns; first light. Shadowy Spitfires and quietness in the tent as we doze and wait. I recall that initial quiet anxiety that we may be scrambled and when the order doesn't come, anticlimax.

Throughout the squadron there is a feeling of girding one's loins for a sustained, supreme, almost superhuman effort in the near future. Everything we have been taught, how we react and respond to intense pressure, will be tested to the utmost. Private thoughts are ever with me. Will I have the courage needed? The chips will be down and the battle will be a battle that has just got to be won. A second chance will not exist. There will be only one way to go and that will be forward into the approaching hordes of German aeroplanes. Except for Wimpey and I, the others know the form. They have won their private battles although, of course, they will now have to start again. I've got to start from the beginning. I've got all that to come and only when my own private battle is over and won will I really be able to join ranks with the others and be a true fighter pilot.

The question obsesses me. I lie back on the grass in the warm sun, hands clasped behind my head, and gaze at the sky.

Towards teatime, Mac turns up at dispersal with a new pilot for 'A' Flight and introduces him as Tommy Lund. Later, in the Mess that evening after we have been released, Mac brings him over to me.

'Geoffrey, would you keep an eye on our new arrival and see he gets to know everybody? Tommy, you remember meeting Geoffrey at dispersal this afternoon? He'll look after you. See you both later.'

Tommy I like immediately. Tall, slim and older than myself, he is a flying officer. He is easy to talk to and obviously intelligent. Before joining the RAF he was up at Oxford reading history and he joined the service as soon as he had obtained his degree. He was posted to us from another squadron up north somewhere, so at least he is not as new to the game as Wimpey Wade and I were. I introduce him to Wimpey among others and they get along like a house on fire. It's a most pleasant evening; I'm going to get on well with Tom. He's quite a good-looking bloke in a mature sort of way and when he grins or laughs he looks like Old Nick himself. Good type of chap to have around, calm and unflappable. About ten o'clock he pushes off to his room. It's been a busy day for him and he wants a little peace and quiet.

Not a bad sort of day for myself, really. I'll phone up dear old Pete for a chat. Haven't spoken to him for about a week and he hasn't phoned me. Guess he's been busy in the front line at Tangmere.

The operator puts me through without delay. There is the usual pause but soon it becomes a longer pause than usual and, in due course, much longer. Probably out in a pub somewhere. Then again, maybe not. Premonition; no, not Pete, not quite so soon. My stomach turns itself into a knot. Please no, not old Peter. Don't mess around, God.

A voice comes on the line and says it is the Squadron Adjutant. 'Who's speaking, please?'

'My name's Geoffrey Wellum.'

'Oh, Geoffrey, I've heard a lot about you from Peter. Look old lad, Peter didn't come back from a trip at first light today. I'm terribly sorry.'

'Oh my goodness. I had a feeling when he didn't come to the phone. What happened, do you know?'

'Well, not really for certain, but we are pretty sure that he was clobbered by 109s over the Channel.'

'Any glimmer of hope?'

'Not really, Geoff, I'm afraid. The squadron was chasing some 88s back towards France and we had one hell of a scrap. There were lots of 109s about. Peter, well we are pretty sure it was him, went into the sea on fire. Actually, we lost two and we haven't accounted for either of them and that's about all I can tell you. He was doing so well, he already had a couple. If we do hear anything, I'll personally see to it that you are informed at once.'

'Thanks, I'd like that.'

I put down the phone. I won't hear from them. Peter is dead.

Well, that's that. Pete's gone, but he was on the right side numerically and so has helped to win the war.

Poor, dear Peter. I recall his look as we parted at Paddington. I wonder if he had any premonition? I remember how withdrawn he became for a while at Little Rissington and how even I couldn't get near to him. I think he might well have done. All I pray is that he knew and felt nothing, that his death was quick and clean. 'We'll meet in London if all goes well, Geoff, won't we?' What a waste all this is.

I wonder if God can give me an answer? I doubt it. In any case, I don't suppose I shall even be able to find Him. Why take young lives like Peter's? What is this life on earth all about? Give me a sign God, anything. Why allow wars?

I imagine Pete still strapped in the remains of his Hurricane now resting somewhere on the bottom of the cold grey

Channel. Peter Sears, my very close and dear friend. Why,
God?

Grief is a private matter. Much as I try not to, I can still see
him in his Harvard keeping formation on me as we fly back to
Kidlington after fooling about over the Cotswold countryside.
Swaying gently in the thermals just off my wingtip.

Thoughts of Leicester. Only two left now.

Stay in position, Pete, and see me through this lot, there's
a good mate.

I'm going to write no more about my friend Peter Sears.
He's gone and that's all there is to it.

The squadron has just landed at Biggin Hill.

Here at our new home the fighting is the hardest of anywhere in the skies over England. If any aerodrome is in the
forefront of the battle and right in the front line, it's Biggin.

Situated on a plateau, it is known throughout Fighter Command as 'Biggin on the Bump'. The whole place has an air of
total war and mortal combat. Broken Spitfires and Hurricanes,
hangars in ruins, filled-in bomb craters everywhere and so
much general bomb damage that one is left in no doubt
whatsoever that all is total war. In spite of all this, the fighters
still fly and the station is still fully operational.

No bloody German is going to knock out this place for
long. He's just not bloody good enough.

This must be England at her most endangered, and her most
dangerous. She is alone. Nobody else in the whole world to
help her. Taking tremendous punishment, her back to the
wall but dishing it out too. We can only go forward. Can't go
back any further. Bloody Nazis. Somebody has got to stop
them.

England is being tested and, with her, my own personal
testing time is about to begin. This is the moment for which
I was trained and the moment that has been on my mind

largely since I joined the squadron. I am down on the order of battle for tomorrow morning at first light; readiness at dawn.

So be it. Soon I shall know what the others already know. I shall be either a man or a coward. I'm afraid of being a coward. If the truth were known, most people are, I should think. I suppose cowardice is the most common of all skeletons in the cupboard.

I share a room with a new pilot. His name is John Drummond. He was waiting at Biggin when we arrived, a quiet retiring sort of chap, a bit of an introvert. As we unpack our kit I get to know a little about him, although he doesn't volunteer an awful lot. It appears he was in a Gladiator squadron in Norway and they were, of course, hopelessly outnumbered and virtually decimated. He has a DFC but obviously doesn't want to talk about it so I don't press him. We get on well enough. He's friendly, so the arrangement suits me, not that I'm in a position to object. Hardly know he's around, anyway.

Lying in bed later that evening, I find it quite impossible to sleep. I'm tense and excited, I know it. There's a Hun overhead droning his way towards London, which doesn't help. What a panic it all was, the move from Pembrey. One moment we were at readiness basking in the sun outside the tent and the next we were put back to thirty minutes, told to pack up and get the squadron ready to move by next morning. So we did. We moved and here we are.

Only a few hours of safety before first light and the testing time, a few hours to think about it before the dawn, and so with jumbled thoughts I drop off into an uneasy and restless sleep. I remember before I do to say a prayer and have a short talk with Peter. At least if things go wrong I know he will be waiting for me and then we will both push off in a couple of Harvards on a formation cross-country to God.

'The whole fury and might of the enemy must be turned upon us. Hitler knows that he will have to break us in this island or lose the war.'

Winston Churchill, June 1940

4. First Light

Oh Lord God,
Thou knowest how busy
I am going to be this day.
If I forget Thee,
Do not Thou forget me.

Navy prayer

Something pushing at my shoulder, a faraway persistent voice I have no wish to hear. Some silly ass put a light on. That must surely be classed as inconsiderate. 'Your tea, sir. Just coming up to four o'clock, like you said, sir, and Mr Kingcombe presents his compliments and it looks like another fine day. Due at dispersal at 04.30. Are you awake, sir?'

'Just wrap up, Frimley, for God's sake.'

I force my eyes open and see the face of Frimley, our batman. He pauses, looks at me for a few seconds as if to make certain and, satisfied it seems, he goes quietly from the room.

Oh, God! Another dawn.

I wonder where they get hold of chaps like Frimley. Always seems to be around when he's needed. Is it two or three weeks since we came to Biggin? Every morning I wake to see his ugly bloody mug. Don't know how I'd cope without him, though. I glance across to see if John is awake but, of course, his bed will be empty; collided yesterday with Bill Williams attacking a Dornier. Silly of me. Well, at least I must have slept last night. Haven't been sleeping too well lately; too much excitement.

Still half asleep, I make a supreme effort. Very reluctantly I get out of bed and somehow I find myself at the wash basin. Hot water for a change. Where's my razor? On the floor and how did it get there? I pick it up and have a sip of Frimley's tea. At least it's hot, sweet and wet. I start to shave and so another day begins. Back to reality. Down to earth. A job to be done. I accept it is September 1940.

Wash and dress quickly and wander across to the Mess. How quiet and still it is in this hour before the dawn. Life at low ebb. Nothing moves, no breeze to ruffle the hair or stir the leaves. All is very quiet and peaceful and perhaps a little sinister. Through the mess hall and ante-room, not yet cleared from the night before, there hangs the stale smell of tobacco smoke. Full ashtrays, empty beer tankards and carelessly discarded magazines litter the place. Subdued voices come from the dining room where a drowsy uninterested steward serves tea and toast; he's seen it all before.

With scarcely a nod I sit down. I glance down the table as the teapot is pushed my way. Tommy, Butch, Brian, Tony and one or two others are sitting too far away to bother me at this early hour. One by one we assemble, men with whom I have lived and flown for the past four months; it seems much longer.

There's a little muted conversation but for the most part people are concerned with their own private thoughts. Some are looking at old magazines, the same magazines that they read yesterday and will read again tomorrow. What day is it, anyway? Except for the occasional clink of a cup, all is quiet.

These precious minutes slip by in thought and meditation. What fun that last peacetime holiday was in Cornwall: fishing for bass, surfing, swimming, my father and mother and my first half of bitter in the Ship Inn; sunsets and dinner in the evenings. Wonderful thoughts; not so many months ago. Now look at me. What on earth is it all about?

I sip my tea and toy with a slice of toast. I'm not hungry. I just relish this time for privacy and my thoughts of the past. Is it a form of escape? Am I fearful of the present? The steward appears in the doorway, almost apologetically.

'Gannic Squadron transport outside, sir.'

Brian, who is leading the squadron since the CO was sent away wounded and Bob Tuck was posted to command a Hurricane squadron, gets to his feet, leaving his toast untouched. He looks at us whilst taking a final sip of tea. My goodness, he looks older nowadays and preoccupied, although always cool and quietly spoken, promoting trust. He also has a good R/T voice, which exudes confidence. His DFC denotes the type of man he is; a fine experienced leader. Hope he gets the squadron.

'OK, men, let's go. Any more for the tumbril? Come on, Wimpey, for God's sake! The way you tuck into toast at this time of the morning rather revolts me. Put a spare piece in your bloody pocket if you really must but just get a move on, yes? Tom, Geoffrey, get the skids under you.'

Tommy looks at me and smiles. Wimpey rises with a persecuted expression on his face, takes a piece of toast and, still eating, moves towards the door. Tommy and I rather take our time.

Tom is a close friend by now. Why do some people become closer than others? He is a charming person with a lovely smile; a man I've got to know really well since he joined the squadron. We just seem to get on together, each knowing what the other is thinking without the need for words, and for that reason our friendship has strengthened. We enjoy our pints together at the end of the day. I would miss that chap if anything happened.

'Look, are you two going to condescend to come to the war or must I prevail on the enemy to cancel for the day?'

Brian gives me a shove and pretends to kick me up the backside.

'What a nasty, rude man,' mutters Tom to no one in particular. We join the others in the waiting transport.

'Ah, here we are then. How nice of you both to turn up.'

The vehicle moves off. It's just beginning to get light; just the faintest tinge. There is something unreal and inexorable about the whole procedure.

Arrival at dispersal is for me always a moment. The drive round the perimeter track, masked headlights, the glow of somebody's cigarette and the squeal of brakes as the transport stops at the hut. No turning back now; committed. Here we go again.

I enter the hut and make for the flight board to check the 'Order of Battle'. Good, No. 2 to Brian. That makes me Red 2, suits me fine. I go to my locker and get my flying kit. It only seems ten minutes ago that we packed up for the day.

I remove my tie and open the collar of my shirt (far less sore on the back of the neck when you keep looking round). Now, where's my silk scarf? Don't say it's been lost. I take my parachute from the locker and, of course, my scarf is where I last threw it. I tie it round my neck, pick up my helmet and, slinging the chute over my shoulder, head for the door and the damp fresh early-morning air. Walk steadily towards my Spitfire, which is dispersed about fifty yards away. The sky is clear. In the slowly strengthening light the ghostly figures of the ground crews work methodically on the aircraft, removing covers and plugging in the starter trolleys.

I cut a corner, walk off the perimeter track and over the grass. Moisture collects on my flying boots from last night's heavy dew. It's going to be a lovely day. There is a strange stillness and artificial peace about the place that is almost palpable; an uneasy tranquillity. The airmen going about their tasks cannot really be heard unless you go out of your way to listen. They don't talk much and then only in subdued tones. In the first place, I suppose, it's far too early for leg pulling and animated conversation when even the birds are still silent. Secondly, they have done this curriculum so often that everything is automatic and there's not an awful lot to talk about anyway.

It is first light and still and rather beautiful; the birth of a new day. Reveries are suddenly and rudely broken. A raised voice comes from somewhere in the gloom, curt and to the point.

'OK. Clear? Contact.'

The engagement of a starter pinion and the clank of a reduction gear as in a not far distant dispersal pen an airscrew turns, flicking over. The engine fires twice but does not pick up, as if loath to shatter the serenity of the moment. Then, giving up the unequal task of combating the primer pump and the starter trolley, it explodes into life with a spurt of flame from the exhaust stubs. The peace and quiet is finished, the silence no more, the day has begun and now to business.

One after the other, Spitfires are starting up. The fitters warm up their engines. Twelve Merlins all at 1,200 revs or thereabouts. The power of the moment is awe inspiring. The still morning air reverberates with the sound of harnessed energy. Slipstreams flatten the grass behind the quivering aircraft. In its way it is exciting, wonderful and not without a certain beauty. It is also tragic; which of us is going to be killed this day?

The ground trembles. A peculiar sense of involvement makes me swallow rather hard. This, yet again, is one of those moments that have an intense effect on me, strange and unexplained. I experienced it when I first touched and smelled an aeroplane. At Father's flying club, it was; a Cirrus Moth. I wonder where that aeroplane is at this moment, assuming it hasn't pranged. I became aware of the strength of this inner feeling again when I first joined the service. The Tiger Moths at Desford and that march to the flights that beautiful morning in company with Nick and Peter; it keeps cropping up. Dare one say it's pride? Just as well the others can't read my thoughts, or do they feel it also?

Dispersal pen and my Spitfire. I pause and look at her. A long shapely nose, not exactly arrogant but, nevertheless, daring anyone to take a swing at it. Lines beautifully proportioned, the aircraft sitting there, engine turning easily and smoothly with subdued power. The slipstream blows the moisture over the top of the wings in thin streamlets. Flashes of blue flame from the exhausts are easily seen in the half light, an occasional backfire and the whole aeroplane trembling like a thoroughbred at the start of the Derby.

The engine note increases as my fitter opens up the Merlin to zero boost whilst the rigger stands with his hand on the wingtip, watching expectantly. I think to myself, 'Don't open her up any more, you twit, or the tail will lift and the whole shooting match will end up on its nose.' The engine note changes fractionally as the magnetos are tested. The fitter, intent on his instruments, red cockpit lights reflecting on his face. Sounds OK, no problem there at all. Throttle back, mag check again at 1,500 revs by the sound of it and then throttle right closed, engine idling, smoke from the exhausts, cutout pulled and the engine splutters to a stop. Peace again.

Bevington, the fitter, looks from the cockpit and gives me the thumbs up. He levers himself out on to the wing and jumps to the ground. I walk forward and hang my parachute on the port wing for a quick getaway; you can easily put it on whilst the engine is being started, saves a lot of time.

Now to the cockpit. Up on to the wing and step in. I hang my helmet on the stick and plug in the R/T lead and oxygen tube. At the same time, I check the bottle contents: full. Fuel? Press the fuel gauge button, reads full also. Now brake pressure. OK, that's fine. Trim? Let's adjust it now and then it's done with. Full rudder bias to help with the swing on take-off, elevators one degree nose heavy, that's good. Airscrew, full fine pitch. That's about it, then, ready to scramble when the time comes. Bound to come sometime. It'll be a miracle if we get through to midday without one.

I climb out of the cockpit and my fitter and rigger are waiting, as always. What stalwarts they are, both utterly loyal to 'their' pilot, dedicated and uncomplaining. They are both smiling and friendly.

'Twenty-five drop on both mags, sir. We found that oil leak last night. Nothing to worry about and in any case we reckon we've cured it.'

'Splendid; so we're at readiness, are we?'

'On the top line, sir.'

'Good men, see you both later, no doubt.'

'We'll be here.'

No need to tell them what is expected when the balloon goes up. It occurs to me and not for the first time, as I walk back to the dispersal hut, that the respect and feeling that these ground crews have for their pilots borders on affection. No standing to attention and shouted orders, we all get on together keeping Spitfires flying. To my mind, the atmosphere in a front-line fighter squadron is something approaching unique and certainly gives an inner feeling that will remain with me as long as I survive. I will never forget. I pause at the hut door and look at the ever-brightening sky. Clear as a bell and I go inside.

As I put on my Mae West* the telephone orderly at his blanket-covered table lifts the receiver.

---

* Inflatable life jacket, so called in reference to the then-popular busty American actress of that name.

'Hello, Operations? 92 Squadron now at readiness, sir. Twelve aircraft. That's right, sir. Goodbye.'

I lie down on one of the camp beds and try to relax. Now all we have to do is wait. If I'm lucky I may be able to get a little sleep.

The light outside is getting stronger. Any time from now on things can start to happen and I wonder if the day will be opened by the normal Hun 'weather recce'. A section will be scrambled but won't get near it, of course. It'll be too high, have too much of a start and he won't come in very far anyway, not with the weather this clear. I suppose we are duty bound to have a crack at it and that, of course, will only leave us with ten aircraft for the main interception. The weather is sure to be all right for him to give the OK for his chums to do their lousy bloody work. In the meantime, we must just wait and sweat it out, never an easy thing to do even though we do get a lot of practice.

Waiting. Thoughts race through the mind. Some read. Some sleep, such as Butch Bryson. He's out to the wide; or is he? Could well be after the amount of Scotch he put away last night. I must say I enjoyed that little party a lot. You get a good pint in the White Hart. Pleasant crowd in there as well. Had a letter from a girl called Grace yesterday, sister of a school friend. She seemed interested; shall have to give a bit of thought to her sometime.

I must have nodded off into an uneasy doze. How long, I wonder. I find myself sitting bolt upright. The phone must have rung. Yes, that's it, the bloody phone again. I swear that if ever I own a house I shall never install a telephone, so help me. All heads and eyes are turned towards the telephone orderly, AC2 Webber. He seems to be listening for an agonizingly long time. He turns his head.

'There will be no NAAFI van until later this morning, sir. It's got a flat battery. OK if I tell Chiefy, sir?'

I lie back again and silently curse under my breath. I could blow my top when this sort of thing happens. Unreasonable thoughts: who cares about the bloody NAAFI van, or its perishing battery for that matter? I'm being stupid, of course. They have a job to do like everyone else and they're doing it pretty well what's more. Tell you what, though, I'll change places right now. I'd make a good van driver.

What's the time? 06.15. That recce kite should have shown up by now if it's coming. Been here for two hours odd. This time yesterday, no, the day before it must have been, we were landing from our first sortie; at least, nine of us did. Not poor old John and Bill, though. Must all be a bit strung up with this waiting. Once you are on your way, well, things aren't too bad. However, as we aren't we'll just have to continue waiting and that's all there is to it. Relax, try to relax. I suppose that's the answer. Don't know the meaning of the word. Nevertheless, let's make a real effort. Hard work, relaxing.

Tommy gets up and walks to the door. He opens it quietly, thoughtfully surveys the scene for a moment and goes outside. I get up and go to the window. I see old Tom walking up and down very slowly. Every now and then he kicks at a stone or a piece of paper; sometimes, he stops and looks at the sky.

The phone rings again. The orderly picks it up and listens intently. Tommy has appeared in the doorway. Nobody speaks, everybody watches. The orderly turns to Brian.

'Squadron Leader Igoe, would like a word with you, sir.'

He hands the phone to Brian, who listens to the Ops Controller, his face devoid of expression.

'OK, Bill. Right away. Yes, I expect so. No, I don't. Of course. OK, old boy. Cheers.' He puts the phone down and turns to us.

'Ops say that a plot has appeared over Gris Nez and it looks like our recce chum. Two aircraft at standby. Tony, take

Tommy as your No. 2 and call yourself Black Section. Off you go!'

They go at once and hurry away to their Spitfires. Intent, they do not look back.

'Two at standby, Chiefy.'

'Yes, OK, sir. Everything's under control.'

It would seem that the programme for today is starting to move at last. I stand watching Butch and Wimpey playing a game of chess. How they can do that at this time of the day defeats me. Five minutes and the phone rings again.

'OK, sir, Black Section scramble.'

There are cries of 'Get them off, Chiefy. Start up, start up!'

Two airscrews slowly revolve. Two Merlins splutter, hesitate and then burst into life. They both taxi, turn into wind, open up the throttles and away they go. No messing about, get cracking. Two rudders flicking as the pilots correct for torque and swing and they race away into the distance. Airborne, wheels coming up immediately and the start of the long climb. Not many watch them go, but I do. I like watching aeroplanes, always have done, especially on take-off and landing. Anyway, it's nice to see them off and silently wish them well.

It won't be long now before the rest of us are on our way. I think I'd better go round the back and have a pee. I return. That's better. So the minutes pass by. There's no doubt about it, I'm a bit on edge this morning. That collision yesterday I expect. I just want to get on with it.

I look around the crew room. Only Brian, who is reading and sucking a matchstick, looks relaxed and at ease but, on second thoughts, when did he last turn a page? I watch quietly and he doesn't. Not that an outsider would notice anything except, perhaps, an air of anticipation.

Black Section has been in the air twenty minutes.

Eventually, it happens and although I have been expecting

it, the ringing phone still makes me jump. We all look up and something tells me that this is it. A shout; yes, it's the orderly, here we go.

'Squadron scramble base angels twelve.'

As one we all make a dive for the door. Cries and curses I have heard so often before: 'Start up, start up', 'Out of the bloody way', 'Move, for Christ's sake'.

I race for my Spitfire. Blimey, out of breath already. Forget it, just run, keep going 'two six'. I look and see my aeroplane now only a short distance away. The ground crew are starting up, the engine fires. There's my parachute hanging from the wingtip where I left it. I make a grab and begin to put it on. My rigger has already removed the starter plug and pulled the trolley clear. He climbs on to the starboard wing and waits by the cockpit. With my chute on I hobble round the trailing edge of the wing and up on to the walkway. With an agility that never ceases to amaze me, my fitter is out of the cockpit in a flash and putting his hand under my arm, almost lifting me into the aircraft.

At once I feel better. The vibration humming through the Spitfire, here we are, home again. Sutton harness straps are held over my shoulder, held there by my two ground crew, God bless 'em. Fix the shoulder to the leg straps and insert the pin and I yell 'OK'. Door closed, helmet on, mask fixed, R/T on and we are ready to taxi. The fitter and rigger are by now standing by the chocks. Wave 'chocks away' and there they go any old where. Brakes off, ease open the throttle and we move, my ground crew looking anxious and excited as they hold my wingtips, eyes fixed on me. Everyone is taxiing at once. I pick out Brian. As his number two I must take up a position on his left. Wave the ground crew clear and they leave go of the wingtips. I am on my own. Bevington gives me a wave very close to a salute. I smile to myself; very Hollywood.

Taxi quickly and take up position and stop, every fibre alert.

I feel composed and reconciled. The squadron forms up. Will
we all see the day through? OK, Brian, ready when you are.
Over the R/T Brian's voice is comforting and quietly confident.

'OK, Gannic, here we go.'

Eyes fixed on Brian's aircraft. It starts to move. Brakes off
with a hiss of escaping air, ease the throttle open and I go with
him. Course corrections on the rudder, keep her straight,
squadron formation take-off. Bumpy ground, more power,
keep up with him; come on, more throttle, still more, acceleration and gaining speed. Tail coming off the ground and yet
more throttle, now we are really beginning to move. Controls
are getting feel. We race across the ground, a bump throws
my Spitfire into the air, catch it on the stick, hold her, we fly.
Eyes riveted on the leader. Brian just leaving the deck.

Change hands on the stick, select wheels up, throttle back
to climbing power and pitch back to 2,850 revs. Now settle
down and hold position; concentrate. The edge of the airfield
flashes by below us and we are away and starting a climbing
turn to port.

Over the R/T: 'Hello, Sapper, Gannic Squadron airborne.'

A very quick glance around and there are the rest of the
squadron tucked in nice and close and so, within four minutes
of the phone ringing in dispersal, ten Spitfires are airborne
and once again in their natural element. A fighter squadron
climbing away in formation on full power. Their flight paths
as straight as arrows from a bow, slender noses pointing
upwards to the sky in the swift, direct flight to join battle;
purposeful and determined. Pilots concentrating and intent
on watching and keeping station, having to correct now and
then with slight movements of stick and throttle. Spitfires
responding as if to say 'this is our environment, our job; this
is what we were built for, we know all about it'. The Merlins
spinning easily in front, their deep-throated sound torn away
in the slipstream, utterly reliable and giving confidence; 'we

won't let you down, we won't pack up'. Their slightest vibration felt through the whole aeroplane.

They are alive, these Spitfires. They live just like the rest of us, they understand. Never, no matter what the circumstances, shall I cease to be thrilled and excited by such a sight and the wonderful feeling of being involved in what I see. My thoughts are apt to stray from the task in hand at such moments. The R/T brings me out of my reverie and almost with reluctance I pay attention. Control is calling. The controller's voice calm, clear and unemotional.

'Gannic leader, this is Sapper. One hundred and fifty plus approaching Dungeness at angels twelve. Vector 120. Over.'

'Sapper, this is Gannic, message received and understood.'

'Gannic, bandits include many snappers.* I say again, many snappers, keep a good lookout. Over.'

'Sapper, this is Gannic. OK, understood. I am steering 120 and climbing hard through angels seven. Over.'

'Thank you, Gannic leader.'

Oh, dear, this looks like being quite a day and quite a party. I swallow hard and find myself both calm and excited. My tummy feels hollow. It's difficult to explain. Anyway, let's just settle down. Presumably one never gets used to the emotion experienced when battle is impending. You just become reconciled, somehow. I glance at my altimeter. It reads 9,250 feet or thereabouts. Turn on the oxygen. Wouldn't do to forget that. Turn the tap to emergency and feel the flow inside the mask against my cheek. That's flowing OK, turn it back to fifteen; there, that should be enough for this trip. The R/T again.

'Gannic, this is Sapper, you are very close now.'

'Sapper, this is Gannic. OK. Tally-ho! Tally-ho! I can see them. They are at least angels one five and what's more there are hundreds of the sods.'

---

* Code name for Messerschmitt 109s.

'Thank you, Gannic leader, good luck!'

The controller's main task is done. All very right and proper!

I look ahead into the far distance, the vast panorama of sky. There it all is, the whole arena for bloody battle, and there they are, the enemy. A swarm of gnats on a warm summer evening. Jesus, there's a gaggle! I'd say there are a hundred and fifty plus and you can say the plus again.

I ease out slightly from Brian and search up above the oncoming circus of Germans. Covering the bombers, sure enough, are the snappers, ME 109s. The whole spectacle frightens yet fascinates me. A few seconds for the imagination to come into play and my mind travels back in time. These are the King's enemies. These are Huns attacking England, our small country, our island, intent upon invasion and eventual occupation. We are on our own against this Teutonic monster, this arrogant bully, this invader of small nations.

Nothing new, I suppose. All this has happened before. Spanish Armada, the Elizabethans; they were a tough and brave bunch, they were. How does it go?

> Take my drum to England, hang it by the shore.
> Strike it when your powder's running low;
> And if the Dons sight Devon, I'll quit the port of Heaven,
> And drum them up the Channel as we drummed them
>   long ago.★

Something like that.

Is there an afterlife? Can it be possible that the Elizabethans are with us now, with us in our cockpits this very minute? Hawkins, Grenville, Frobisher, Raleigh, and Drake; who's to say? How the rest of the squadron would pull my leg if they

★ After Sir Henry Newbolt, *Drake's Drum*.

could read my thoughts and their theatrical meanderings; or would they?

I glance round at the ten brave little Spitfires and a strengthened resolve flows into me. Well, there's not many of us but we'll knock shit out of some of you, at least for as long as we can. One thing to say that now but, in amongst that lot, things may turn out to be different. Must be some other friendly squadrons about somewhere, at least I bloody well hope so, but I'm damned if I can see them. How the hell can ten of us cope with this lot? Where do we start? Only one answer, attack and get stuck in and trust in the Lord.

This is interception. Good God, I've never seen so many aircraft in one bit of sky before. It's absolutely breathtaking. Not long to go now. Brian's voice is in my earphones.

'Gannic from leader. OK boys, in we go. A good first burst and away. Watch for 109s.'

Voices over the R/T. Urgency.

'109s above the first lot coming round to six o'clock, 3,000 feet above.' 'Six more at four o'clock high.' 'I see them, they're starting to come down, here they come, watch 'em, Blue Section. Break into them, Blue, break starboard, break, break for Christ's sake.'

Things are starting to get rough. Automatically I have followed my self-imposed drill that I always do at times like this. Reflector sight on; gun button to fire; airscrew pitch to 2,650 revs; better response. Press the emergency boost override, lower my seat a notch and straps tight. OK, men, I'm all set. Let battle commence. Please, dear God, like me more than you do the Germans.

I hold Brian's Spitfire in view some thirty feet away and look ahead for a potential target and at the same time I assess the situation. This will be a head-on attack from below and it'll be bloody hot work. The lower lot are Dorniers; can see them very clearly now and closing rapidly. Pick my target. A

Dornier slightly out of formation, you'll do. A quick glance above and behind. No 109s immediately behind but that bunch up there might be troublesome. Just a mix-up of aeroplanes; in fact, bloody chaos. Now for my target. There, I see you, you sod. Back in tight formation now, however; never mind, have a crack at him.

All at once, crossfire; heavy and pretty close at that. Bloody front gunners. My target, concentrate, the target. Looking at him through the sight, getting larger much too quickly, concentrate, hold him steady, that's it, hold it . . . be still my heart, be still. Sight on, still on, steady . . . fire NOW! I press the gun button and all hell is let loose; my guns make a noise like tearing calico.

The tracers from my De Wilde ammunition cross with other tracers, return fire, very close, ignore it. I get the fleeting impression of hits and explosions on the glass nose of my Dornier and of Brian's Spitfire breaking away, its oil-streaked belly visible for a fraction of a second. Keep firing, Geoff, hold it. For Christ's sake break off or you'll hit him; too close, this. I stop firing, stick hard over. I even hear his engines as he flashes by inches overhead.

Bloody hell, this is dangerous!

Stick over and forward and a touch of top rudder and breaking downwards, some side slip. Sorry, Eddy Lewis, but I'm frightened. Most brutal, not in the handbook, this, not at all. Still downwards, I've survived. I'm sweating, that's over. Not a bad burst, although I say so myself. I bet he knew he'd got that one, bloody Kraut. Now let's go back and do it all again. How and why on earth do I find myself in this situation?

In less time than it takes to think about it, I am 3,000 feet below the main battle and moving at real speed through the air. Stick back and I pull up, feeling the G loading and, using full throttle, regain the level of a real old mix-up; everybody split up, each man for himself, a Great War dogfight. Aeroplanes everywhere, coming and going in all directions. Keep turning, Geoff, throw her about, don't fly straight for a second. Fly like hell. Good little Spitty; she responds, she's on my side.

The R/T is alive with shouts, warnings and odd noises. Too busy to listen. This is some fight, real and serious, no quarter asked or given. The effort required is tremendous. Strong arms hurling Spitfires around the sky, unreality, fear, anger, reconciled.

A 109 crosses my front. I fire a quick burst and I manage to fasten on to him but a Hurricane gets in my way and I have to break off. Where the hell did he come from? Keep twisting and turning, search for an opportune target. Someone in a parachute and yet another one over there. An aircraft of some sort in flames; a 109 out of control. A Dornier in a vertical dive, thick smoke coming from somewhere and as it turns on its back the starboard wing breaks off. Poor devil, serves him bloody well right.

Confusion: more yells on the R/T, 'Watch 109s at eight o'clock high.' I look up and see them as they half roll and start to come down into the dogfight, fresh for the fray. God, is there no end to them? The sun glints on their wings and bellies as they roll like trout in a stream streaking over smooth round pebbles. Trout streams, water meadows, waders, fast-flowing water, the pretty barmaid at the inn. Dear Jesus, why this? I am hot and uncomfortable.

'Watch that bastard behind you, Yellow 2. He's close, boy, real close. Break Yellow 2, break you clot, break!'

There's even humour over the R/T and I laugh hysterically, confused and lonely.

'Blue leader, can you give me a hand? I'm just off to your starboard somewhere.'

'Sorry, old boy, I've got three 109s on to me but don't worry, I've got 'em surrounded.'

A formation of Heinkel 111s turning away and splitting up

in confusion. I latch on to another 109 but I think I miss him with a quick burst as he turns under me. There's tracer behind me and very close indeed. I break down hard and a 109 I hadn't seen overshoots and pulls up, flying at terrific speed. He goes way up above me. Turning in a wide circle and still flying fast I take a look around. Things are thinning out a bit. However, there is an aircraft way below and I see that it is a Heinkel 111 going like a bat out of hell and between me and the coast. You fat sod, now where do you think you're off to?

Instinctively, I turn towards him, losing height. As I catch up I can see thin dark grey smoke coming from his exhausts as he overboosts his engines in an attempt to get away. He is heading for Dungeness, now some ten or twelve miles distant. Obviously he's detached from his formation and is beating it back home. I take a look around and behind. Still something going on a fair way above. Possibly 109s and our chaps but nothing near me as far as I can see.

Ease the stick forward, throttle open and I drop out of the sky after him. There goes my fox. I find myself gulping with excitement and tension. I'll give you something to take home with you, you stinking great Kraut. You'll know you've been in a fight even if you get me in the attempt.

I catch him fast with so much height in hand. Ease the throttle back a bit to settle things down. Now come in for a quarter attack. Nicely positioned off his port side and getting into range, lay off deflection, ignore the return fire, steady, hold it, open fire. It's a good steady burst and I can see hits on his fuselage and I think, in fact I'm sure, his port engine. Yes, no doubt about it. There is a large puff of black smoke from somewhere, oil smoke I reckon. Good show. That's encouraging. His return fire is a little too close for comfort and as I break down under him, three holes appear in my port wing. The cheeky bastard!

I pull up on his starboard side and looking back over my

shoulder start another quarter attack. Firing in short bursts, the quarter attack becomes an astern attack. Sights on, never mind the return fire, steady, fire again, a long burst this time. I surely must be hitting him. The return fire stops; that's better, give him another squirt, Geoff.

Certainly I hit him on the first attack because considerable black smoke is coming from that port engine and getting thicker all the time. The propeller is slowing down as well. I continue to fire into him, short bursts but good ones. There's another large puff of grey smoke, this time from between the port engine and the fuselage; looks promising.

The rear gunner has certainly stopped firing and the nose of the Heinkel has dropped. He starts to lose height steadily as I notice that the port airscrew has almost ceased to rotate. I'm getting a bit excited but this is no time to become over-eager. With difficulty I force myself to calm down. I stop firing and watch the enemy aircraft as it banks to port, turning into his now-feathered airscrew, not the best thing to do in any case. His engine is still smoking badly. This chap is definitely badly hit and is slowing up in spite of the ever-increasing fall away to port. I have to throttle back a little to avoid overshooting. This is looking good. I think he's going. Yes, I've got him. And since you're going, take that for luck, you bloody son of the bloody Fatherland.

My guns fire a few rounds and then stop. Try firing again. Nothing. Sod it, out of ammo. Not a very intelligent thing to do, to leave yourself with nothing. Should always keep something in hand but, no matter, he's had it, I'm sure.

I watch him losing height fast and on fire and, in a leisurely fashion, I break away. Home, James.

A flash, bright like magnesium and a sharp, very loud explosion. Something red streaks past the cockpit from some-where astern. Very distinctly I hear the hiss as it goes past. I can even smell something: Cordite? Phosphorus?

More explosions behind me; a frightening noise I can't place as more tracers go tearing past. It is only a fraction of a second before it registers, but even that delay is too long.

I've been hit.

I've behaved like a beginner, bounced from behind. My own fault, shouldn't have relaxed after I'd finished with that bloody Heinkel. Elementary rule number one: never relax vigilance. I asked for it and got it; caught napping, well and truly bounced. So this is how a fighter pilot dies.

These thoughts go through my mind like a flash of lightning, summing up the situation. I instinctively duck and at the same time yank the Spitfire round in the tightest and roughest turn ever. It is the sort of thing you do without thinking when you have that frightening realization that you could well be about to die and must fly and fight for your life.

Looking back over my shoulder, an Me 109 is sitting on my tail not thirty yards away, or so it seems, and turning with me. I see the flash from his cannons and puffs of greyish smoke as he tries a quick burst. Not a bad one either as I hear more hits somewhere behind down the fuselage.

A feeling of hopelessness and despair threatens to swamp me and I hear myself say, strangely enough in a normal voice, 'Oh God, I'm going to be killed.'

What a way to go, allowing myself to be surprised and out of ammunition as well. What a bloody, bloody, bloody fool. I'm going to die just like Laurie, Nick and Peter.

I keep turning, keep going, and the 109 tucks in behind me in a very determined manner. Round and round and still he sticks there, glued to my tail. This chap can fly, I fancy; an old hand. Thank God my controls appear to be intact and the dear old Spit is responding. What a kind forgiving aeroplane, even after I let her down so badly.

I hold on to the turn for all I'm worth and even tighten it. A quick glance at the gauges. How seriously has he clobbered me? Glycol temp at 105 degrees, a bit high. Oil pressure not too bad at 75 lb. That's possibly lowish but the oil temperature is on the high side. It fits, actually. Since the fight started I've been flogging the Merlin like mad; too bloody frightened to do anything else. Still tighter with the turn if possible, Geoff. I start to black out. Must be pulling six G. Mustn't go black if I can help it. Lean forward, raise my feet on to the rudder pedal extensions; God, they're heavy.

The Spit judders, a high-speed stall. You can hold a Spitfire on this judder if you're good. Hold on, Geoff! Hold on to this turn. Fly her like hell. How long will I have to go on like this? The physical effort required is tremendous and the perspiration starts to pour off me. As I watch the 109, I now know the meaning of the word 'fear', real stark staring fear, the sort of fear that few people possibly ever experience. I find myself yelling at him. Goodness knows why, I suppose it helps.

Round and round we go. Who's going to be the first to give up? Don't ask bloody silly questions, Geoff. It's got to be him. The Hun fires at me again. No noise of any more hits. Missed me.

Maybe I've gained a little on him. Try and get a little height on him as well if you can, Geoff. Clearly and plainly I see the mottled paint is peeling from the leading edge of his wing. Gracious, but he must be close. Keep going as I am and it won't be easy for him to hit me. I can't be an easy target. I lean forward again to ease the G loading. Don't black out, mustn't do that; a silly thing to do at this stage. Keep going and you must gain. A Spitfire can turn inside a 109 and, anyway, he's on the wrong side of the Channel and must be getting short of fuel.

I'm starting to calm down and think logically. I think I've now got the situation more in hand. Maybe when he sees he's not getting very far he'll make a move and then I may get a chance to shake him off and beat it. I only hope that none of his chums butt in to help him out because that might make things more difficult and they're quite difficult enough already. In the meantime, fight the bastard.

I reckon I'm a little above, just a fraction, and therefore gaining. God, I hope so. Coupled with fear, I now also feel a sense of anger. What right has this German to fly his snotty little aeroplane over our England and try to kill me? Who invited him? Just because he's stupid enough to believe his bloody Führer and his master-race-dominating-the-world crap, he flies for his wretched Fatherland and tries to impose typical Teutonic bullying on our country. The bloody arrogance of it! Well, you'll not shoot me down you black-crossed sod.

The German pilot is trying to tighten his turn still more to keep up with me and I'm sure I see the 109 flick. You won't do it, mate, we're on the limit as it is. I can see his head quite clearly and even the dark shape of his oxygen mask. Yet again, I imagine that the 109 gives a distinct flick, on the point of a high-speed stall. He has to ease his turn a fraction. The Spitfire gains slowly. I exalt and yell at him. Sweat starts to get into my eyes. I must be losing pounds; fear and exertion, I suppose. I'm tiring but still I yell at him. Perhaps I've gone off my rocker.

The 109 finally comes out of his turn and pulls up, trying to gain height on me. As he climbs he goes into another steep turn, very steep, well over the vertical. I look up at him but he has made his effort and failed. I've gained too much and now I'm more behind him than he is behind me. The chance has almost arrived for me to make my break and I watch him intently. He stops his turn and pulls right up and away.

This is it, now get the hell out of it! Stick over and roll on to my back; let her go. Stick centre, take off the bank and pull through hard into a half roll. Throttle still open and hold the vertical dive. Now stick over again and aileron turn down to the deck. All this is instinctive, done without thought as I search for my attacker but I can't see him. Where is he? Dear God, not behind me, please not. Mind you, that Hun would have had to have been bloody quick to have followed me and even if he did, I'm a difficult target. Well, we'll soon know.

Speed is building up at a tremendous rate. Stick forces increasing. Ailerons getting as heavy as hell; hold it, hold the stick over, desperate straits need desperate remedies; strong arms, strong nerves. Blimey, we're shifting.

How badly damaged are we? Look at the altimeter: 5,000 feet. Gosh, that was quick. The noise is terrific. Swallow and shout to clear my ears from the rapid change of pressure. Ease off the bank and stop the turn. Now, start to ease out of this incredibly fast dive. I've never flown as fast as this before. Careful use of trimmer.

Everything is screeching, a thousand banshees, thoughts of poor dear old Laurie on that horrible night at Kidlington. Close the throttle a bit. How do they build aeroplanes to stand such a strain? Perhaps this one won't. My mind is beginning to wander. Now come on, Geoff, pull yourself together; more effort, laddie, more effort. It looks as if you may be getting away with it and if you do, you'll be bloody lucky. That 109 pilot might have been able to fly all right, but he must have been a lousy shot because you were cold meat whilst you were watching that blasted Heinkel of yours going down. Too damned pleased with yourself by far. Let it be a lesson; you won't get away with it again.

Thank you, God, you're a pal.

I take the Spitfire right down to ground level, flying very, very fast. Ease the throttle back to plus 4 boost, revs still at 2,650. Take a quick look around, still clear, thank God. OK, let's go home.

Right down on the deck, even below the level of the tops of the taller trees. I'm a difficult target. Tearing over the

ground at terrific speed built up during the dive. Check the
compass, the DI has toppled. Compass all over the place as
well but it's somewhere about 290 degrees. That will have to
do for the moment. A small farm with a barn flashes by;
high-tension wires ahead. Now don't be a split arse, none of
the underneath stuff, pull up over the top and down the other
side. Confidence is increasing. If you can fly yourself out of
this mess then there's hope that you can fly youself out of
anything, so just fly.

There is rising ground ahead with two large woods a couple
of hundred yards apart and just off to starboard. A slight turn
and right down between the two. The ground slopes away,
down we go and the woods are behind me in a trice. Down,
down a bit more, keep right on the deck, follow the contours.
A cluster of cottages ahead, smoke rising vertically from one
of them, in September as well. There's someone waving and
a dear old lady looks up as she crouches against a hedge. I am
past and away; sorry if I frightened you, my love. The noise
of a Merlin on full song and the rush of a low-flying aircraft
must have terrified her.

Another village and a church tower, a larger village than
most. I am level with the top of the tower but this is now
behind me. Good heavens, my poor old engine. I've given it
one hell of a thrashing. A quick glance at the instruments. All
temperatures and pressures OK. Oil still a little on the high
side but that's only to be expected. A railway line ahead. Ah!
That must be the main line to Redhill and London; goes
straight for miles, can't miss it. I begin to feel safe.

Pull up to 300 feet and take a good look around. Not a
thing in the sky. Bring the boost back to zero and the revs
down to 1,900. The engine runs dead smooth at these settings.
Blimey, what a morning. Quite a party, that one. I'm beginning to unwind a bit by now. I search all round the great
expanse of sky, peering towards the sun, searching behind and

above. The sky is clear except for a few dispersing smoke trails way up at 20–25,000 feet or so. Not another aeroplane in sight. Where on earth has everyone got to?

I look around my aircraft. My port wing has a large hole in it and several small ones. That must have been the red flash that I saw. Poor little Spitty; bit knocked about. However, probably nothing serious. Don't know what the damage is like behind, though. Let's get up to 1,500 feet. I pick out a couple of landmarks and set course for base, now only five or six minutes away at most. There's thirty gallons of fuel left, no worries, plenty. Ahead I can see aircraft circling. They are Spitfires in the circuit prior to landing at base. The airfield comes into view very clearly and quickly. Nice to see you.

A peculiar sensation comes over me, a feeling almost of self-pity. I can't really explain it but I realize how lonely I felt up there and I get an overwhelming urge to talk to somebody. What's more, I can't wait to get on to the ground. It must be right away. Now. This minute.

As I enter the circuit I call control.

'Sapper, this is Gannic Red 2 coming in to land.'

At once there is a reply. I am not alone.

'Red 2, this is Sapper, come right on in. Nice to hear you, Red 2.'

Thank you, Bill. I feel on top of the world. This is a reaction I suppose. Anyway, I feel good and I'm home.

Speed down to under 180 mph. OK, wheels down, select and wait. A reassuring clonk, clonk, and green down light on the panel; pitch fully fine and turn crosswind. Now turn in for the final approach, flaps down, a braking effect just like a dozen men sitting on your wings, trim her out, speed 90 mph, that's nice. I look ahead over the long nose, open and slide back the hood, just a trickle of engine. The hedge of the airfield passes under my wings and the ground comes rapidly closer. Check her. The rate of descent slows, speed dropping away, second check, ease the stick back a bit, a little lower, concentration needed, throttle closed, stick back, don't let the nose drop, stick still back, a wee bit more. The speed drops off, near the point of stall and everything has gone quiet. The nose points upwards and the airscrew idles over in front of me, I can almost count the blades as they pass.

The aircraft sinks and we touch, wheels and tail wheel together. Not bad that one, not bad at all. No time for self-congratulations, though, keep her straight, easy on the brakes. We stop. Turn crosswind and take a look around before taxiing in. Another Spit is landing behind me and to one side and, as I watch, Tony rolls to a halt not twenty yards away.

I undo my oxygen mask, push back my helmet from my head and let the cool slipstream blow my hair and face. By God, that feels good.

Tony looks across at me, also takes off his helmet and waves. He wipes his brow in an exaggerated mock gesture. I wave back as if to say, 'me too, mate'.

Well, that's over for an hour or so, I hope. Flaps up, radiator shutter open and taxi in with Tony. As we do so, I realize that it's turned out to be a gorgeous day.

5. Mars, God of War

Bevington and Davy are obviously worried. No sooner is my Spitfire safely back in her dispersal pen than they both make a dive up on to the wing to the cockpit. This is quite normal and would not have excited my curiosity except for the urgency with which they did it. I've never seen them move so fast as I hang my helmet on the stick ready for the next scramble. I still have a feeling about today. It's going to be one of those specials and we've only just started.

'Are you OK, sir?'

'Just about. Why?'

'You should see this bleedin' aeroplane.'

'Shot up is it? Well, I got caught by a 109.'

'I'll say.'

'Did you get anything, sir?'

'Yes. I'm pretty sure of a Heinkel and I gave a Dornier 215 something to think about, I seem to recall.' I don't want any more questions. 'Now, do you two mind if I get out of this bloody aeroplane?'

'I'm glad you can, sir and I've a feeling it may be for the last time. She'll have to go away. I don't think we can repair this lot.'

Talk in dispersal: stories of individual battles to Tom Wiesse, the 'Intelligent Officer', as he calls himself. He's Norwegian. Combat reports are being written. I can't really be bothered with mine. It's all over for a short while so why on earth write about it? There's a more relaxed feeling, like opening the innings and surviving the first over from a notoriously fast bowler. I finish my combat report, such as it is, short and concise, dash off my signature and hand it to Tom Wiesse.

'Just a minute, Geoff, didn't you tell me something about a Dornier?'

'Yes, that's right. Oh, haven't I put that bit in? Sorry, Tom, I just plain forgot.'

'Well, come on then, get your finger out.' He pauses and looks at me. 'Look, I'm sorry young Geoff but it's got to be done. I'll tell you what, just jot down what happened on any old piece of paper and I'll get my clerk to type it out on another form and then you can sign it later. Bit of a bugger, wasn't it?'

'Yes, it was a bit fraught, to say the least. Most trips seem like it these days. Sorry about the report.'

'OK then, that's settled. I like the sound of your Heinkel, by the way.'

I feel tired, don't want to talk, just want to be quiet and recharge my batteries. The others have started to settle down in their chairs. Wimpey has closed his eyes and appears to be asleep as usual. They all probably feel as I do. The excitement is over, for the moment.

The tea comes in. Good for Tom, I didn't hear the NAAFI van arrive. Organizes things in a quiet sort of way does Tom. The tea is hot, sweet and wet, just like Frimley's, whenever that was. I catch Tommy's eye and he winks and smiles; nice chap, my mate Tom. By the way, where's Butch? I look around the hut but he's not here. Oh, no.

I must have dozed. My tea is only half consumed. Brian is talking to me. 'Geoffrey, move your things into "G" will you? It's a nice shiny new aeroplane especially for you. "G" for Geoffrey. Apt, isn't it? Watch out more next time, you should know that. Good men are scarce.'

As I head for the door that bloody phone rings. I pause. It appears that six aircraft are wanted for a convoy patrol. Brian is talking to the Controller. 'I'll take my six, Bill, what time do you want us airborne? OK, 10.30 it is. We've had no breakfast yet by way of passing, so I'll send the rest to get some and have them back here by 11.00 if that's OK with you. Thanks, Bill.'

I make my way to my new Spitfire.

What Brian's conversation means is that I shall get no breakfast today. I'm bound to be wanted for this patrol. Doesn't matter, I'm not in the least hungry. I've got no bind. Brian calls me from the hut door.

'No. 2, Geoff. Take-off 10.30 hours.'

'OK, Brian.'

Looking at my watch I see that it is already 10.15. There's no sense going back to the hut again so I stay talking to Bevington and Davy and take my time strapping myself in and getting settled comfortably. Bevington and Davy are happy with their new aeroplane.

'Let us know what this new 'un is like, sir. We'll soon get her into shape.'

The sun is warm, the sky is blue and little fluffy white clouds float lazily over the English countryside. Now where on earth . . . ? I know, walking down Kingsway for the interview. Good God!

I sit strapped in my tiny cockpit and allow my mind to wander. Wouldn't it be lovely to lie in the grass by a fast-flowing trout stream in Hampshire or Wiltshire, just me and waving reeds, water meadows, buttercups and grazing cattle? Perhaps a nearby pub with good English ale and chunks of bread and cheese. Yes, and pickled onions, a whole bloody great jar of them and it wouldn't matter a damn if I didn't catch any trout.

Time? 10.25. Ready to go. Pity.

I start up and taxi to join Brian. We take-off and climb up towards the estuary. The sun is hot through the perspex hood and it is a bit hazy but the Germans seem to have gone home to take at least a breather. The new Spit is a beauty; the engine lovely and smooth.

Time passes as we drone up and down. I see some aircraft high up above and report them to Brian. They are 109s, he says, and would I keep my eye on them. Too bloody right I will. They don't seem to take any notice, however, and make one wide sweep round and push off back out to sea again. Wonder what they were up to? Checking the weather, the convoy? It's a little strange. It could mean a busy afternoon. The weather is wide open; it's a wonderful day to suit the Hun. If I get sinister feelings in the early morning, they are invariably right.

'Gannic Red leader, this is Sapper.'

'Sapper, loud and clear.'

'Gannic, pancake, pancake. Your relief is taking over. Thank you.'

'Sapper, received and understood.'

Another job done. What's the time? That was a quick hour and a quarter and we dive away back towards Biggin.

On the ground again I feel hot, sticky and tired. It would be nice to get this Mae West off for a few minutes. Perhaps they will let us go and have a spot of lunch. I'm not really hungry but at least I could have a wash.

I walk on the peri track along dispersal towards the hut. Shan't forget this hut in a hurry. Come to think of it, I'll never forget for as long as I live what is happening to me now. I wonder how long I will live, anyway? At least until the next scramble with a bit of luck. I look at the parked aircraft waiting patiently like tethered horses. It is an uneasy patience for this is high noon, halfway through a gorgeous summer's day of total war. First light, high noon, evening, dusk and then the quiet hours until the next dawn and first light again. It is a relentless ritual which will continue until this bloody war is

won and then what are we going to do? Listen to a lot of
ignorant politicians, I suppose, who, having got us into a war,
will have no trouble at all in making a balls up of the peace.
They'll cock everything up again; they always have done. As
I enter the hut Brian is just putting down the phone.

'OK my merry men, we're at fifteen minutes available and
we can go to the Mess for a quick bite of lunch. We may have
a busy afternoon.'

We haven't been back in the Mess very long, just long
enough for me to have my wash and go into the dining room
for a bowl of soup, when aircraft are heard taking off. One of
the other squadrons is on the job. At least they will have had
breakfast. I bet we'll be brought back to readiness to cover
them and once that happens we'll be there for the rest of the
day, as sure as God made little apples.

The soup I find pretty tasteless. It's no good, I'm just not
in the mood for eating, which is just as well for the tannoy
clicks on. A diabolical and terrible invention, the tannoy! A
speaker on the wall with an unknown impersonal voice:
'Attention, attention; 92 Squadron to readiness immediately;
92 Squadron to readiness immediately.' All right, for Christ's
sake, I heard the first time.

I'm on my way. I find myself leaving the dining room with
Tommy and Roy Mottram. Tom smiles one of his 'just for
you' smiles.

'Good afternoon, Geoff.'

'And a very good afternoon to you, Tom. Lovely day, isn't
it?'

Back at the dispersal hut I put on my Mae West again. This
is where we came in. There is nothing else to do now but
wait; for the time being at any rate.

'B' Flight goes off to escort the convoy but returns after
only forty-five minutes. That sounds like a waste of time.

Refuelled, all is ready for the afternoon's battles. Normally the Hun has been putting on some kind of show round about teatime. He would. Today, we gather, a maximum effort on the part of our antagonist is expected so 'B' Flight was recalled early so as to be ready for the mass Teutonic onslaught. Presumably a squadron from up north must have been called down to cover the convoy.

As the afternoon drags on I become restless. How I hate waiting for that bloody phone to ring in this wretched hut. I go outside for a stroll in the fresh air. The sun, now just beginning to descend in the sky, is still warm. There are no clouds to be seen. Gosh, what a lovely day it's been. There's a lot more of it left as well; a day to suit the purpose of the Hun. God must like him.

I hear the telephone ring in dispersal. Instinctively I know that we are about to be scrambled and so, without waiting, I turn and run to my Spitfire. The klaxon makes its raucous blasting noise. Here we go again. The same yells of 'start up, start up'. I clamber into the cockpit.

Again the squadron forms up on the ground ready for take-off. The same as before except that Butch isn't in the line up. Sergeant Don Kingaby, recently joined, takes his place. Poor Butch. Wonder where he ended up? He may be OK, of course, but it's doubtful. It's all rather ghastly when somebody you know well gets the chop. The system, the war. Who next?

'OK, Gannic, here we go again.'

The squadron accelerates over the ground as one. With me, as always, great exhilaration and pride in being one of a squadron formation taking off to give battle.

Airborne and the start of the long climb. Clear the top of the afternoon haze at about 1,500 feet. The green fields of Kent start to unfold beneath us as we climb way on up, climbing hard for all the height we can get before battle is joined. Vaguely I hear the Controller talking to Brian. The same pattern. One hundred and fifty plus; snappers up to 20,000.

Apart from a 'let's get on with it' sort of feeling, I am more relaxed than on the first trip this morning. Perhaps I've got confidence from evading that 109. I won't allow myself to get caught like that again if I can help it. Anyway, I feel I can cope. The Hun that is going to get me is the one I won't see. If I see him in time then I know I can fly myself out of trouble.

No amount of training can prepare you for mortal combat. One has to realize before take-off that in order to have any chance of surviving and coming through you must remember a simple, straightforward golden rule: Never, but never fly straight and level for more than twenty seconds. If you do, you'll die.

When tracers are seen flashing past don't pause, even to think 'Aren't they pretty?' Break hard and fling the aircraft all over the sky. You are flying for your life and you had better realize it.

If you want to shake someone off your tail you have to fly your Spitfire to its limits. In a tight turn you increase the G loading to such an extent that the wings can no longer support the weight and the plane stalls, with momentary loss of control. However, in a Spitfire, just before the stall, the whole aircraft judders, it's a stall warning, if you like. With practice and experience you can hold the plane on this judder in a very tight turn. You never actually stall the aircraft and you don't need to struggle to regain control because you never lose it. A 109 can't stay with you.

Off to port a squadron of Hurricanes is climbing all it knows in the same general direction as ourselves. As we gain height we draw slowly ahead of them. There is another gaggle of aircraft further off over the Thames estuary and coming in from the north. They also look like Hurricanes but I report them to Brian nevertheless.

Looks like the big build-up for a real party and a half. Our side seems to be throwing everything in and so, presumably, must the Germans be. This action is going to be a big one, no doubt about it. The Controller reports another large formation of Huns building up over Gris Nez and starting to come across but he doesn't go into how many. Perhaps he thinks we've enough on our plate as it is. Where do all these bloody Germans come from? There seems to be no end to them.

'Gannic, this is Sapper. You are getting close now. Should soon see them slightly off to your starboard.'

'Yes, I can see them, Sapper. OK, Gannic. Tally-ho! Many bandits ahead level. Watch out for snappers and don't all rush at once. There's plenty for everybody.'

A great mass of German aeroplanes. Little chatter on the R/T. It's quite obvious what's required. For what we are about to receive.

Within seconds we are in among them, split up and each man for himself and fighting his own private battle. Things moving terribly quickly. There seem to be literally hundreds of aeroplanes with everybody shooting at everybody else. If we can split the Hun formations, well, at least that will be something.

For some odd reason I am taken by surprise at the sheer size of this battle in this truly tremendous arena. Wherever I look the sky is full of a mix of aircraft and the ferocity of our attack is almost frightening.

The bombers, Heinkels mainly in this batch, are in rigid formation and a milling mass of small gnat-like fighters battle it out around them. I try to latch on to a vic★ of three Heinkels slightly on their own. They are away from their

---

★ A V-shaped formation of three or more aircraft; the word derives from an early phonetic alphabet.

main formation but, before I can get near enough, a pair of 109s come in at me from the port beam. I see them in good time, turn into them and pass underneath. They go by overhead, pretty close, and as I look up at them I can see oil streaks on the bellies of their fuselages. They have yellow noses.

Another 109. Bastard. I reverse the turn and try to get on to him but he is going too fast and I miss out. Some tracer goes over the top of my hood, not all that close but I have to break. I don't even see who took a pot at me. I must be difficult to hit as I throw the Spit about, never still for a second. What on earth is going on? There is great confusion and I am in the middle of an almighty bloody mix up and I haven't even fired my guns yet. Obviously I came bounding into the middle of this lot without bothering to think exactly where on earth I was going or who I was going to have a shot at. A bit immature that; not very bright at all.

But half a moment. There's a thing, all is not lost, a couple of Junkers 88s flying very tight together about half a mile distant and a fraction below. I've got my eye on you, you buggers. Just you hold on a bit mateys and I'll have your guts for garters. Even as I watch they drop their bombs and start a slow turn away.

Below is fairly open country, only a smallish village and a few scattered houses or cottages. Pray God that the bombs miss them but, at least, it's not a built-up area such as the East End of London. Presumably they chucked their loads off in a bit of a panic.

A pair of 109s sail above and behind them but they have not seen me. Where on earth do all these bloody 109s come from? They must have hundreds of the blighters. They still haven't seen me. Perhaps I can get a burst at the bombers and get out of it before they do. Astern of the four of them I have a little height in hand.

Throttle open, dive under the fighters, a quick burst and away. Come on then, let's get it over with. Ease the stick forward, feed on more power and down we go. A quick look around. Clear behind, but there is so much going on who can tell?

OK, now watch the target. Speed building up too quickly. Ease the throttle back slightly. The 109s still haven't seen me. I begin to swallow hard and my left knee begins to tremble for some bloody stupid reason. I'm getting excited again, although tensed up. Wish I was the cold calculating type with steely blue eyes.

There's no time to consider anything but those 88s. Astern of the bombers. They come towards me at an astonishing speed; too fast. Shit! Sight on. Oh, damn, I'm still miles too fast. Bloody hell! Overtaking like a rocket, open fire. The guns going, trembling Spitfire, smell of compressed air or cordite or something. Hold it a fraction longer; hits on the left-hand one, lots of them. Christ, Geoff, you're going to ram him. Stick forward, a thump. Either you've hit him or it's slipstream. Hope it's slipstream. Blimey, we're going vertically towards the ground. This is rather off putting, but I think it's all right. You didn't hit him; you broke away a bit late and hit the slipstream. Strewth, that all happened quickly; bloody close as well.

Pull up and start to climb for another go. The sky is still full of aeroplanes. This is one hell of a battle, everybody mixing it. Each man for himself. I find myself just a little off to one side as I clamber for height and I have an uninterrupted view. It is magnificent and yet appalling. No fewer than six parachutes float lazily towards the ground. Friend or foe it doesn't matter, at least they're out of it.

Junkers and Heinkels split up, their formations largely decimated as they head back towards the coast. A Junkers goes down well and truly on fire. Mine? Like to think so, but I can't possibly claim it. Yet another 88 plummets to the ground.

Three of the crew bail out and only one chute opens, the other two Roman candle. I can see the man at the end of one of them quite clearly, arms and legs thrashing as he plunges earthwards. A Spitfire spins down and a Hurricane dives away, a long trail of black smoke behind it and, at its base, a bright angry red flame. I am transfixed. I don't see anyone bail out. The dive steepens. Poor sod. Yet another aircraft goes down in a steep dive. A large one, looks like a Heinkel. My God, he's shifting for a big plane and, oh my goodness, streaming out behind is a man on the end of a parachute, caught up somewhere round the tail of the aircraft and flailing about like the tail on a kite. Well, he may be a Hun but I wouldn't wish a death like that on anybody.

The battle is not letting up for a second. Dear God, fancy allowing this sort of thing to happen. What are You up to? It's ghastly. They'll probably tell me it's not You, it's the Devil.

I see a 109 heading back to the coast on my port side. I latch on to him for a second or two and give him a good burst but another Spit crosses in front of me and also tags on to the German. I have to stop firing. Seem to be surrounded again. How the hell did I manage to get back into the middle of this lot? A steep turn to the left. Now, let's see. What the blazes is happening? A fat Heinkel; a quick shot. Too late, missed; shots went behind. Another Heinkel or something, anyway it's got bloody great black crosses on it; another quick squirt, no time for more. Better, that hit him. Tracer from behind; sod it. A 109 up my chuff. Turn hard starboard. He doesn't follow. Thanks very much. A formation of five Junkers 88s being attacked by a collection of Spits and Hurricanes. The 109s seem to be pushing off home. Short of fuel, I bet. I join the party and get a good burst in at one of the 88s on the left. I have to break down under him to avoid a collision. I again don't know if it is mine or not but an 88 pulls away, turns over on to its back and heads for the ground. One of the remainder has an engine on fire but there are so many Spitfires and Hurricanes attacking that I just can't get a look in. Anyway, I wonder how much ammunition I've got left. I don't expect there is all that amount. I pull out of the mêlée as everybody is getting in everybody else's way and even as I do so yet another bomber falters.

I feel exhausted and ache in every limb. I'm not cut out for this sort of thing. Perspiration trickles down my back. The sun streams in through the perspex. It's still too hot, too bright and the sweat gets into my eyes. They feel sore. The oxygen mask is horrible, wet and clammy. If only I could unhook it. What's my height? Angels ten. I can unhook it at this altitude if I want, so I do and it feels a lot better.

At last things are thinning out, thank goodness. Anyway, I've had enough for a little while. There's twenty gallons of fuel left. That's not too bad but I've used a lot. Let's get out of this. Stick over and down we go. Watch out behind, though; it's not quite finished yet. Down to 1,000 feet and taking stock of the situation. First of all, where am I? That airfield over there looks to me like Detling. How's the fuel? Still almost twenty gallons; that's the second time you've checked in thirty seconds. It's enough to cruise quietly back to Biggin. Looking around and high above, scores of dispersing vapour trails and that's all that's left of that terrific and ferocious battle. The killing is over, for the time being anyway. Half-time everybody; you can have a rest now.

Search as I may, as far as I'm concerned there's not another aeroplane in the sky. Well, you got away with that one, Geoff old boy, but for how long?

Be nice to get back on the deck again. Throttle back a little more and take another look around. There is nothing about down there at least. Half a turn to starboard, nothing behind. Let's go home.

God, I'm hot. I must be getting some kind of reaction because I feel a nausea coming over me. Some fresh air would be a good idea. I struggle with and finally open the hood. Immediately, I feel better. I refix my oxygen mask and enjoy the slight buffeting from the slipstream. And so we cruise home and base shows up ahead after a short time. No messing about, let's go straight in. As I land I notice a crashed Spit sitting on its belly but, as I pass on my landing run, it's a case of out of sight, out of mind.

Back at dispersal I switch off. The quietness is deafening. I feel completely knackered; just like a wet rag. Davy and Bevington undo my Sutton harness and help me out of the cockpit.

'Any luck, sir?'

'Not really, possibly a Junkers 88. Have to call it a probable. I just seem to have sprayed thousands of bullets all over Kent.'

As I climb out of the cockpit, I feel totally drained and grateful to have my feet on terra firma again. Jesus, I'm weary. It's been a long day. How many more times am I going to say that to myself? I hope to goodness we're not sent off again; not just yet, anyway. I could do with a bath and a rest. At least I can *get* a bath, which is more than some poor sod in the army fighting in the trenches or whatever they fight in these days. Thank goodness I'm not a soldier but, at the same time . . .

For how long will it go on at this pace? Indeed, how long can it? Something has got to give soon. It's such a near-run thing.

I wander slowly towards dispersal unaware of the activity of rearming and refuelling going on around me. One of the first people I see as I enter the hut is Wimpey. Both astonishment and disbelief are on his face. His hair is all over the shop and he's obviously had a hard time. There are beads of perspiration on his forehead and round his nose. I can see where his oxygen mask has been. He looks absolutely whacked. I wonder if I look like he does. Possibly; most of the others do.

'Geoffrey, I thought I saw you going down on fire near Detling. Nice to see you.'

'Did you indeed, Wimpey? Not me, mate, thanks to God's mercy. I don't suppose I was all that far off it though at sometime or another. As it happens, I did end up over Detling.'

'Well. I was quite convinced that it was our Geoff. Anyway, I certainly saw one of our aircraft going down, at least I think it was one of our Spits. I thought it looked like you.'

'Your faith in me is touching, Wimpey. Thank God you were wrong. You look as if you've had a bit of a bellyful yourself.'

'I'll say I have. I feel absolutely buggered. I had one hell of a battle on my hands. I reckon it's the worst yet, or should I say best and get a medal? That's the remains of my kite in the middle of the aerodrome.'

'The one on its belly?'

'Yep.'

'Are you OK?'

'Think so. I've still got two of everything.'

'Well then, that's all that matters. By the way, who's missing then, if I'm not?'

'Tom,' Wimpey asks, 'is anyone adrift?'

'Yes, it would seem that Sergeant Crawford is still unaccounted for.'

'Who on earth is Sergeant Crawford?'

'A new lad. He arrived yesterday morning.'

Brian is speaking to the Controller. 'OK, everybody, that looks like it for today. We're at thirty minutes and I'm off to the Mess. Anyone want a lift?'

'Be right with you.'

'Come on, then, let's get cracking.'

I clamber into the back of the Humber with Tom, Wimpey and Roy and off round the peri track. The dispersal has a more settled look about it. Some of the ground crew have done their jobs and the Spitfires are waiting for us as usual. Not required this evening if we're lucky, but certainly at first light tomorrow. In several pens, the aeroplanes are being worked on. With cowlings off they look a bit naked. The riggers are patching bullet holes.

I've had enough for one day. Can't speak for the others and I don't much care either, I just know I've had it.

'I think,' says Brian, 'a pint or three at the White Hart tonight will do us all the world of good. Transport leaves the Mess at 8.30. Don't be late, anyone, and, Geoffrey, don't drink more than three pints and get tight again because we shall have to call you the "Boy Drunkard" if you do.'

What it is to have a dominant leader but, thereafter, I was always referred to as 'Boy Wellum', the boy. I work out that I am nineteen years old.

> The tumult and the shouting dies,
> The Captains and the Kings depart.
> Still stands thine ancient sacrifice,
> An humble and a contrite heart.

> Rudyard Kipling, 'Recessional'

6. Brief Encounter

A character. A new pilot arrives on the squadron.

As it turns out, he is also called Tommy. His real name is Sebastian Maitland-Thompson. The day he arrives I spend a most entertaining time talking to him in the bar and later in the White Hart.

During the course of the evening, the other Tom, my old mate, comes into the pub, having been somewhere or other with Tony Bartley and Bob Holland, and I introduce them. They click at once and we all of us get along like a bush fire. Both Tommys are obviously intelligent. There are periods when I feel I am no more than a bystander but, such are their manners, I am not allowed to feel left behind or in any way neglected. I enjoy listening to their conversation.

The new man is a huge chap. Six foot plus the rest; a front-row forward, it seems, and what a formidable one he must have been. He is also a successful amateur boxer. Thank God he's on our side. In private life he is a barrister; 'just deny all knowledge, old boy'.

How he talked his way into the cockpit of a Spitfire good-ness only knows. I would have said that his mere size would have made it quite impossible. He exudes an old-world *Barretts of Wimpole Street* Victorian courtesy and politeness that is totally engaging. Phrases such as 'I do declare', ''Pon my soul', 'Quite capital' and 'A stoup of ale would be most acceptable' all come out in a natural and quite charming manner. Already he is known as 'Big Tom' or just 'the Big Man' but never that 'big bastard'.

A smallish fresh-complexioned face, wispy receding blond

hair and eyes that somehow look right into you with a lazy, easygoing but sometimes deceptive smile. Easygoing he may be but, as we get to know this character, it becomes obvious that very occasionally he says he is going to do something. His mind is made up and his smile does not hide the fact that he intends it to be generally known that he has made a profound statement. He does that something, no ifs, buts or bloody arguments. It's final and that's all there is to it.

Obviously, the day arrived when he decided that he would like to fly a Spitfire, so he would just have told the poor bloke who was his boss something like: 'I'm going off for a few years and I'm going to be taught to fly a Spitfire. Good day to you.' He went, he did and now he's in a squadron to prove it.

The Big Man settles into the way of life of 92 Squadron quickly and easily. Now, content with his lot, he takes the whole thing in his stride with the nonchalance of a founder member. I seem to amuse him for some reason and, after he has been with us for a couple of weeks or so, he volunteers to loan me three pounds towards the purchase of a small motor car.

I address the assembled company as we sit in the comfort of the ante-room at fifteen minutes available.

'You know that little car I borrowed from that friend of my father last week?'

'The little Ford Ten job?'

'That's the one. Well, this bloke says I can buy it for five pounds. What do you think?'

'You can't very well go far wrong at a fiver, can you?'

'That's the way I feel about it. It can seat four . . . five at a pinch. Ideal for pub crawls and it could be a sort of pilot's passion wagon.'

'In a Ford Ten. Ridiculous suggestion.'

'I don't know. I can imagine it –' Wimpey cuts me short.

'I'm sure you can, Boy. What this is going to lead up to

and what it really means of course is that Geoffrey has no money as usual and, therefore, is not in a position to take up the offer. So watch it, comrades.'

It seems that I have convinced nobody and that my ploy has been rumbled.

'Of all the pathetic bloody flannel. What happens if you get the chop, Boy?'

'Boy, you really are growing up to be a crafty young bugger. You really are.'

Big Tom comes to my defence: 'I don't think so at all. It appears to me, as a Johnny come lately, that Geoffrey has been set standards of craftiness and one hundred per cent pure flannel seldom surpassed in the glorious history of the Royal Air Force by the present members of 92 Fighter Squadron.' He rummages in his pocket. 'There we are, Geoff, three quid any help? And greater love hath no man than he should donate his last few pounds at the expense of his beer. There you are.'

'Thanks, Tommy, you are most considerate. I'll pay everybody back on the first of the month.'

Hands search trouser pockets and in no time the total sum of five pounds finds its way into my clutches.

'Well, Geoff, when are we going to see this high-powered projectile?'

The conversation gets no further. The distant tinkle of a telephone is followed by the appearance of the telephone orderly.

'Flight Lieutenant Kingcombe, sir, Operations on the telephone.' Brian leaves the room. A sinking feeling; now where have I enacted this little scene before? No car today, that's for sure. It's not long before Brian returns.

'OK, men, "B" Flight have just been scrambled and Ops want us at readiness right away. It seems things may get busy. Boy, Toms one and two, Tony, Wimpey, we're on our way.

No bloody procrastinations, so wrap up before you start and look lively!'

That's final enough, I suppose. The brave Flight Commander has spoken.

Climbing up through the late-afternoon haze, the Spitfires take on the colour of burnished copper. Heading towards the south coast and climbing hard with the sun behind us on the quarter, the reflection on the spinning airscrew gives the appearance of a solid disc of copper. Shadows move and flicker first one way and then the other across its face; it's lethargy making. I feel warm, resigned and not unduly alert. The glare makes it difficult to differentiate the camouflage on Tom's aircraft as he flies on my left and slightly behind. He sees me looking at him and waves a hand. How many times have the two of us enacted this little scenario? Strange it would seem if one day he couldn't be there for some reason.

It really is a remarkably thick haze. All that filthy foggy smoke from London. Fancy having to breathe that into your lungs every day of your life. I suppose you don't notice it; I didn't that morning as I walked down Kingsway for my interview. I wonder what on earth I would have done if I had been turned down? Wasn't all that long ago, really. Now look at me; a Spitfire pilot. Whoever would have thought it? I'm a lucky bloke.

Only directly beneath me am I able to see anything of the ground and then it's not easy to pick out detail. May be a bit tricky getting back into Biggin, although visibility should improve somewhat when the sun falls below the horizon. At least, let's hope it does.

There is an inversion at 2,000 feet and, as we climb and break through into clear air, the haze stretches away as far as the eye can see. It blankets everything and from where we are it looks as solid as any cloud. My feeling of lethargy is shattered when the Controller comes on the air to tell us we are being vectored to the Eastbourne area to investigate some believed hostile plots. The effort to rouse myself is almost too much. It appears that for most of the latter part of the afternoon, 109s have been making a nuisance of themselves all along the south coast. I wonder why these wretched Germans always seem to cause a disturbance just when any civilized fighter squadron is thinking of packing up for the day. Given any excuse, no matter how small, Operations will call you to readiness and, of course, leading on from that it takes only a little cunning thought to send the whole squadron hurtling into the air. All the Controller has to do is pick up the nearest phone and yell 'scramble' and even if he can't be bothered to do that he has a little blonde WAAF assistant to do it for him. Hard lives those chaps lead.

As far as this afternoon is concerned, whoever had this brilliant idea I don't consider it a particularly good one myself, but Ops must have some notion that there may be mischief brewing up on the part of the Germans this evening and we are to be on the spot to get in the way, as it were.

The haze below is still hopelessly thick but at 15,000 our small formation levels off, throttles well back and rumbles its way steadily onward on the vector given to us. Directly beneath me I am just able to make out a coastline and what appears to be a reasonably large town. The Controller comes back to us and says it's Hastings and would we please turn west on to 270 degrees for Eastbourne. He says further to exercise a certain amount of caution as some Hurricanes have been reported in the area by the Observer Corps. Possibly from Tangmere, I suppose. They must have a patrol airborne at the same time as ourselves, unless we are to relieve them. Why didn't Tangmere, or whoever, get on to Biggin Ops and say they had a squadron in the area? Somehow it all seems a little vague to me. Bearing in mind the poor visibility, I should have thought the Observer Corps would have had quite a job on their hands to identify aircraft at height.

Flying a westerly heading the sun is now low enough to make seeing a tricky business. To some extent the situation wakes me out of my previously lethargic attitude and I sit up and take a little more notice.

Our formation spreads out a little as if everybody has the same thoughts. I carry out a personal search over the Channel. That's the direction they have to come from in the first place. However, my thoughts are suddenly switched elsewhere. The Controller comes on the air.

'Gannic leader, this is Sapper. There are some bogeys to the west of you, vector 285 and investigate with caution.'

'Sapper, this is Gannic, I think I can see them, am proceeding.'

Like hell he can see them. I'm buggered if I can.

'Gannic aircraft, this is leader, aircraft at one o'clock 2,000 feet above and heading inland. I think they are Hurricanes.'

Ah, there they are. I can see them now.

'Gannic leader, this is Blue 1. I've got them, they are starting to turn to starboard.' Having said my piece I keep my eyes glued to those dots and for a moment I catch a glint of sunlight on perspex. Watching them I'm damned if I would like to say for sure that they were Hurricanes.

Almost without realizing it, my eye has been attracted by a movement below the suspects. More aircraft are standing out clear for all to see. Now where on earth did they come from and how could we have possibly missed seeing that little lot? Concentrating too much on the ones above, I suppose. That's bad, very bad indeed. I catch a good view of the lower formation and there is no doubt whatsoever that they are Hurricanes, six of them streaming away towards the west.

A nasty ugly mistrust infiltrates my thinking and observation. I'm not sure I like the way this situation is developing.

We might have to be a bit careful here. The Hurricanes are now getting well away and obviously have no idea of the presence of that top lot of aircraft, whoever they are. In any case, those aeroplanes are now turning in a large circle that will eventually, if continued, take them round behind us and out to sea again. I draw Brian's attention to the Hurricanes.

'OK, Blue 1, turning towards this top lot,' and then, almost immediately, 'They are starting to lose height; they are coming down but I don't think they have seen us. Watch it, everybody.'

By this time there is no doubt in my mind that these are hostiles. As if to confirm my sentiments a voice says, 'They are 109s, leader.'

'So I see, let's go and try and get 'em.'

As the enemy aircraft turn out towards the coast, they are well spread out. We are cutting them off nicely and, being underneath them, we must be difficult to see. They are moving pretty fast, however. One of them is well out to the right of his formation. 'Yes you bastard, I reckon I might just be able to do something about you.' I'm in the best position of our chaps and so I break out towards my selected opponent. Looking behind, I am gratified to see that my number two, a new sergeant pilot called Gaskell, is sticking tight and coming with me. Good lad.

I cut the corner still more towards the diving 109. Going to need all the speed I can get for this situation. The Huns have got quite a start on us. I go into fine pitch, press the boost override and open the throttle. With all my attention now focused on him I can tell to the second when he at last sees me. He steepens his dive and straightens from his turn, heading directly out to sea and home. Obviously he thinks he can outrun me and is relying on the start he has. Well, we can only wait and see because I don't think he has made a very smart move. He has no advantage from his fuel injection. I open the throttle wide and make certain that the boost override is fully pressed. Ease the stick forward and as the nose drops away I plunge after my quarry. Reflector sight on. The Spit accelerates very quickly. Didn't have to half roll to follow him this time and the general noise of the rushing air around the cockpit and the stiffening of the controls seem to impart a tension in me. The excitement of the chase, because that's all it is. This chap is not turning to fight, he's just getting the hell out of it back across the Channel. Know the feeling well, mate.

Curving slightly in towards him I am conscious only of the target. I concentrate hard as I lay off deflection through the sight. Hope Gaskell is still behind and nobody else, like one of this chap's mates, for example. Gaskell should know what to do even if he is new to the game. This bloody German is going damn fast. No time to worry about what's behind too much if I'm to get in a burst at him, but it's going to have to be a quick one. He's diving at terrific speed but I should be able to get something off and tickle him up a bit.

Tighten the curve of pursuit slightly. The nose comes through and starts to get in the way of my view. No matter, nearly there . . . fire now. The noise of tearing calico again, recoil, the 'take that you sod' feeling and curving tracers. Only a fraction of a second; cease firing. Bugger, he's still getting away. It's now a stern chase. Another burst, no more than a long shot. That one could be termed as fairly accurate but the range is opening up the whole time. What a pity he had those few precious seconds' start on me. My speed is building up the whole time, but at this rate we will be over France before I can get really close to him.

Take a quick look round, nothing, I seem to be alone. Where have all the others got to? No matter, where's my bird is more to the point; my God, he's on fire! No, it's not fire, I think it must be coolant. I must have clobbered his cooling system. You jammy old sod, Geoff. Away ahead, his dive, if anything, has steepened. I plunge after him and slowly now I begin to catch him, my speed still building; come on, little Spit.

What's the height? The top of the haze appears to be rather close. If I remember rightly, the top was at about 2,000 feet. Barely 4,000 on the altimeter. Got to watch this; it's unwinding like a mad thing. Hun or no Hun I'm going to have to think about pulling out of this. Got to be pretty quick about it as well or I'll be in the 'oggin' with that bloody Hun and that would be stupid.

Ease the throttle, back on the stick, come on, pull firmly. The stick force is fairly heavy and Spits have light elevators. Use the trimmer. Steady you ass, you'll have the bloody wings off. The G builds up and I lean forward to lessen the effect. The haze tears towards me and into it we plunge. Keep the pressure back on the stick. Here we come. OK, Geoff, take it easy, you are going to have about 1,000 feet to spare. I level out and describe a wide circle, the Spitfire flying very fast. I don't quite know where I am. Had a busy twenty seconds back there. Visibility is shocking. Straight down I can see the reflection of the last rays of the sun on the molten coloured sea. Of my Hun I can see nothing, not a bloody sign. Since he went into the top of the haze in a very steep dive indeed – and I should know – I would put his chances of pulling out as not very high. Putting it another way, I started to pull out quite a bit earlier than he did and all I had left to play with was barely 1,000 feet and that's not very much when you start off from 15,000.

Even here, off the south coast, the poor visibility prevents a reasonable search. The situation is fruitless and hopeless. In my own mind I'm certain that my Hun went into the sea. I can't see how he could possibly have got away with it, and even if by some miracle he did pull out, he was still losing coolant at a hell of a high rate. I suppose he might have got a couple more minutes' flying. If only I could see or get a sight of an oil patch or something it would help. I search for a short while but it's no use, the weather is too thick. Now that's annoying, just my sort of luck.

I'll only get a probable for all that effort, Tom won't give me more if I know him; tight old bugger.

Well, it's no good messing about down here over the sea. I suppose I should start thinking about trying to get back home. It's getting latish anyway. The light won't last all that much longer so there's no point in hanging around. I presume I am somewhere off Eastbourne. That being the case, the approximate course home must be, well, let's say just west of north; so steer 350 degrees and we can get down to more accurate detail later. Climb up a bit and get clear of this bloody haze. It's been a damn nuisance ever since we took off. As I get on top there is nothing else in the sky. Settling down on course the glassy sea is still directly beneath me but soon the coast comes up beneath the trailing edge as we cross inland. No sign of a big town. Anyway, we're on the right lines, all roads lead to Rome but, in this case, Rome could be anywhere.

Clear of the murk and well throttled down for a quiet unhurried trip back to base. Steady on 350 degrees. I could always call up and get a vector but, perhaps not, not yet anyway. Just carry on with this heading and in a short time I should be able to see the balloons over the Thames estuary if they are being flown sufficiently high to get above this smoke. As time passes, I don't see them, so presumably they are somewhat below 2,000 feet or else I'm way off in my calculations.

The sun is now below the horizon and the whole world in which I find myself is one of purple mistiness. Nothing appears to be alive. I am alone in a strange still environment. No movement at all. My aeroplane is stationary. Even the Merlin, sensing my mood, has become very quiet in its running, working smoothly and easily and in no great hurry. This is a type of peace and tranquillity that, to my mind, is utterly beautiful. It is a shame having to think about the ground and having to get back on it. If only I could go on flying like this for ever.

A short time ago I probably killed a man. I was excited and elated, totally taken up with the chase and the kill on a 'him or me' basis, and now this terrific sense of peace. What a strange life we pilots lead. This is the sort of moment that only those who fly can fully understand. I wonder how this compares with the peace of God? How does the blessing go? 'The Peace of God that passeth all understanding.' Surely, at moments like this, alone and lonely, one must be very near to Him, even though there is a war waging and I don't understand why He allows it to happen. What a pity that all men can't share these moments because they are out of this world.

It could make a splendid painting; a Spitfire slipping along the top of the plain unbroken surface of the evening murk. Only a line of red and another of orange in the western sky to show where the sun has finally called the end of the day.

Back to reality, Geoff. Reverie is all very well but you've got to get home so extract the digit. I don't particularly want to but I know I must. What a great shame. It's so glorious up here alone.

There's only one thing to do and that is to see what the visibility is like nearer the ground. It should have improved now that the sun has gone below the level of the horizon. Throttling back, we slip quietly down into the haze. The altimeter slowly unwinds. Below are fields. Down at 1,000 feet things stand out a little clearer. Visibility is just about a couple of miles, I should guess. Fractionally off to starboard and almost dead beneath, the long straight railway line that comes up from Ashford. I turn slightly and follow it up to

Redhill. Lucky that I know the area. Should do, of course, I've been around here long enough. Longer than a lot of my mates. Actually, I've overshot slightly. Turning to my right and on to a course of 030 degrees should do the trick. Not long afterwards Biggin Hill appears out of the evening mist. We may well get some fog tonight.

Coming in to land I can see another Spit taxiing in. Not quite so late back as I thought I was. We land and, turning, taxi back to dispersal. Even from this distance I am able to pick out Davy and Bevington as they wait patiently.

Another day gone, Geoff. You've survived; until dawn tomorrow. I can't really be bothered to think about my combat report, let alone write it, but I've no doubt Tom will insist. To be honest, I haven't got over that sense of lonely peacefulness that came over me back up there above the misty gloom of the ground. It was strange and wonderful and I feel a great contentment. Only men who fly will understand.

What on earth shall I find to do when I am not able to fly a Spit any more?

7. Parting Day

The approach of autumn, as always these days, brings a misty haze which hangs over Biggin Hill. October and we have a new CO, John Kent, a tough Canadian. Just what the squadron needed.

I leave my overnight kit in my room and head for the Mess. It is just coming up to 12.30 p.m. Things appear to be fairly quiet on the aerodrome. Can't say I feel any better for my forty-eight hours off, although I suppose it must have done me some good. Could have done with a month, let alone two days; at least, that's how I feel at the moment. I phoned up Grace and took her out dinner-dancing. She was delicate and yielding and as we danced closely, moving as one, thoughts of war in the blue skies vanished.

What would I have done with a whole month's leave? The money situation permitting, of course, I could have gone away deep into the country and got lost, to the type of place I sometimes dream about, somewhere with sun-drenched water meadows and grazing cattle, hedges, meandering streams and so forth. However, all I had was two days and so I went home. Had to, really. After taking Grace out I'm woefully short of cash until the first of next month.

Possibly going home for such a short time was a mistake. It was wonderful and secure to see Mum and Dad again but, I don't know, things weren't quite the same for some reason. Thoughts of Grace? Don't think so. No doubt it's the war and also the fact that I had to return to it so quickly. Perhaps it was just me. I found I was fidgety and unable to converse easily; an effort was required when it should have been all so easy. I wanted to be quiet and left alone, which was selfish of me; after all, it's been some time since I was in my home, especially overnight. I expect I have changed. Would Peter have felt the same if he had still been alive?

I recall how my mother would look at me when she didn't think I'd notice. My room just as I had left it all those months ago, excited at the possibility of becoming a pilot in the Royal Air Force. As always, the room was ready for me, not a thing changed. I find it difficult to comprehend all that has happened since I left home.

It's a strange situation. When I'm away from the squadron I want to get back again and when I am on my way back I want to turn round and go far away. But squadron life has such a strong hold over me. That would probably mean that my imaginary month in the deep country would be a disaster unless, well, I wonder if Grace would come with me? Perhaps not; as I say, somehow it's always Spitfires and 92 Squadron. Grace might be worth a try, though. My thoughts are jumbled and inconsistent.

I think my trouble is that subconsciously I appreciate that with the posting to a fighter squadron I have possibly reached my peak by satisfying a burning ambition to fly in the RAF as a fighter pilot. To be with 92 Squadron in the front line at such a period in the history of the world and the Royal Air Force is to be in Fighter Command during its finest hours. This is what 'fighters' are all about, defending Britain and clearing British skies of the King's enemies. This is why I think that this period could well be the pinnacle of my life, although to think along these lines when one is only nineteen years of age is crazy. I've seen so little of life, really. Is it possible that nothing will ever reach such heights again?

What of the others; the two Tommys, Wimpey, Brian and co.? Do they also try to analyse things as I do in my more broody moments? If they do, do they arrive at the same conclusions?

Nobody, I don't care who he is, will ever be able to forget such times as these if they survive. It won't take long for those not involved to forget, though. After all, they're safe, there's been no invasion, as yet. Then what, after the war is over?

How many will remember or give a thought to, apart from the next of kin, of course, in twenty years' time, or twenty months, for that matter, the battles that are going on over their heads at this moment? They will just take for granted that German storm troopers are not parading up and down The Mall or changing the guard at Buckingham Palace for bloody Hitler. We fighter pilots are all very popular at the moment and no hostess can fail if she has some of us to her party. People want to know us and talk but, you wait and see; when we beat the Germans it will be convenient to forget and because the RAF officer is not quite the one to know, we will be right out on the pavement. If we should fail, however, and not beat the Germans, then we will be blamed. Young men die for these options. Nobody wants reward, just a quiet thank you would be fine. Perhaps this is a chip on my shoulder. A lot of people have them, I'm told. Fair enough, but what effect will all this have on those of us who survive; what effect on our lives as we grow older? Fancy living long enough to grow old.

What a jumbled mixture of thoughts. Tell the others about this and they will think I'm round the bend; nuts.

I arrive at the entrance of the Mess without realizing it but once inside my odd mood vanishes; home again. The atmosphere in this place I understand. This is much better. The little WAAF behind the reception desk gives me a smile.

'Good afternoon, sir.'

'Hello, Gay, any mail?'

'One, sir, heavily scented.'

'I don't believe it.'

She hands me the envelope. It's from Grace. I'll read it later, quietly, and go for a lunchtime drink first. The squadron, as usual, seems to have taken over most of the available bar space. Brian and the two Toms are there among others; Tony, Roy and Allan Wright of all people, a charming chap and a steadying influence on all of us. Their smiles are warm and friendly.

'Hello, Boy, enjoy your break?'

'So-so. Could have done with another month.'

'What do you want a month for? Didn't you manage to hop into bed with her in the time available?'

'Now don't bring the level of the conversation down to normal quite so quickly. Anyway, what's the form?'

'Thirty minutes until four o'clock, then readiness for the rest of the day.'

'Pity, what's it been like?'

'Quiet, standing patrols mainly, we've got to do one later, possibly about five o'clock, and you're on it, so cheer up, Boy, and have a swift drink.'

'That's mighty magnanimous, half a can, please.'

'We're taking ours into lunch, coming?'

'Right away.'

It doesn't take long to get back into the fold.

'Hello, Ops, this is 92 Squadron now at readiness.'

Pancho Villa, a recently joined Flight Commander, is heading us this time. John Kent is away getting a Polish medal. Brian has just left on forty-eight hours.

Sitting around waiting, so what's new? Half an hour to go before our standing patrol if we're not scrambled. People are sitting quietly reading or dozing. I just sit and then I remember Grace's letter. Of course, I would remember it when I'm all trussed up in my Mae West. It's a nice letter. She ends it 'All my love' and two little Xs as well. Grace has been more in my thoughts recently than I might care to admit. I don't seem really to follow things up in that direction. Perhaps I should. When I had my forty-eight hour stand down, I gave her a ring and she turned up as arranged looking cool, relaxed and pretty. I recall at the dinner-dance standing at the bar talking quietly with her and as the crowd increased she had to stand nearer. I felt the slight pressure of her shoulder. We looked at each other and understood. What simple innocent things give pleasure, in this case physical touch. I've never slept with a woman, it hasn't really worried me all that much, but I would like to sleep with Grace and, what's more, she knows it; after all, I virtually told her. She didn't laugh at my clumsy directness and inexperience, she just smiled and said, 'Yes, Geoffrey dear, I know.' I wonder if that means what I hope it means.

The late-afternoon sun streams through the windows of dispersal. One or two flies buzz around and an enormous bee is bashing its head against one of the panes. I get up, walk to the window and open it and let the thing out. As I return to my seat, Tommy grins at me and gives the boy scout salute. I laugh at him and settle down to rest and wait. I'm finding waiting much easier these days and in any case I've got a letter to re-read, and so the time passes.

An airman brings in some tea, someone puts a record on the radiogram and we sip our tea to the strains of Tommy Dorsey 'Getting Sentimental Over You'. Blue cigarette smoke rises slowly over the rafters.

The phone rings. Webber, the telephone orderly, takes the call.

'Ops confirm they want us airborne by 17.30, sir. Maidstone patrol line at 20,000 feet.'

'Thank you, Webber, tell the flight sergeant.'

'Right, sir.'

'OK, merry men. The time by my watch is one minute to 17.00; press tits at 17.20. We'll not rush things so get to your aircraft in good time. Any questions? I assume not, your silence is deafening.'

I finish my tea.

'Pancho, I'm going on up to my aircraft now. I've synchronized my watch.'

'OK, Boy.'

I walk slowly up the dispersal. The same old smells, oil, high-octane petrol and aeroplanes. Late hazy sunshine, dusty flying boots and everything has a copper colour about it. What a lovely summer it's been weatherwise. Reaching my dispersal pen I see a crowd of ground crew sitting about talking. Davy and Bevington get up as I approach.

'That's all right, lads, plenty of time, we get airborne at 17.30.'

The other airmen get up and wander slowly to their aircraft.

'Well, I'd better get down and check my kite again, just in case. You never know.'

I sit down with my two stalwarts and talk to them. I get to know all their problems that way and they seem to like telling me, which is more important. The time passes quickly.

'Well, I suppose we'd better get cracking.'

'OK, sir, back in about the usual time?'

'Guess so. Could be about dusk, I suppose.'

I clamber into my Spitfire and settle down in the cockpit. Without really thinking, I run through the drill. Time to start up. 'Contact'. Airscrews turning all along dispersal and engines breaking into a crescendo of noise. Taxi out and form up on Pancho Villa's 'N' and the remainder of the squadron positions behind and on either side. Twelve Spits ready for the off. I glance round at Tommy and he gives me a wave. Two minutes to 17.30 and we are all ready.

'OK, Gannic, here we go.'

How often have I heard those words through my earphones? As one, the Spitfires start to roll forward, throttles opening and away over the turf and into the air. Maidstone bloody patrol line here we come, again.

Climbing steadily through the late-afternoon haze, the sun, red and rather angry looking, throws its last rays on the gently swaying aircraft, bathing them in a brown golden colour. It reflects on the spinning arc of the airscrew as I look ahead and ease away from Pancho and take up battle formation. Look around and automatically search above and behind and down towards the ground but it's too hazy to see all that much down there. Height reached, we drone up and down our patrol line. It's all very quiet and peaceful.

'Sapper, this is Gannic leader, anything going on anywhere?'

'No, Gannic, nothing on the board of any consequence. The odd plot over Gris Nez but they have been there for some time now.'

'OK, Sapper, thank you.'

Well, that's that. With any sort of luck we will soon get the order to pancake and that will be the end of another patrol and another day. Just like I said, nice and peaceful. The minutes pass away and the sun sinks lower. Another five minutes and it will be touching the horizon. I look down into the haze but there's nothing to be seen except a momentary glimpse of a glinting window reflecting the last dying rays of the setting sun. There it is again, strange but . . . just a second, hold on a bit, if from up here at 20,000 the sun is already touching the horizon, it must be below the horizon at ground level, so how on earth could windows on the ground possibly reflect the rays of the sun? It's all a little odd, to say the least.

I fix my eyes on the spot where I last saw the flash. Now there, there it is again and yet a second time. Surely that looks rather nearer. Maybe, but we are cracking along a bit too of course. Nevertheless, how can the reflecting object possibly be on the ground? Yet another flash, but more prolonged. Could it be the reflection from the perspex canopy of an aircraft? Suspicion enters my mind and now, thoroughly alert to something odd going on, I find myself leaning forward and tense in my cockpit. Concentrating on that part of the sky I sense rather than see movement. There's definitely something going on down there, but what? Christ yes, now I see it, an aircraft, quite positive. Hell fire, there's another one alongside it. Jesus, there's a whole bloody formation.

I'm far too excited. Now calm down, Geoff, just for a second. Don't start getting all het up like a new boy. The Controller said there was nothing on the board but there is, right down there below us, two, four, five, six, ten, twelve – that'll do for a start. I can see one quite clearly for a brief second and it's an Me 110, no possible doubt at all, twin rudder and fins. Instinctively, I press the transmit button. 'Gannic leader, this is Red 2. Ten plus bandits at one o'clock, estimate about three to four thousand feet below.'

I see Pancho's head turn in the direction I indicated.

'Where away, Red 2? I can't see them, are you certain?'

'Quite certain, they're 110s. Follow me, I'll stay up sun, such as it is.'

'OK, go ahead.'

I pull out in front of the squadron, turning to starboard as I do so. Almost immediately Pancho's voice comes up on the R/T.

'OK, I can see them now. Re-form on me, good show.'

'Will do.'

'Sapper, Gannic leader, tally-ho!'

'Really, Gannic, how many?'

'Sixteen or thereabouts, they are 110s.'

'How very odd.'

'OK, Gannic, stand by to go in in about thirty seconds. Do not attack yet, wait for it. Echelon starboard . . . GO!'

Pancho is taking us into the best possible position and the squadron looks terrific and in good order. A lump in my throat. I can't help gulping. Come on, Geoff, earn your fourteen shillings a day.

I feel a savage delight. Right, you sods, you're going to catch a packet. We have the height for a change and what a jolly nice change it is too. What was it that Mannock★ used to say? 'Always on top, seldom on the same level, never underneath.'

I wonder what on earth these Huns are up to. What is their purpose? Sixteen 110s stooging quietly over the fields of Kent at about 10,000 feet out for a quiet evening stroll no doubt. I search the sky above and behind but it appears to be clear. It's no trap, these Huns are on their own.

'OK, Gannic, let's sort this lot out.' Pancho peels off. I catch a glimpse of the oil-streaked belly of his aeroplane. Stick over and I follow. The squadron falls out of the sky behind the 110s and it doesn't appear that they have seen us. I pick a 110 two removed from the leader. He's a little wide. It's obvious I'm closing my target too fast. Mustn't let my speed build up too much if I can help it. Ease back the throttle; must reduce this overtaking speed or else I shall make a balls up of the whole attack. I am still well up on Pancho. Back with the throttle a little more, that's a bit better. Now line him up, sights on, hold it steady. He's growing bigger quite rapidly. Hold the line, Geoff, hold it, not quite there yet; right, you bastard, now's the moment and I press the gun button. Vibration, noise and recoil. Take that little lot. This is a damn good burst, quick now or you'll collide with the bugger. Stick forward, flung against the straps and I pass just underneath his tail. Blimey, that was a shade close. No return fire and I have at least hit him well and truly. I glimpse a gush of smoke or

★ Major Edward C. 'Mick' Mannock, the UK's leading First World War fighter ace with 73 victories. Killed in action over France 26 July 1918, aged thirty-one.

something from somewhere around the centre section wing root and then he is past and gone.

Pull up, regain height, come on, Geoff, open the throttle, give her all she's got. Up we go, that's nice, roll over and looking down I see two 110s going down, one with black smoke. Hope it's mine.

The remaining Huns have split up and a mother and father of a dogfight is developing. Without knowing how or why, I find myself back in the general mêlée. I manage to latch on to a Hun who seems to be making a break for it. You're not getting away with it as easily as that, my friend, not if I have any say in the matter.

A quick look around above and behind again. All over the sky 110s are being chased by Spitfires. My particular Hun takes violent evasive action and I follow. I fling the Spit all over the sky in order to stay with him. This chap is no fool. I'm on to a good one here, he's like an eel, blast him. I manage one quick burst and I'm sure I see strikes on the fuselage. I don't think I imagine it. Doesn't seem to have slowed him up any, though. Warm work this. Stay still, you stupid bugger. Another snap shot. These 110s are being well flown, no doubt about that. We have a bunch of Hun pilots who really know their job and how to chuck things around.

Now that was a better shot, Geoff, that last one. My Hun stops his gyrations and dives steeply away. No trouble in following you now, old chap, and take that to help you on your way. Think I've got this one. His dive steepens and he starts to turn on his back. I take a quick look round before finishing him off in a nice tidy manner and am just in time to see a 110 diving down on me, opening fire as he does so. Jesus, I've seen him just in time, another fraction of a second . . . I break towards him and his tracers go harmlessly over the top. That was a bit of luck, Geoff. Don't dwell on that one too long. Something made you look up just in the nick of time.

An aircraft spinning down to my left and from the way of the spin I would say out of control. It is a 110 and, to my amazement, its tail twists off and hangs in the air for just a fraction of a second, then flutters like an autumn leaf towards the ground. Hun aircraft appear to do this sort of thing quite often. The fuselage snapped like a carrot just in front of the tail assembly, leaving the front half to plummet to earth and, even as I watch, it starts to break up as it does so. Bad luck, chum, shouldn't have joined. Another 110 is being attacked by two Spitfires and I go to lend a hand but, before I can get to the scene, a small blob detaches itself from the Hun aircraft and a parachute opens. The aircraft curves down, way down, until it is lost in the evening shadows. There'll be a few empty chairs in the 110 Mess this evening.

Only one got out of that aeroplane. I wonder if these chaps are carrying rear gunners? Can't recall seeing any return fire and I don't think they could have seen our first attack. I stay with the mix-up in a rather aimless sort of way, looking for a target or somebody to help. It's getting rather warm. I'm sweating and I realize I'm gulping; must be excited still. Mustn't let that worry me. Just keep going and keep a bloody good lookout up your chuff. Another 110 streaming glycol flashes past but I have to avoid colliding with a Spitfire and I can't do anything about him. With luck, he won't get far, anyway. Got two engines, though.

Isn't it an odd life? Last night and this morning at home in my own room once again, Mum and Dad, where I grew up, the night before with Grace and now look at me. Lucky they don't know what I'm up to right now, that's the main thing.

I look around and I'm alone. Now where the hell has everybody got to? They were about a few seconds ago; I was in the middle of the buggers. The sun has almost set and everybody must have decided at once to call it a day, had enough. Turning in the direction of base, I pick out a Spit diving away into the haze over to starboard, obviously going home. Somehow and for some unknown reason, I hang around. Amusing and distant R/T conversation, the speaker unseen and unreal as his voice comes over the ether. The voice is clear and very Oxbridge accent.

'Black 1, this is Black 2, can you still see me?' A pause . . .

'Black 2, yes, I've got you in sight.'

'Well, where the bloody hell am I, then?'

Possibly one of the two Tommys or it may be Wimpey. I'm not too sure, difficult to tell. This sort of thing makes for a little light relief.

'All Gannic aircraft, this is Sapper. Pancake; pancake. Good show, lads.'

I look around, I don't want to be hurried. The rusty yellow haze has turned to a sort of mauve colour. Over to the west a long angry red line shows the passage of the sun beyond the horizon and the gathering of evening shadows; passing day. Ten minutes of organized and legal murder. I have what almost amounts to a sense of guilt at my involvement and the excitement I experienced during the chase. How many Germans did we kill in that short space of time and how many of us did they clobber? Whoever understands, I hope He is satisfied.

'All Gannic aircraft, this is Sapper. Pancake, pancake.' The Controller sounds a little anxious. We must be split up all over the shop and taking time to get back and, of course, it's getting a bit dark down on the ground. I'll give the old lad a call.

'Sapper, Red 2 returning to base.'

'OK, Red 2, transmit.'

'Sapper, Red 2 transmitting . . . Mary had a little lamb, its feet as black as soot, and into Mary's bread and jam his sooty foot he put. Over.'

'Very amusing, Red 2, but vector 285 for base and beer. Confirm bar open.'

'Immediately, Sapper. Thank you.'

Turning on to course far over to the right I am just able to make out the balloons of the Thames estuary barrage sitting on top of the haze. They are barely discernible; it's getting late. I'm off home a bit smartish. I wonder if we all are. Let the nose drop away and down into the murk. Level off at 1,000 feet and I see another Spitfire also losing height. I switch on my navigation lights for something to do. It's well into dusk so I join up with him. It's Wimpey. His helmeted head turns, he's seen me so I close in and fly tight on his port side. Let him take me home, I almost can't be bothered. His navigation lights flick on. 'I bet this looks good, Trevor. Take me home.'

He gives me a thumbs up.

> The busy world is hushed,
> The fever of life is over
> And our work done.

> *Book of Common Prayer*

8. Snappers About

A cool afternoon, rather dull and lifeless with rain in the air. I huddle in my Irvin jacket* as I trudge back to the dispersal hut. Just been to check over the old Spit. Fancy being called to readiness at three o'clock in the afternoon. We were beginning to hope that we had got away with it for the day, but oh dear me no. Not on your Nellie. The man got on the phone to the Mess. 'I'm going to bugger up 92 Squadron's otherwise peaceful afternoon,' he said. 'Send one flight to readiness right away, got it?' We got it right enough and, of course, it just had to be bloody old 'A' Flight. Plenty of people in the flight at the moment so I make out I haven't heard a thing, but it doesn't work.

'Boy, you jolly well heard and in any case you look too comfortable in that chair by far. Come on, let's get on our way.'

'I've got an awful toothache.'

'Balls.'

'Headache, bad nerves, weak heart?'

'Move it.'

'OK, I'm coming. Don't rush about. Worth a try.'

It's one of those afternoons when everything looks drab and grey. Lots of cloud, layers of the stuff. Nothing too low, however, so I suppose there's no reason why the war should not continue. At dispersal it is all automatic. Parachute and

---

* The upper half of a two-part thermally heated insulated flying jacket. In warm weather fighter pilots often wore the jacket only, unless in exposed conditions such as open-cockpit flying.

helmet from the locker and hump it to the waiting Spitfire. Pass the time of day with Bevington and Davy; all ready to my liking and so the stroll back to the hut.

A NAAFI van clatters past on its way down the dispersal and stops outside the crew rooms. I quicken my pace. A cup of the finest tea courtesy of NAAFI is the only answer. Smartly into the hut and grab the biggest and nearest mug I can lay my hands on followed by a rush to the counter before the lady has time to pull down the shutters and push off.

'Good afternoon, would you fill that with tea, please?'

'Certainly not.'

'But I'm gasping, have all my very 'igh-class mates polished off the lot?'

'No, it's not that, there's plenty left, but just look at your mug or whatever you like to call it. Where on earth did you manage to find such a thing?'

'It's not mine. I've just borrowed it. Anyway, what's the matter with it? It won't leak, will it?'

'Size, has the mere size occurred to you?'

'Not really. I suppose it is on the big side.'

'Well, you'll just have to pay more, that's all. It will cost you tuppence, I'm sorry.'

'Oh, Lord, I don't think I have tuppence on me. There's one, though. I'm very poor, have to live on my pay.'

'Give it here.'

'Ah, thank you. Would you like a cup?'

'And how do you intend to pay for it if I did?'

'Well, actually, I've found another penny and I'd like to reward you for filling up my very large mug.'

'Give it here, you poor hard done by soul and thank you, but I don't quite know what for.'

'Thoughtfulness.'

I take up my mug, which is as full as it ever could be. 'Thanks, that really is wonderful.'

'OK. Now clear off please and let me get on. I don't know what's the matter with you people this afternoon.'

I take a sip to save spilling any. 'OK, then. Bye bye, see you tomorrow, maybe.'

'Please just go away.'

That seems final enough; what a kind lady. A wave of my hand and with my steaming great mug of tea, wet, warm and sweet, I enter dispersal and find a vacant seat. The big Tom gives me a long hard look.

'Geoff, I do declare you must be a truly wonderful chap. How on earth did you manage to extract that positively bloody great urn of tea out of the NAAFI?'

'Overwhelming personality, cheery good humour and charming manners.'

'And it's not a bloody great urn, sir, it's my mug wot I've been looking for.'

'I'm sorry, Webber, I didn't know.'

'Yes he did, Webber, and he doesn't deserve it. It's improper possession, a crime under air-force law. Make him give it back to you, full.'

'It's all right, sir, I've got another one.'

'Really, Webber,' says the big man with interest. 'Where do you keep it, may I ask?'

'Don't tell him, I forbid you.'

'If you say so, sir, orders is orders.'

'Thank you.'

Big Tom grins, gets up and takes his own small mug of tea to the window, looking up at the sky. I'd like as many pennies for the number of times I've seen chaps doing just that. I find myself standing beside him.

'This stuff is lifting quite a bit, Geoff. It's getting slowly better the whole time.'

'Um. I don't somehow reckon on it clearing completely, though. It's still looking a bit mucky out to the west.'

'Maybe you're right.'

'Mind you, Tom, this sort of weather might well suit the Hun tip-and-run boys. They've been doing rather more of that sort of thing lately.'

'I bet Group think so too, they wouldn't bring us to readiness straight from thirty minutes just for the hell of it.'

'Wouldn't they? Don't you believe it. They're highly trained in the art of disturbing released squadrons are those controllers. They all go on a course, a special disturbance course, it's for squadron leaders and above, so we can't volunteer yet.'

'Now you're getting flippant again. Aren't we a funny little Geoffrey.'

He slaps me on the shoulder. My knees buckle and I decide to return to my chair. I shall be safe there from his comradely gestures. It seems I am just not destined to have any peace and quiet this afternoon because in a very short time the phone rings. Webber picks up the receiver. I don't like it. I've got that peculiar empty feeling. He looks at Brian.

'It's for you, sir; the Controller.' Brian takes over the phone.

'Yes, Bill, what can we do for you?' A pause. 'I see, how many aircraft? Four? OK. I'll send Geoffrey Wellum and Ronnie Fokes each with a number two. When do you want them off? Now? OK, right away.' Brian turns to us.

'OK, lads, you heard the gist of that, standing patrol North Foreland to Dungeness at 10,000. Each of you take one of our newer blokes. Boy, you can take Tommy Thompson and Don Kingaby for you, Ronnie. Off you go.'

That sounds a very final order. There's positively no arguing with a bloke like that and I get up and move without too much enthusiasm towards the door.

'I'll keep station on you, Ronnie.'

'OK, Geoff. Right, Don, you're with me. Keep your eyes skinned and stay close. If we run into any trouble, stick to me like glue, right on my tail, understand?'

'Understand.'

'Let's go, then.'

On the climb up there is quite a lot of cloud about and Ronnie calls up Ops and tells them about it.

'OK, Blue 1, thank you. Reduce to angels five. Keep the ground in sight if you can.'

'Received and understood. Anything happening?'

'Nothing at this very moment, but 109s have been active bombing all along the south coast and we expect them to have a go up North Foreland way. They have been at it somewhere or other for most of the afternoon, on and off.'

'Thank you, Sapper, understood.'

'Just a minute, Blue 1, talk of the Devil, I have a message for you.'

'Standing by, Sapper, pass your message.'

'Buster, buster Margate. Bombs have just been dropped on the town. This is Sapper, over.' He sounds a little excited.

'Sapper, this is Blue 1, received and understood.'

We arrive at the scene after the birds have flown. I have a good look at Margate and can see nothing untoward, no smoke, no fires. It all looks very peaceful so let's hope little damage was done. Ronnie tells Ops as much and they order us to patrol below cloud, in this case about 1,500 feet. Visibility is not all that brilliant as there appears to be a mistiness over the sea. Not a very good afternoon really and it's always a problem to catch these hit-and-run boys. Sapper comes up on the air again.

'Gannic Blue 1, bogeys reported over Broadstairs and Ramsgate.'

'Received, Sapper, any height?'

'Sorry, Gannic, reported at 1,500 feet.'

'Sapper, that could be us you know.'

'Don't think so, they're not reported as Spitfires.'

'OK, Sapper, thanks. Let me know if you get anything definite.'

'Will do, Gannic.'

I call up Tommy. 'Yellow 2 this is 1. Spread out a bit, they must be around somewhere.'

'If they're here, Boy.'

'Quite.'

Searching and straining my eyes I can see nothing to arouse any suspicion but Ops keep calling us up with reports and I begin to feel inadequate and uneasy. It must surely be our formation they are plotting. Now, let's have a think. If I was a German how would I go about dropping a bomb on a coastal town in this afternoon's conditions? Easy, come right in on the deck, every fool knows that. Under the radar. Then pull up to say 1,500 feet or even less, drop my bomb, down to the deck again or pull up into cloud and bugger off smartly. I fancy on the deck. That's the answer, then. That's where the sods are most likely to be, at ground level, and we are too high.

'Yellow 2 here. Is that something below and over the coast by that little bay there?'

'What do you mean "there"?'

'Sorry, Geoff, at eight o'clock, sorry, they're low.'

Little bay, he must mean . . . Christ, yes. I can see what he means. There is something down there. Can't see them now, though. They must have gone over the land, if they're aircraft.

'Sapper, any other friendly aircraft in the area?'

'No. Only you.'

'Understood.' I rivet my gaze on the area in the vicinity of the bay. There it is, that movement again. It's more of a feeling than a sighting but it can only be aircraft of some sort, surely. There it is . . . no, there *they* are. A pair.

'Ronnie, this is Geoff. Two aircraft nine o'clock low, almost on the deck.'

'OK, Geoffrey. I can't make them out; you lead, we'll follow.'

'Turning port 90 degrees and diving.'

'Carry on. Still can't see them, Boy.'

'Ron, I can just make out their movement . . . seem to be turning and heading out to sea. Dead ahead now, see them. Right down on the water, just off the coast.'

'OK, I've got them now. Well done, Yellow 2. Carry on, Boy, I can't catch you yet, you've got a head start.'

A quick glance behind and I see Ronnie with Blue section following on. My number two quite nicely placed. 'Stick close, Yellow 2.'

'Just behind, Yellow 1.'

'Tally-ho!'

I can see the two aircraft quite plainly now. They are flying fast and very low indeed, not more than a hundred feet is my guess, and their course is straight as a die for the coast of France. I recognize them. They are ME 109s. We are dead astern and they haven't seen us. Ronnie gives a brief call on the R/T as we start the chase.

'Sapper, this is Gannic Blue 1. Tally-ho! Two 109s.'

'Received you, Gannic. Go to it, lads. Good luck!'

Wonder who the Controller is? Probably a new bloke under training. It's not Bill Igoe, that's for certain. This chap's very excited. We're the ones who should be like that, not him.

Closing steadily we drop down into a thin layer of haze sitting on the sea and the 109s are just in the top of it. Four lethal determined-looking Spitfires are closing in behind them looking for the kill. Pilots hunched forward in their cockpits, concentrating and intense. The roundels on the Spits standing out clearly as if to say, 'we're British and we're going to clobber you for coming over here to kill our people uninvited'.

I feel excitement. The same as the hunter must feel as the field gets towards the end of the chase. Never went much on this hunting lark myself. Seems a bit one-sided to me. Chasing

German aeroplanes is another thing entirely. I peer ahead
through the spinning disc of the airscrew and steady myself
down. If we're sensible and do the job carefully and properly
then both these Huns are cold meat. They haven't seen us.
Gun button on to fire. Reflector sight on and set the range
scale to 109 wing span. Still pulling them into range nicely.

God, this is relentless. Ronnie has come level with us on
the starboard side. Looking through the sight I ease the dot in
the middle on to the top of the left-hand 109's fuselage; no
deflection, straight dead astern. Don't worry about the other
109 now, Geoff, Ronnie will look after that, I hope.

'Take the one on the right, Ronnie.'

'OK, Geoff, already on to him.'

My whole concentration now revolves around the target.
Slowly my 109 grows into the cross bars. The spot of the sight
is still dead on. I suddenly have become horribly calm. That's
the idea, Geoff, steady, don't get worked up again and cock
it all up. A little closer . . . take your time just this once . . . he
doesn't know you're anywhere near . . . a shade more . . .
that's nice . . . you're there, Geoff. The guns fire. I must have
pressed the tit.

A huge puff of white vapour explodes from the entire centre
section of the 109. Glycol. Masses of it. The whole area of the
cockpit is enveloped in one great mass of steam. What a burst.
That's really clobbered him and almost before I stop firing he
turns quickly on to his back and goes straight into the sea like
a gannet. A truly terrific wonderful splash, so great that I just
clip the top of the spray, or at least I fancy I do.

'Good shot, Boy, and there goes the other bastard.'

Out of the corner of my eye I catch a glimpse for just the
merest fraction of a second of another large splash. That's
settled their hash. At least it was quick. Ronnie calls up Ops
but we are too low for anything like good reception at this
range. However, they get the gist of things. The section pulls

up to just above the haze, re-forming as it does so in a steady easy turn back towards England.

My goodness, things don't half happen quickly at this game. Less than a minute ago two German pilots were contentedly heading back home after another tip-and-run sortie on our south coast and now, in just sixty short seconds, they are both dead, still strapped in their seats at the bottom of the Channel. A lot can happen in sixty seconds. I wonder what sort of chaps they were? God knows, but I suppose they are in good company. How many others are down there? Peter for one.

As we approach our coast I look back in the direction of their last resting place. The sea under the haze and cloud is a sullen metallic leaden grey. It looks cold and hostile. An area of constant restless movement, brooding and ready to ensnare the next aeroplane to come within its reach and crash into it; or the next ship to sink. There's no mercy, no satisfying of its appetite. The sea can be terribly cruel and unforgiving. It's a horrible and lonely place in which to die. Peter knows.

What a world. Geoff, you've just killed a bloke, a fellow fighter pilot. I'm getting some sort of reaction. That was just about as callous and as calculating as you can get, just plain cold-blooded murder. The bloke didn't even know what had hit him. On the other hand, if he had just dropped his bloody great bomb on a house, and they're not in the least discriminating these Germans, the people in that house, old, young, male or female, wouldn't have known what had hit them either. It's all bloody wrong somehow, that twentieth-century civilization should have been allowed to come to this. Just total war, I suppose. What's it all about, for God's sake?

As we fly over the Weald of Kent, safely on our way home to Biggin, I look across at the others. There seems little elation, no thumbs up signs or anything like that. Each with his own thoughts. We're all lucky, at least we're on our way home. The section closes into a tight formation. Must look pretty tidy from the ground. What good company, Ronnie Fokes leading us.

I look over at Tommy the Big. His head is turned towards me as he concentrates on keeping formation. I can see his eyes over the top of his face mask but, seemingly, from this distance anyway, they appear devoid of expression. Biggin approaches out of greyness ahead. It is a different greyness from that over the sea. I can still see in my mind that water back there. There's such a hell of a lot of it. What a terrible and frightening place the sea can be when it wants to. 'The lonely sea and the sky.' Masefield knew what he was talking about.

Ronnie leads the section in a shallow dive across dispersal and breaks away in a Prince of Wales Feathers. A very tight circuit and into fine pitch. Wheels and flaps, slip off some height, not too much, over the hedge, throttle back, stick back and the rumble, rumble of wheels over the turf. Safely on the ground.

I'm back home. One day perhaps . . . now that's enough of that. Don't be a total bloody fool.

Turning crosswind at the end of my landing run I watch the others all safely down. Who would ever guess at the damage we have done in our little Spitfires?

Nothing to do now but taxi in. Approaching dispersal, my mind a bit of a blank as usual, I notice Tom Wiesse, the Intelligence Officer, appearing from behind our primitive dispersal-point toilet doing up his fly. That reminds me, all that NAAFI tea is giving me hell.

9. Convoy Pair

Mid-January 1941. It has been raining steadily and relentlessly the whole morning. Six armchairs ring a large log fire, and each chair is occupied by a fighter pilot. Lunch is over and 'A' Flight are in the Mess on thirty minutes' availability. Except for the occasional rattle of a coffee cup or the rustle of a newspaper page being turned, peace reigns and an air of contentment prevails.

The September battles are behind us and the squadron is at Manston, the forward base for the winter months. Situated close to the south coast and the Thames estuary, it was a peacetime aerodrome. During the summer months' bombing, to which all our fighter airfields in the south-east of England were subjected, it had suffered heavily. Among the buildings destroyed was the Officers' Mess, and so the pre-war house used by the Station Commander has been taken over, suitably equipped and used for the purpose. It is a warm and friendly place and we enjoy its homely atmosphere.

I look out of the window as a flurry of rain, hustled by a fresh westerly wind, dashes itself against the glass. The cloud is unbroken with its base not much more than 500 feet and below that wisps of driven stratus hurry across the rain-sodden landscape. If anything, the weather seems to be lowering the whole time; dull, threatening and unfriendly.

Settling down further into my chair, I relax and ponder jumbled thoughts. This is the sort of weather we could have done with for the odd day back in September. At least it would have given us some small respite from the undoubted strain of daily combat flying. I look at the occupants in the other chairs. Bill Watling is fairly new to the squadron. Tommy, Brian, Wimpey, Tony and myself are, I suppose, the survivors out of the original 'A' Flight that first went into battle in August. Brian was shot down and wounded in October, he says by Spitfires, and is just getting back on song again. How unreal and remote it all seems. Did we really go tumbling into all those Huns? Less than eighteen months ago I was still at school; what an eighteen months.

I wonder what's going on there at the moment? Who has my old study? Whoever he is, has he changed that duff lock on the door? Never realized how I liked the place and how much it all meant to me. The large dining hall with its oak panels, the high table for the gowned masters with the portraits of the founders and past headmasters peering down from the walls with apparent disdain and distaste. Then there were the cloisters leading to the chapel, playing fields on a fine summer day with cricket and ice creams from the grub shop; peaceful England at her best and now look at us, really having to fight for our very existence. There's an awful lot I don't understand.

We all say 'Please God, give us victory over the Germans, our cause is just', and the Germans likewise pray for victory over the treacherous British . . . are the Germans allowed to believe in God these days? Presumably God favoured us during last summer; or did He – with the glorious weather that must have suited the purpose of the Hun? In any case, why does He allow this sort of thing to happen? Whatever He decides, many thousands of people, 'His children' we are all taught to believe, are going to be slaughtered before it is all over. There is an awful price to be paid.

My thoughts meander on. The RAF will bear the brunt of this war for some time yet; the bomber boys at night, poor sods, and we fighter chaps during the day. I think of my friends who are no longer with us: Butch and Howard were both shot down and killed and Gussie did not return after he took off leading a section one glorious summer evening and ran into a bunch of 109s. His body was found some time later still in his Spitfire in the middle of a wood. John Drummond, with whom I shared a room for those early days at Biggin, collided with Bill Williams and I gather is still not found. There are many others.

Since being at Manston, it has been possible to unwind a little. We have not been doing all that much operational flying except for a few standing patrols. With the onset of winter and the poor weather, enemy air activity during the daylight hours has been greatly reduced. No doubt they are licking their wounds; after all, we gave them something to think about during those long, seemingly endless summer days. In fact, we won that battle insofar as we were able to deny the Huns the command of the air over the Channel. That was essential, of course, if they were ever going to mount a full-scale invasion. Fighter Command inflicted the first setback or defeat that these wretched Nazis have suffered. We gave them a bit of a beating, but not without paying a price of course.

I look at Brian reading his paper. Still composed and relaxed but looking very tired and a lot thinner. Wimpey is asleep and I would say that he has changed the most. Gone is a lot of his gaiety and boyish pranks. He started operational flying with great nerve, dashing into the thick of the fight regardless. A natural pilot, he seemed to like flying upside down more than the right way up. People said he was asking for it and that if the Hun didn't get him it would only be a matter of time before he killed himself. In fact, he was shot down twice, but got away with it and retaliated by shooting down eight, so they gave him a DFC. Make no mistake, Trevor Wade has suddenly become much older. The lines on his rather drawn face tell their own story. Dear old Tommy number one appears to have changed the least . . . except maybe he is a little quieter. We are, of course, very close friends and invariably with the Big Man spend happy and relaxed moments talking together over our evening tankards of ale.

These men have etched themselves on my memory for all time. We have lived, flown, fought, experienced danger, felt elation, sorrow and fear, taken leisure and done our drinking together. We are now a closely knit band of pilots who trust each other when in the air and are happiest when in our own company on the ground.

There is a mutual respect and a sense of comradeship that will make these days supreme in our lives, days that we will remember always, or for as long as we live. Such, I suppose, is the atmosphere in any battle-experienced front line operational fighter squadron and, as my thoughts continue, I know that I am thankful and have great pride in being here. Last year and this must surely be Fighter Command in its finest hour and I certainly wouldn't swap places with anybody, even though, at times, things get a little rugged.

My reveries are broken when a mess steward comes into the room and puts a couple of logs on to the fire in a blaze of sparks, just like the sparks from a Spitfire exhaust when you throttle back at night. Funny how everything still seems to revolve around Spitfires.

More beating rain on the windows and I wonder how long it will be before we are released and told to stand down for the rest of the day. I should have thought that Ops would have done so already. It's unusual not to have heard something from them in weather like this. The minutes pass by and my eyes turn towards the window again. Surely they can't be thinking of sending any of us off in this stuff?

I experience that feeling, not exactly of apprehension or even excitement – it's all very difficult to explain – an emotion, a sensation of having to boost oneself to meet a challenge that may be flung down at any moment.

It must be telepathy. Brian looks up from his newspaper, glances out of the window and then at his watch. Putting the paper on the floor beside his chair he rises, picks up his empty coffee cup and moves quietly over to the small table where he refills it from the pot on the hotplate. Milk, two spoonfuls of sugar and he walks slowly to the rain-spattered window where he surveys the dismal scene outside with professional interest. Leaning close to the glass he looks up at the ever-lowering cloud base.

I watch him and I know what is going on in his mind; surely not in weather like this. As he turns, I catch his eye. We are both in accord, our thoughts in unison. Tom has woken up and is staring into the fire, his face expressionless. What are his thoughts? The others all appear to be dozing, empty coffee cups and newspapers cast aside.

Coffee consumed, Brian places his cup on the table with slow thoughtful deliberation, glances once again out of the window and moves towards the door. It is just after 2 p.m. and I know he is going to phone the Controller.

Some minutes pass. He seems to be taking his time and I sense that the conversation covers more than just getting our release. As he still does not return the feeling that something is cooking grows stronger, although it does occur to me that any controller would think very carefully before sending aircraft off in these conditions, particularly as a further deterioration is likely. This is what the conversation is all about, I'll bet a pound. One thing is for certain and that is that if we are sent off it'll be for only a very good reason.

It seems an age before Brian re-enters the room, walks over to the fire and stands with his back to the flames. He says nothing. Tommy stretches, stifles a yawn and looks at him.

'You have our permission to speak.'

'Ops may want us to send two aircraft off. They'll be ringing back shortly.'

So that's it! I damn well knew it and what's more I've got a feeling that I shall be one of the two to go. Oh, Lord! Why did yesterday have to be my afternoon off when I missed a simple standing patrol? I glance across at Tom. The expression on his face is one of utter disbelief.

'Good God. Are they really serious?'

'They're serious, right enough,' replies Brian. 'When I first spoke to them they asked if I thought we could get a whole flight into the air. I said anything was possible. To get something into the air was one thing, but to get them all back again was quite another. I told them in no mean terms what sort of weather we have and they finally settled for just two. Apparently, our weather conditions are the best in all 11 Group at the moment.'

'Well, all I can say is that the rest of the country must be bloody awful if we're the best. What do Met have to say?'

'I spoke to them first and they hold out no hope of improvement for at least another twelve hours and, as far as today is concerned, the chances are that it will get even lower as the day goes on towards dusk.'

'Did you tell Ops that?'

'Of course I bloody well told Ops that. What a damn fool question. No, Tom, they realize the situation and are getting on to Command to see if our journey will really be necessary.'

'What's it all about, anyway?'

'There is a large convoy going up the east coast tonight and it would appear that there are one or two plots milling around over the Dutch coast and the navy are getting worried. If those plots start to move out into the North Sea then I think we will be asked to make an attempt and obviously we will have to go and show willing.'

Well, now we know. The contentment and peace that prevailed a few minutes ago have gone. Everybody is sitting up and taking notice, excepting Wimpey, who hasn't stirred.

'Come on, Trev, wakey, wakey, you've heard. You're not asleep, anyway.'

'Indeed, I am asleep and, what's more, I haven't heard a bloody word of what's going on, not a single solitary bloody word.'

'OK, Brian, who is it to be?'

'Well Geoff m'boy, would you go as number two to Tommy?'

My heart sinks. If only I could say 'certainly not'.

'Why yes, of course.'

That's it, then. I could have said that I had a cold or made a fatuous excuse of some sort or other. After all, having got through the summer, why stick your neck out now? However, I'm going and that's it. Tommy looks across at me and grins, most infectious.

'You'll go, Tom, all right?'

'Yes, Brian, and I'd like to take Boy with me, if anyone. Have to keep an eye on him, of course; he's too new to let out alone.'

'Quite,' from the recumbent Wimpey.

'Oh, go back to sleep and wrap up. Brian, where is this so-important convoy?'

'I'm not too certain, but our esteemed Intelligence Officer is waiting by the phone now and if they decide on going he will get all the gen required.'

Tommy gets up and crosses to the window on which the rain continues to beat without let-up. I join him. It is not an inspiring view. Only the sky looks alive with constant movement. The low slate-grey clouds chase each other across the rainswept countryside, which looks completely saturated. Apart from the swaying trees and the tumbling overcast there is little movement. Nobody is about. A quiet voice behind us: 'Yes, I know all about it and so does the Controller. He doesn't want to send you but, somehow, I'm sure we will be asked to try, in which case that is exactly what we'll do. It won't be a picnic, but we are supposed to be up to this sort of thing. It's bloody borderline, I know.'

'Well, I'm thinking whether we will see anything.'

I stand and listen to the conversation. I haven't much to say.

'Take a look at the visibility. What do you reckon it is?' says Tom.

'A bad 2,000 yards, if that.'

'I agree and, bearing in mind that the Met say it's probably going to get worse, getting back may be tricky and we have no diversion to go to, it seems. What do you think it will be like over the sea?'

'Well, obviously, it won't be any better.'

A slow but delightful smile; understanding.

'Ops will want to know all the pros and cons before they finally decide and I'm on your side.'

Tom Wiesse, the Intelligence Officer, arrives and joins us. Known to all and sundry as 'Spy', he looks more hot and bothered than usual.

'Operations are on the phone again, Brian. It looks as if the show is on.'

My heart sinks and a feeling of total resignation bordering on despair comes over me. Brian goes to the phone, only this time it is not long before he returns.

'Well, I've told them what I think and how I assess the situation. They understand but they want us to have a go, so there it is. If it really turns out to be utterly impossible then give them a call on the R/T and they will tell you to return to base, we hope.'

'At 500 feet or less they may not even hear us.'

'Then you will have to use your judgement.'

'OK.'

'Those plots are looking a bit offensive. It appears that the

Hun airfields are not too bad at the moment, weatherwise.'

'Really? That's fine, we can divert there, then.'

'A typical Boy remark. Come on then, let's get going. It'll be dark a bit earlier tonight and it's already half past two.'

'Come into the office when you're ready,' says Tom, 'and I'll tell you all the latest on positions and what the opposition is doing.'

'OK, Tom, we'll go down to dispersal in the brake, see you there.'

Tommy and I follow Brian to the door and leave the others to their fireside. Well that's that. Let's get cracking and get it over with one way or another.

The drive round the airfield to dispersal does nothing to ease the tension. The rain is still being driven by the wind and the clouds continue to scurry after each other across the sky. They come out of the west in an endless procession of distorted angry shapes. Altogether a horrid afternoon. Filthy. No vestige of a break is visible. It is with us for the rest of the day and we are lumbered with it.

We enter the deserted dispersal hut and not even the telephone orderly is at his table. At the door I pause. We are a lot of untidy louts. Flying gear and discarded parachutes, scarves, empty cigarette packets and all sorts of personal rubbish litter the place. On the wall the pin-ups look at us with cynical amusement. The squadron artist ones are the best. I turn and look out to the, as yet, silent airfield. In the distance my ground crew in their black sou'westers are pulling a starter trolley towards my aeroplane. Near by, another Spit stands lonely and silent, its engine and cockpit covers on and the wheels chocked. Rain drips off the trailing edges of the wings and elevators. From being a live trembling vibrant thoroughbred it looks utterly miserable and forlorn, resigned to being tethered in the open, unattended with nothing to do but get wet.

I get geared up: Mae West, gloves, flying boots, helmet and muffler. It takes but a short time to get dressed, pick up my parachute and with an urgency of commitment follow Brian and Tommy into Tom Wiesse's little office, where he is studying a wall map. The flight sergeant puts his head round the door, water dripping from his oilskins.

'All OK, sir. Both aircraft ready when you are.'

'Thanks, Chiefy, ten minutes at the most.'

As usual Tom is sticking pins in the wall chart. We stand and watch for a moment or two without enthusiasm. The moment has come for our Intelligence Officer to expound: 'This is the situation. A convoy which assembled in the estuary off Southend is proceeding north up the east coast during the hours of darkness. At the moment it is in Barrow Deep and moving at seven knots.'

'We should be able to catch up, then. Barrow where?'

'Barrow Deep.'

'And where, might I ask, is Barrow Deep?'

'If you look you will see it is where I have my finger.'

'It's a change to see your finger there.'

'Look, cut it out. Now listen to me. Your humour, Geoffrey, is often misplaced and always untimely. Barrow Deep is a channel in the Thames estuary. We are to patrol along a line approximately north-east to south-west, ten minutes each leg and five miles to seaward of the convoy. The position, I suggest, is here to here.' Tom runs his finger along a line of pins. 'Put it on your maps; pencils and rulers on the table.' We do it in silence, concentrating and assessing in our own minds the task before us. We won't see a bloody thing.

'R/T silence?'

'It doesn't matter all that much. If the Hun pick up your transmissions they will at least know you are about and you never know, it may deter them. After all, they won't know the names of our pilots.'

Cheeky bugger.

'Perhaps it would be as well if we don't talk about the weather too much as it may be of use to the Hun if he gets to know what cover he's got over this side.'

'I expect he knows already and, in any case, it may be rather too low for his purpose.'

'Well, don't give him anything he could use.' Trust Wiesse to have the last word. 'Anything else? No? Then off you go and good luck.'

'Cheers, Brian, see you later.'

'Yes, get going. Keep an eye on this bloody weather, Tom.'

Tommy waves his hand, pats me on the back and without a word makes his way down the peri track. I walk towards my waiting Spitfire, parachute over my shoulder and helmet on my head unstrapped, the oxygen mask hanging to one side. Rain on my face; this bloody, bloody, bloody rain. I round the end of the dispersal pen and there they are waiting, as always, ready and no last-minute panics. My ground crew come towards me, the Spit stationary, silent and patient.

'What a day to pick, sir.'

'I quite agree. Bloody, isn't it?'

The water runs down the side of the fuselage over the RAF roundel. I hand my parachute to Bevington who holds it ready by the shoulder harness. I put it on, clamber on to the wing root, slide open the hood, open the access door and step into the cockpit. Once again, as soon as I am in the aeroplane and seated, I feel better. Confidence returns, let it damn well rain. Fitter and rigger help to strap me in and Bevington closes the door.

'How long, sir? Any idea?'

'At least an hour, I should think, probably more like an hour and a half.'

They jump to the ground and, resigned, I start my cockpit checks. I am conscious of the incessant rain lodging on my shoulders and face as I fit my oxygen mask, R/T lead plugged in, also oxygen tube, that's OK. Release the Sutton harness lock and check the fuel gauges, full of course. Oxygen on and the needle flicks up to the full mark. Shouldn't need oxygen today but you never know. Elevator trim one degree nose heavy, full rudder bias, pitch full fine and controls free. A quick double check round. Everything looks good. Radiator shutter open, all right then, fuel on, ready for starting. Throttle open a little. Coolant temperature? Shows dead cold, OK so we will have to prime her. Give her six pumps on the Ki-Gas; I lean out of the cockpit.

'All clear?'

A thumbs up from the two stalwarts. 'Clear, sir.'

'Contact.'

'Contact, sir.'

Mag switches on, press the starter button and booster coils at the same time and the starter engages with a metallic clang. The airscrew turns slowly, the engine fires, hesitates for just a second, kicks back and then starts with great puffs of smoke from the exhausts which momentarily engulf the cockpit. I adjust the throttle and the Merlin settles down and runs evenly as it warms up. The needle of the temperature gauge comes off the cold stop and the whole aircraft seems to tremble in anticipation. The slipstream blows the raindrops round the windscreen in moving lines of minute bubbles. Water is blown off the wings' upper surfaces in avenues of movement only to disappear off the trailing edge. What does that remind me of? Lemmings.

Thoughts are cast aside and I become conscious only of the Spitfire and myself. We are part and parcel, as one. Spits impart that sort of feeling. No need to check the magnetos, Bevington does that every morning anyway and Merlins are very good in that department as a rule. Let's go then, if we must. No point in prolonging the inevitable.

Wave away the chocks, open the throttle and we start to move, edging forward out of the dispersal pen; take your time, no need to rush. The ground crews walk at each wingtip, don't want to make them run. Even Flight is standing by watching as we slowly taxi by. He gives a wave. A signal from me and Bevington and Davy release the wingtips and I am left to my own devices. They join the flight sergeant and stand in the rain, watching.

I look around as I taxi along and one of those strange feelings comes over me. I wonder why I often feel like this. Here I am, on my own, in control of perhaps the finest fighter aircraft in the world, certainly one of the most advanced. Hundreds of young men even as I taxi along are striving to get where I am and thousands more wish it but will never achieve it. I am lucky, very lucky. I get a kick out of such thoughts and feel good; sod the weather.

Tom has been taking his time but is moving at last and the rain, as if in a final attempt to dissuade us, intensifies. A gust of wind rocks the Spitfire on its narrow undercarriage, the clouds overhead seem to glower at us threateningly and the whole weather scene looks ugly and sinister. I wish the visibility was a bit better. It's odd that it should be so poor with the wind as fresh as it is. I've got about as far as I think we might want to go so I turn the Spit into wind and wait for Tom and try to relax. He arrives, turns into wind about twenty yards away and gives me a thumbs up. I reply and without more ado away we go; no sense in hanging about. I keep my eye on his Spitfire, not too near, no point.

As we accelerate along the runway the spray, thrown up from his wheels and blown by the slipstream, trails away behind like the wake of a speedboat. We both leave the ground together. I keep my eye on him. Wheels coming up,

throttle back a shade, adjust the pitch, rad shutter and close
the hood. We level off just below the cloud base at 600 feet.
Even so, I notice the odd wisp of stratus below us.

'Hello, Sapper, Gannic Red Section airborne.'

'Gannic Red, this is Sapper, received and understood. Vector 010 degrees.'

At least, I think he said 010. That would be about right but
the reply was distorted and rather faint. Odd. Possibly we are
a bit low for good reception. No matter, follow my leader in
a slow turn to port and settle down on course.

It is pretty turbulent and we are in and out of the cloud
base, so we lose a little height. I ease out from Tommy and
almost level with him. It would seem to be the best place. He
can keep tabs on exactly where I am in relation to himself,
important in this sort of weather. In order not to overshoot I
have to throttle back still further to minus 2 boost. Obviously,
we are going to take things nice and steady.

For the first time I take a look around. The rain makes it
difficult to see ahead through the windscreen but it is not too
bad out of the side of the hood. Can see just about a couple
of miles, certainly no more.

The coast comes up quickly, some chalets and beach huts,
the breakers and out over the water. The testing time is about
to begin. On the beach a bystander would see two Spitfires
flashing by just below the overcast and out into the inhospit-
able murkiness of the estuary and the North Sea.

Immediately, what little horizon there is disappears as the
greys of the sea and sky blend into one. Only below and out
to one side can the sea be seen, the waves angry and unsettled,
tops breaking into white horses, their movement slow but
powerful as they move in almost soldierly formation towards
the north-east. View through the front panel is absolutely
damn all! How on earth could you shoot anything down in
these circumstances? I glance across at Tom but he doesn't

look my way. He seems to be concentrating in the cockpit, no doubt on the blind-flying instruments. It can't be easy for him. A wisp of stratus passes between us. I snatch a quick glance at the altimeter. It reads 400 feet. Jesus Christ, this is just plain bloody.

We hold course. The seconds pass and become minutes. I stick to the other Spitfire like glue. It is bumpy and I watch Tommy's aircraft as it lifts and sways in the turbulence. Even now, in these tense and wretched circumstances, it is a thing of beauty.

We must surely be about there. I ease out a little further and take a look around, searching; after all, that is what we are here for. It appears to be just a shade lighter out to sea, a pastel toning of the dull grey of sea and sky which still blends into one. What a day to go flying. The rain is making it a hopeless task; sod the Germans. I call up Tom on the R/T.

'Red 1 from Red 2, it may be a bit better over to starboard, it looks lighter.'

I see Tom turn his face towards me. 'Say again Red 2, you are very distorted.'

That's odd, I can't hear him very well, either; hope water hasn't got into the R/T somewhere.

'Red 1, I say again, the weather looks better to starboard, the weather . . . lighter . . . starboard.'

'OK, understood.'

We make a slow turn towards the break but the improve-ment is only marginal. There is nothing for it but to stick it out. I follow Tom down to 300 feet and we start our patrol. At the end of the patrol lines I find the turns a bit tricky. There's not much room at 300 feet and the visibility really is shocking. I keep as good a lookout as I can and at the same time watch Tom and the grey sea beneath. If only this incessant rain would stop. The longer we go on the more it would appear that an element of self-preservation is coming into the equation. All I feel I want to do is to be able to see ahead, but since I can't I might as well forget about it. One point to remember and that is that this westerly wind will be blowing us further out to sea the whole time. Hope Tom remembers to allow for it but, of course, he will. He comes up on the R/T.

'Red 2, how's it going?'

I hear him through heavy static and background noises and I can only just make out what he says.

'Red 1, I can see very little and I am most uncomfortable, over.'

'Say again Red 2, you were almost unreadable. Is your R/T OK?'

I hope so. Of all days, today is when you want good communication.

'Red 1, I say again, I can see very little, I am most uncomfortable and I think my R/T is going on the blink. R/T very bad.'

'Received and understood, Red 2. Stick to me, then.'

I sure will. There is nothing for it but to settle down until this bloody stupid patrol is over and we can get back to our fireside. I find it difficult enough watching the other Spit and those hideous angry looking waves without searching for Germans. I must not lose orientation or I shall be a dead duck. Another check on the altimeter and I note we are flying at barely 300 feet.

I hear Tommy calling control. I can barely make out what he says. He sounds terse. His tone of voice seems to denote that he is not prepared to put up with any nonsense; something about 'this farce'. He asks for a reply to be repeated, a reply I do not hear at all. If anything, my R/T is getting worse. What a time to have a duff set. Sod's law. Tommy again comes up on the air.

'Red 2 from Red 1, did you get that?'

'Red 1, no.'

'Understand. No.'

'Correct.'

'Red 2, a bandit ten miles to the east is approaching, do you receive?'

'Red 1, received and I understand a bandit.'

'Sorry Red 2, say again.'

I can only just get the gist of the conversation. I close on Tommy's Spitfire and I see him looking across at me enquiringly. I point to him and give him a thumbs up. I then point to my microphone and my earphones and give a firm thumbs down. He nods.

'OK, Red 2. Understand.'

I sheer off and follow him round in a turn towards the north-east. Maybe he's had a vector from Operations. I look at my watch. We have been about thirty minutes. Just about half time, I reckon, unless Ops recall us, and with a Hun about that's not very likely. The rain is forcing its way through every little gap between the frames and is dripping with the consistency of a Chinese torture over my knees and soaking into my trousers. All the time the Merlin runs without faltering, utterly reliable. What an engine! Thank the good Lord for Rolls-Royce.

I think Tom talks to Ops again because we alter course slightly. We're on an interception or I'm a Dutchman. He takes a quick glance at me. Yes, Tom, I'm still with you. I search out of the sides of the hood. Only the disturbed water, almost calculating and waiting greedily for a lack of concentration so that it can reach up and draw you down. Easy to fly into the 'oggin' in this sort of visibility. Been done before, many times. Don't know about Tom, but I'm beginning to feel a bit of strain. We're on our own, Tom and I. Tommy with his head in the cockpit a lot of the time, he has no horizon to fly by, checking on instruments. He must be feeling it a bit. My job is easy compared with his and I'm beginning to feel sorry for myself. Must pull myself together.

We start a slow turn to the right out to sea. The turn seems to go on and on and a quick glance at the gyro shows that we have nearly completed 360 degrees. It would appear that we are orbiting. I hear Tom transmit but, my R/T being what it is, I don't understand. For sure he is able to hear control replying. All I can do in these circumstances is to stick tight.

It seems we have entered a nasty squall, as if things weren't difficult enough already. The cockpit hood is now virtually opaque. To hell with it. I take a grab at the hood handle and with an effort I open it and slide it to the rear. Open-cockpit flying; a bit of buffeting and rather uncomfortable but at least I can see a bit better, a lot better in fact.

Tommy straightens out and a quick glance ahead shows me why. Another heavy squall of rain and every other sort of crap seems to reach right down to the sea surface itself. There is no visibility and I instinctively close right up to the other Spitfire. Straight and level right through the curtain of rain at 300 feet. Sod this for a game of marbles. Eventually, a lightening of the oppressive and glowering overcast and we are through the worst of it. Not much visibility ahead but at least we can see out to one side again. Thank God we are out of that muck and I ease away to one side and take a quick look around. The weather has definitely cleared a fraction. Can't last though, darker stuff is all around us.

Looking out to sea it is then that I feel rather than notice something happen. Nothing solid, but an impression of a disturbance just in the cloud base ... something odd ... not quite right. I am thoroughly alert to something sinister. Without thinking I turn slightly towards the point of interest. A quick glance for Tom. I can still see him. I transmit whilst I watch him.

'Red 1, this is 2. Follow me, easing off to port,' and again very slowly and deliberately, 'Follow me, Tom.'

I return to my searching out to seawards and I get a shock to end all shocks. There, its dark green paintwork contrasting with the slate grey of the sky, is a Junkers 88. The swastika edged in white stands out vividly on the tail fin. It looks menacing and evil as it streaks along just under the cloud base. How far away is he? Not that far, can't tell, everything is happening too quickly, though why it should be such a surprise to me I can't say. This is the reason we're out here.

My astonishment is increased as he very obligingly turns across my nose in towards the land, the direction one may presume of the convoy. Automatically, I turn to follow as he fades from view into some extra-low stratus. Blast it, I shall lose him if I'm not quick. I curse the rain and visibility and cloud and for some reason I think of Wimpey in front of the fire and I resent him being there as I stalk this wretched Hun.

Closing the distance I am not conscious of being in an aeroplane, merely an awareness of a target and a feeling of growing excitement, which I always have difficulty in controlling. This is a lonely business. I hope Tom is around. The Junkers emerges from the cloud, losing height towards the waves beneath, and almost immediately disappears from view again. This is going to have to be a quick burst, if indeed I get a chance at all. I will have to be smart on the draw. Reflector sight on . . . too bright, no matter. Gun button to fire. I try to peer ahead through the rain-covered screen. There's a trace of oil on it which does nothing to help. However, I know where you are, you stinker!

The enemy aircraft finally breaks cloud, still easing downwards. He can't be more than 200 feet if that, and I don't think he's seen me yet. Can't see Tommy. Forget about him but, for a moment, I feel like shouting and yelling at him 'a little help, mate . . . this is where he is . . . I've got a bloody

German over here'. Good God, that reminds me, I've forgotten to tell anybody. I press the transmitter button in case anybody is still able to hear me or understand what I'm saying.

'This is Gannic Red 2. Tally-ho! Tally-ho! A Junkers 88 heading westerly, tally-ho!'

I close, tense and trembling a little. I want to be sick. Why after my experiences do I continue to feel so? Some sort of strain? The weather? Don't know, but I should be thoroughly ashamed of myself. Have a go, Geoff, don't waste time or he will see you and pop back into cloud like a dose of salts. Closing, a little closer, Geoff, and still I don't think he has seen me. Astonishing. Must be looking for ships. I've calmed down. Lay off deflection . . . just a shade . . . not too much. He's no more than a blurred image through the rainy oily windscreen. Draw the bead through the line of flight . . . that's about it. Press the button. The Spitfire shudders as each of eight guns pours out 1,200 rounds a minute.

Almost at once somebody in that 88 sees me. He goes into a steepish turn away, turning back out to sea. I follow, firing short bursts at him the whole time, spraying lead all over the sky. If only I could see just that little bit more. Easing in astern of him I am quite close and flying automatically. I'm sure I can see hits; hope it's not imagination. There are no tracers from return fire as he eases out of his turn and pulls up towards the cloud base. Only time now for a quick snap shot . . . a fraction of a second. Very close, my fire must be reasonably accurate. Too late, he pulls up into cloud and disappears. Bugger it. That's that.

Did I see his starboard undercarriage leg drop out of the nacelle, hanging uselessly? I'm sure I did. Anyhow, he has turned from the convoy, that's the main thing. I am feeling robbed. There may be a gap between some cloud layers a little higher up and, without really thinking but conscious only of the disappearance of the 88, I pull up into cloud, following as near to his course as I can estimate. Another world, outside a void, like driving a car in a really thick fog except that, in a car, you at least have your wheels on the ground. Here in an aeroplane, in thick cloud, you are three dimensional and have no such assurance. Automatically, I open the throttle and ease up into the climb concentrating on the instruments. This is a bloody silly thing to have done. The turbulence possibly helps a bit insofar as when the aircraft is thrown off altitude or thrown off course, the constant corrections needed to counter-act any deviation help to keep you on the ball and alert and so I find myself utterly absorbed in the task and conscious only of the instrument panel in front of me.

Hold the rate of climb. Eyes scan the blind-flying panel. All very well to talk about this sort of thing in the lecture room and in the Link Trainer but, for real, I realize that to use and interpret these instruments requires self-discipline and a determination to believe the story they tell. One must be able to fly relaxed.

Eyes read the information and send the message back to the brain and from the brain eventually to the hands and feet, feeling, correcting, real flying. A challenge. Your eyes never cease roving, scanning the instruments; artificial horizon . . . rate of climb . . . speed and speed again, terribly important is speed . . . directional gyro . . . artificial horizon. It must never stop. I feel like a spring. I am tense again and I try to relax. Stick to the instruments and the climb continues. I've settled rather more to the task and start to take stock of the situation. It is time to collect my thoughts and think logically. I wouldn't say no to Eddy Lewis being around.

This is a serious situation and it's developing every moment. It is a situation that presumably we were trained to expect and cope with. Well, I suppose so, but only to a certain degree. Being in a Link Trainer is one thing; being in this bloody aeroplane right now is another. Better assess the situation. In thick cloud climbing after a Junkers 88, which is probably miles away by now. My R/T is next to bloody useless. What a jolly prospect.

Now that I have a spot more height it's possibly a good idea to give a call just in case I can be heard. I speak slowly.

'Red 1 from Red 2. If you are receiving me I am climbing through 3,000 feet in cloud after a Junkers 88, which I think is damaged. My course 055 degrees. Suggest you stay below cloud. Over.'

Not a peep in the way of a reply. Only heavy static. Well, that's that. A check on the course . . . 055, yes that's near enough. Left wing is way down; come on, Geoff, correct quickly, keep the concentration going, watch the rate of climb or you'll do a Laurie.

I am conscious of a horrible feeling of uncertainty that is starting to make itself felt. It is a sensation with which all pilots are familiar. Are the instruments telling me the truth? Doubt. Horrible doubt. The seat of my pants tells me that the altitude of the aircraft is totally different from the story that the instruments are telling me. Self-discipline and training, stick to the instruments whatever you do. Once you lose control of the situation things go from bad to worse in a matter of seconds and then panic sets in. After that it becomes merely a matter of time before the ground gets in the way. The gyro has processed and I reset it to coincide with the compass. Ease back on to course 055 degrees. That's it, but quite what I'm hoping to achieve by this escapade in these weather conditions I'm not too sure. Obviously I'm a prize bloody fool.

At 5,000 feet I find myself still climbing in dense cloud and concentrating as I have never concentrated before. I seem destined to just go on and on. It's almost as if I just can't be bothered to think and plan ahead. Possibly I'm getting frightened; certainly I feel lonely. For some reason I turn the oxygen control to 20,000 feet and get the flow into my face mask. I find that I start to take a more logical appraisal of things. The chances of seeing my quarry again by now must be very remote. Therefore, if I don't get any breaks in the cloud by, let's say 10,000 feet, I shall pack it in. The speed's a bit low; adjust. Not too violently, you twit. Relax and concentrate. That's more like it. Now, where was I? Oh yes, abandoning the chase at 10,000 feet.

The question will then arise as to how to get back to base in one piece. If I hold this course and let down through the cloud slowly and carefully, I will at least be heading out to sea . . . no high ground to fly into. With luck I should start to see the waves at something like 500 feet on the altimeter. After that turn on to due west and make it gently back towards the coast which, eventually, I'm bound to reach. Query . . . how long will it take? How far out to sea have I flown, bearing in mind that I've had a westerly wind up my chuff? It will be dead on the nose on the way back. Must bear that point in mind and try not to be too impatient. Yes, that's about the best plan. It seems reasonable and it's simple; a procedure, a plan, so let's make up my tiny little mind to stick to it and no bloody arguments.

Extra turbulence brings me back to the task of the climb. I am suddenly feeling cold. You know, this little caper wasn't a very smart thing to do. It's too late now. At 6,000 feet I finally reach some sort of layer in the clouds, not all that much but enough to bring some relief. I can see a slight horizon, wonderful.

I take a look off the sides. I can see fairly well, considering. Thank goodness I left the hood open. I search around but no sign of the 88. Hardly expected it. Obviously he stayed in the cloud. Let's hope he just kept going eastward and is damaged as well, the bastard. I take a glance behind but there is nothing to be seen, only various shades of murky grey cloud. Well, at least we presumably put that Hun off searching for the convoy and possibly attacking it, in which case we have achieved what we set out to do and it follows that Operations were justified in sending us into the air, weather or no weather.

The static in my earphones is getting on my nerves. I'm now flying just below a layer of heavy cloud that looks solid and full of turbulence. Automatically I level off and throttle well back to about minus 2 boost and trim her out. I think I'll stay here. No real point in going on with this. Let's have a last try with the R/T. May be able to get a reply or, if not a reply, at least get a message through to them, especially from this height. What height am I, anyway? Just about 7,000 feet; let's have a go.

'Sapper, this is Gannic Red 2. Over.'

'Sapper, this is Gannic Red 2. Are you receiving me?'

Nothing. Absolutely sweet damn all, except static. That's that, then. I'm well and truly on my own and no help from the ground can be expected. It's up to me to get home if I can. Why on earth did I ever join this goddamn firm? Ahead the cloud layers merge; I'll shortly be in the clag again.

This isn't good enough. I'm going home if I can get there, should be all right if I stick to my plan. There is a tremendous urge to see the ground again, in fact, anything. Even the sea would be better than nothing. I look about at the curved wings that alone support me in the air. Sturdy little Spitfire. I can see through the rain-covered windscreen, the long sleek nose enclosing the non-faltering Merlin. I even find myself talking to the aeroplane . . . 'Come on, little lady, we've tried but we have both nearly had enough. Let's get out of this and go home.'

Look out again and then back into the cockpit. Soon be in cloud again. Put my head back in the office and check the instruments. What a friendly little aircraft she is. Re-adjust the gyro, settle down, relax, now throttle back gently and reduce speed to 180 mph. There, that's nice and stable and so we start to sink towards the cloud just below us. Here it comes and in a trice we are in it. Down into the grey turbulence.

The changes in noise level and visibility affect the imagination. Once again, I get the feeling that the instruments are not telling me the truth. It's an odd and unpleasant sensation. A fixation on the instrument panel. I am sure that we must be left wing low but the artificial horizon tells me this is not the case. It takes willpower to ignore the feeling. Down we go through 5,000 feet and I am aware that it is getting much darker. Everything is dull and dirty grey. The light is going. There'll not be an awful lot of daylight to spare by the time I get back to base. I correct for an extra large bump. A real effort is now called for. I think I'm getting a little tired; I shall feel a great deal better when I get free of this cloud. It would be a shame to go and mess things up at this stage and end as a splash in the sea, cold and wet; horrid thought.

The altimeter continues to unwind and we pass 1,500 feet, open the throttle just a shade, keep the speed at 180 and reduce the rate of descent. The effort that I am having to put into the business of flying on the instruments for any length of time in such bad conditions makes me uncomfortable. In spite of the open hood I am sweating. Possibly I'm getting a bit anxious or even scared. A thousand feet on the clock and still no sign of a break. Alert and aware that the sea is pretty close underneath me I know that I am tensed up like a spring. A quick glance outside as we pass 800 feet and I am still in it. The cloud looks as solid and unrelenting as ever and it's still raining like the devil. Seven hundred feet and then, at about 600, another glance outside and downwards . . . I swear I saw something flash by that time, I'm sure of it. Must be nearly there. There is just a glimpse of waves beneath, which instantly disappear again. I am in and out of what obviously must be the cloud base. No visibility at all at the moment but I relax. That split-second orientation has done wonders for my morale and at 400 feet I am finally in the clear, if you can call this clear. Thank God for that.

I let the aircraft drift down to 300 feet where I level out. At least at this height I am able to see a bit further, but the leaden sea looks mighty close. Open the throttle to minus 2 boost and I start an easy rate 1 turn to the left. It seems to be taking a long time. I am getting impatient as the gyro shows that I am passing through north. Ten degrees before due west comes up I start to come out of the turn and we straighten up dead on 270 degrees. Not bad that, not bad at all; on the ball, in fact. At least we are now heading back towards the English coast. Double check on the compass to see that I have got red on red. Wonder how far out to sea I am. Keep going, engine.

The weather never lets up for a second. In places the clouds seem to be reaching down to the very surface of the water in long hostile fangs. The deluge draws down the cloud base itself till it blends with the dull grey of the sea. Wonder how Tom is getting on and where he's got to. If I could only ask him and get a reply. Let's just have one more go and see if I can raise him on the R/T. It's a long shot but it's worth a try.

'Gannic Red 1, this is Red 2. Are you receiving me?'

Not a thing, not even the smallest peep. Let's try Sapper. Any information they could give would be helpful, such as a nice little course to steer for base! It would be pleasant to hear a voice as well. Mind you, we're too low anyway but, never mind, let's try and clutch at a straw.

'Sapper, this is Red 2, are you receiving?'

Nothing, it's quite hopeless. Just the sort of day when you really need the bloody wireless, it has to go and pack up. I'm furious. Switch the thing off and have done with it. I do and the release from the continuous static and background noise is a wonderful relief.

Time passes. It seems much longer than it really is. The sea, rain and cloud, blending as they are, seem to mesmerize me.

The turbulence is getting me down and I feel that I am tiring somewhat. I take note that I am sitting hunched forward and tense like stretched elastic, just not relaxing. I reckon I have been on course now for about six minutes and although I peer ahead as much as the rain allows me to see, I know that I must have a fairish bit to go as yet.

Constant reference to the instruments, can't afford to be inaccurate at this height. Check my course: 270 degrees. Just hold it at that, must be OK. The compass again . . . red on red . . . the directional gyro has processed a little . . . I reset with the compass and we proceed. Well, at least we have got clear of the cloud and can more or less fly contact. The worst may be behind us. I've become more resigned to the situation. Lots of pilots have been in worse predicaments, much worse. Mind you, this will do me for a bit.

Twelve minutes have gone. That's a longish way in a Spitfire. Let's do a little sum. Say the speed at these power settings is 200 mph that's what . . . three and a half miles a minute as near as makes no difference, I think, and that means something like about forty miles covered on a heading of due west. Must allow for the headwind of course. It's pretty strong, judging by the sea state, in which case I could well have ended up nearer the Dutch coast than ours. I bet I was at least half way across.

Another couple of minutes and I am unable to prevent myself from fidgeting. I check the compass again . . . yes . . . we're on due west . . . just keep going, you're doing all right, take it easy. With such thoughts do I reassure myself. If only I could see a bit further. Hold on, though . . . what the hell's that? A line of white ahead and away to starboard. Surf and quite definitely a coastline. I'm almost on top of it, what's more. Turn parallel, keep out to sea, quickly Geoff, the cloud is right on the deck and there may be high ground. Turn, not north you silly sod, south. There, that's better. Now, what's going on? I look to starboard and throttle back still more. Where on earth am I? Lose a little height and edge in towards the shoreline. A point, or whatever the nautical men call it, and there appears to be a lighthouse of some sort. The coast starts to bear away westerly. Follow it, and keep it in sight for Pete's sake.

A bar of shingle with a river immediately on the landward side and running in the same direction as the wave-lashed beach. Now that rings a bit of a bell. I wonder if this could be . . . Yes, I know, this could be Orford Ness. The Lord be praised, but I think I've got a fix. That was lucky.

Pull my map out from the side of my flying boot, must make quite sure. Orbit, if I can. The clouds are right on the very ground inland, it would appear, so that's out. Only one thing for it, a 360-degree turn out to sea. Starting the turn I desperately try to keep the coast in sight but to no avail. As we come round I look quickly over my shoulder, nothing but rain and low cloud and the leaden sea 200 feet beneath. Mucking about like this the chances are that I'll get shot down by our own coastal ack–ack.

Keep the turn going nice and steady, Geoff; don't hurry things. A check on the directional gyro. We are just passing through due east. Now north, here we are coming up to north-west and as the DI moves lazily past the heading and through west on to south so the line of breakers appear white and turbulent off my starboard wing. Get in a little closer, let's check on the map. OK, there's the lighthouse and the river . . . the shingle bar turning away slightly towards south-west . . . it all fits. I've made a landfall at Orford Ness and that river is the Alde. I'll follow the coast down as far as Felixstowe then, if the weather agrees, I'll lob in at Martlesham. I've had enough of this bloody lark, it's dangerous. If I can't make Martlesham then I'll just have to have a bash at getting back to Manston, there's no other option open to me. Should be all right, providing the weather has held at base and hasn't worsened. That'll be the plan, then. Are there balloons at Harwich? Must watch out for that.

Down the coast at 180 mph and the weather inland is hopeless. A river going inland, the Deben so it says on the map – I think – and this start of a built-up area is presumably Felixstowe. Martlesham is out in this weather, I'm afraid. So near, too. Or shall I have a go? Make up your mind, Geoff. No, it's quite obviously hopeless. Try getting back to base as planned. I curse and start to feel sorry for myself and annoyed. This battle isn't over yet, not by a long way.

Away to my right I can see where Harwich harbour should be but I'm going no nearer than I am already. Harwich with its trigger-happy bloody matelots. Cut across this bay or whatever it is to the Naze. I turn to cross the bay. It's not all that far, should see the opposite shore in a second or two. Watch your map. Yes, here we are, here comes the coast again, keep it off your starboard . . . lovely. You're winning, chum.

The surf curves away westerly again. This must be where it leads round to Clacton, which should be coming up shortly. Such is my preoccupation, I've almost forgotten the clouds and rain. I glance around. There is little sign of improvement and, what's more, the light is starting to go. That's all I need. Mustn't waste any more time. Hope the weather is holding at base.

Now, what have we here? Houses and a town . . . Frinton? That's it, Frinton. We want the next one down, Clacton. Mustn't get too near to the Thames estuary, they've got balloons all over the place, so if I make Clacton a starting point and turn on to about 190 degrees that should take me well clear across the mouth of the estuary to the Kent coast at about Herne Bay. Hope I don't miss the North Foreland completely and go stooging off down the Channel. Anyway, that's what

I'll do; 190 degrees at Clacton for Herne Bay. I don't relish the idea of flying over the sea again, but there is no real alternative. Here is Clacton coming up now. There's the pier. Having made up my mind, I automatically turn on to 190, but it takes one hell of an effort to give up my sight of land, even though I haven't seen a solitary living thing, not even a gull, but then gulls are sensible creatures and would have grounded themselves on a day like this.

The coast vanishes from sight. Once again on my own over the disturbed grey sea. I suppose this is the right thing to do. Too late now, mate, you're doing it. Just stick to the plan, Geoff. Dither now and you could be in trouble. The light is definitely deteriorating; I can just detect the exhaust flame. It would be just my luck to fly over the convoy or a flak ship and get myself shot down by the navy. It could happen, it's the sort of bloody silly thing they would do, shoot down one of their bloody silly mates. No man in his right mind should be out flying on a day such as this.

I should think the convoy is off to port and well north of my position by this time; always assuming there was a convoy in the first place. Should be well clear. I suppose ships are more important than Spitfires and their pilots. Wonder where old Tom has got to. Rambling on, talking to myself like a prize twit. Snap out of it, for God's sake, and concentrate. Just keep on going, Geoff. Take it quietly and don't go and cock it up now. You haven't done too badly so far.

Right, what's the distance to the Kent coast? Looks like about thirty miles on the map. Speed? My speed over the ground is, say, 200 mph, give or take a chunk, so I can expect to be somewhere near in about eight or nine minutes. Watch out after seven to be on the safe side but, for now, settle back and keep an eye on the instruments. The blue flames from the exhausts are now plainly visible. Time's getting on.

Seven minutes and I sit up and take notice. I find myself

tense and I can do nothing about it. Altimeter reads 300 feet. Visibility can't be more than a mile, though it's difficult to tell over the sea; just about enough. Any second now and I throttle back a little. We seem to be flying on a fair way. Surely any minute now . . . and, indeed, there is something just ahead and off to the left. The coast, turn quickly, keep out to sea, Geoff. Two bloody great towers emerge from the gloom. Turn, for Christ's sake. They pass by just to my right. That can only be the Reculvers. Lucky I saw the shore in time. The ground rises quite steeply inland and the cloud is on the deck. Keep tucked in to the coast. Getting near to home but can't see a thing landwards. Have to be bloody careful and watch your height, you're down to 200 feet. Get back up a bit, Geoff. There's the shoreline, stay just to the seaward side and take things easy. You're nearly there, nearly home, just keep going . . . a final effort. Dear God, please hold the weather, just a little longer. I may be in need of extra help on this last bit.

Things seem fairly settled for the moment so let's get ready in good time to go on to land the moment I sight base. I throttle back a little more and reduce the speed to around 160 mph and I'll have fine pitch. Come on, wheels, let's have you as well. Select down and a reassuring green light comes on; undercarriage locked. I can always retract if I decide that I will have to belly it in.

We crawl down the coast, hugging the shoreline. Margate shows up through the mist and rain. It's time to turn inland. Now watch it, this is going to be tricky. I know this area, of course, so, if I steer west of south, I reckon I should end up very near to the aerodrome. Not far to go now, Geoffrey old mate.

Getting very dull and the exhaust flames stand out clear and bright. Turning on to course the sea is left behind. We creep over the land towards base. Where is that aerodrome? It must

be somewhere hereabouts, dammit. Don't say I'm going to
end up in any old field after all that's happened, because I'm
damned if I'm going to lose sight of land again. In five minutes
I shall be on the deck in some form or other and that's final.
A check on the speed, OK, nice and comfortable. I find myself
gripping the stick and throttle far too tensely but there is
nothing I can do about it. I look out either side of the tiny
cockpit; only fields shrouded in a clammy horrible mist. Just
off the port wing I can make out a house. It has red bricks.
Now I've seen that place before. As it slides by I take a good
look . . . yes, I recognize it without a doubt. It's only just off
the airfield, I fancy, but I can't see the wretched place. Where
exactly am I? A feeling of hopelessness, almost despair, floods
over me. I almost feel like giving up. Just happening to glance
directly beneath me I get a shock. Sitting on the edge of that
field is a Spitfire. No, not just *a* Spitfire, there are at least half
a dozen of them. It's the airfield and I'm bang over the top of
it. I feel like yelling to the heavens.

Keep it in view, Geoff. Don't lose it, for goodness' sake.
Turn port quickly, watch your speed, there's the hedge and
the old disused hut, get your flaps down, you clot, there we
are, trim her out, good, the windsock standing out, don't lose
sight of it. What's my speed? A bit high at 130 mph, throttle
back a bit, reduce height, keep the turn going. A low curved
approach, easy in a Spit. Look out to one side, not too tight a
turn, watch your speed, you're too fast and too low. The nose
starts to come up and block out the view forward. Still too
fast, over 100 mph. Never mind, I'm going on in this time no
matter what; that is my home down there. Round we come,
there goes the hedge beneath the wings, start to take off the
bank, throttle back, right off. I give it a strong tug to make
quite certain, there's a parked Spitfire, straighten out, hold her
off, bang into wind, thank God, but still too fast by far, swish
tail.

We float across the sodden turf, I have to lift up the starboard wing, the wind still on the strong side, which should help. Slowly it seems the speed drops away, hold her off, stick back, she starts to sink and we touch. I'm on terra firma. But we're running out of space; brake carefully now, don't turn her on her nose. Pity Spits are nose heavy on the ground. Brake as hard as you dare or the whole caboodle will end up in a heap in the next field. The speed reduces, it's all going quiet and we stop twenty yards short of the hedge.

It's over, the engine idles in front of me and I just sit there. I loosen my oxygen mask and feel the rain, lovely cool rain on my face and I lean out of the cockpit in order to feel it more. The slow turning of the airscrew almost stalling brings me back to the present. Open the throttle a shade, select flaps up, radiator shutter open and still I just sit. There's some sort of reaction because I'm trembling and almost tearful. Good God, what on earth's wrong? I must have been really het up. Mustn't tell anyone about this, keep this skeleton well and truly in the cupboard.

I chastise myself. This is bad, a stupid way to behave. Obviously I'm not cut out to be a pilot if I can't accept this sort of thing from time to time. I'm supposed to be experienced and well able to look after myself and take the odd difficult situation in my stride, not behave like a two-bit temperamental bloody ballerina. Now taxi back quietly and pull yourself together.

Brakes off, play the throttle, round we come. It's a long way back across the aerodrome and as I feel the Spitfire beneath me I enjoy it. We waddle over the bumpy ground like an old goose, occasional bursts of throttle and we move quietly along. No snappy fighter-pilot business. I've had enough for one day. Nearing dispersal, I can see Tommy's aeroplane. Good show, Tom. I feel much better. Bevington and Davy run out to meet me and grab my wingtips. Here's my dispersal pen. Turn the tail towards the opening. Davy holds back on one wingtip as I apply brake and we swing round. We stop, I look at him and he gives a thumbs up. Parking brake on, pull the engine cutout and with a last kick and backfire the Merlin stops. No noise. Peace and quiet. How wonderful.

'Brakes off,' calls a voice.

I am jolted back to reality and release the parking brake. 'Brakes off.'

A whole bevy of armourers has appeared as if out of a hat and they help to push the Spitfire back into the pen. A shout of 'Brakes!' and I reapply the brake. I lean back in the seat, relax and take off my helmet. I listen to the ticking of the hot exhaust stubs as they cool and the metal contracts. I'm pleased to hear it.

The armourers swarm over the wings to re-arm the guns and Bevington is up on to the walkway and already has the door open. I notice it all but I still don't feel like moving just yet. That's a bit odd, but I suppose I must. Tommy stands at the entrance of the pen with his hat on the back of his head, his Irvin jacket open and his hands in his pockets. I wonder what he wants?

'Where have you been, sir?' asks Bevington.

'Why, what's the matter?'

'Mr Lund has been back for half an hour or more, sir, and you had me starting to get worried.'

'Thank you, Bevington.'

He grins at me, 'That's all right, sir, good pilots are hard for erks to come by.'

I take the pin out of the Sutton harness, knock the quick release on my parachute and lever myself out of the cockpit, on to the wing and then to the ground. It feels so good. I feel better, more relaxed; we did our best. The flight sergeant turns up and I tell him about the R/T. Then I turn and walk towards Tommy.

14. The first time I went into serious action was against 150-plus enemy planes, most of which were Heinkel 111 bombers.

15. Dispersal hut.

16. 'B' Flight scrambling.

17. A flight of Spitfires scrambling.

18. Biggin Hill, 1941. Celebration party for the record number of enemy aircraft shot down. The party was attended by Noël Coward, Laurence Olivier and Vivien Leigh among others. The photo appeared in *Tatler*.
Front row, left to right: Johnny Kent, Tony Bartley, Mrs Wade, Bob Holland, Trevor Wade, two unidentified ladies. *Back row*: Sebastian Maitland-Thompson, Tom Wiesse, me.

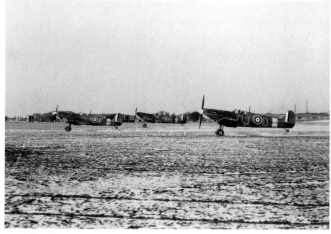

19. Take-off in the snow from Manston, winter 1941. We were going on a sweep over northern France.

20. Our tally board, Manston, 6 February 1941.
Left to right: Allan Wright, possibly myself behind Tich Havercroft, Brian Kingcombe in the cockpit, unknown, Jock Sherrington, Sam Saunders (at back, wearing cap), Bowen-Morris, possibly Bob Holland, Tommy Lund.

21. Hammering up into the wide blue yonder.

22. Bob Stanford Tuck

23. Johnny Kent and Tom Wiesse. Tom was Norwegian and a most supportive intelligence officer. Very fond of Scotch when he could get it. We called him 'the spy'. Johnny was a tough Canadian and a fine commanding officer. When he said 'Jump' you jumped! We were great friends.

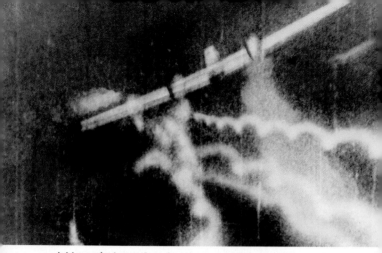

24. A Messerschmitt 110. I was in action many times against Me 110s. One evening we attacked a squadron of sixteen of them. I shot at a couple, damaging one quite badly, rather like this photograph. Cameras loaded with 16mm film were fitted on to the Spitfires' wings alongside the guns and automatically registered a record as the pilots put their guns into action. Every time a picture was taken, therefore, the pilot was actually firing at an enemy aircraft. Both the engines of the Me 110 are on fire and the port engine is bursting into flame. The curling white streak marks the path of a tracer bullet.

25. Group on an aircraft at Biggin Hill.
Top row, left to right: unknown, Bowen-Morris, Ellis, Lloyd. *Bottom row*: Tommy Lund, Bob Holland, Wimpey Wade, Jack Sherrington, Bastian Thompson, Bill Watling, Tich Havercroft, 'Monty'.

26. In summer 1940 Cecil Beaton turned up at Biggin Hill with the Station Commander, as I recall. He took photographs of all and sundry but said little. The top picture is of the waiting room. I am leaning against the mantelpiece. Bottom left is of Sailor Malan – my 'top' boss. The one of me asleep was posed. Beaton said, 'Close your eyes,' which I did with reluctance!

27. HMS *Indomitable* seen from the deck of the *Victorious*, Operation Pedestal, 1942. A Sea Hurricane is in the foreground.

28. The tanker *Ohio* arriving in Valletta harbour, Malta. Her cargo of aviation fuel saved the island.

'Geoffrey, where the bloody hell do you think you've been?'

Somehow that's all I needed and something snaps. Obviously I'm not quite so unwound as I thought I was.

'Chasing a bloody German. Where the hell were you?'

I know that is an unreasonable reply but I just cannot help it. I walk straight past him towards dispersal. I don't want any bloody fool questions. He turns behind me and linking his arm through mine pulls me back to walk at his side. He looks at me with an expression of concern and surprise.

'Take it easy, Geoffrey, we were all getting somewhat worried, that's all. You've been a fair old time you know, mate.'

'Sorry, Tom, but that wasn't a very pleasant trip and I feel a bit peculiar, more so than usual.'

We look at each other and grin. All is well. We walk in silence for a few yards.

'Do you know, Tom, I didn't like that one little bit and I'm pleased it's over. Someone else can have a go next time.'

'Believe me, Geoff, I know exactly what you mean, it was sheer purgatory, but where on earth did you get to?'

'Not now, Tom, let's wait until we get into the hut. I shall only have to explain twice.'

'Sure. You know, you were more than lucky as it turns out. We were ordered to pancake because of the weather mainly and I got back a good twenty-five minutes before you, just before it really clamped. We were watching it because you were still out and I knew that you had a duff R/T. Thank God it lifted just enough to let you in. You certainly wouldn't have made it five minutes earlier, and look at it now.'

In spite of the wind, with the onset of dusk, the rain, now more of a hard steady drizzle, going with the wind has blanked out everything. I would never have made it in this stuff. Perhaps there is a God after all. If so, thank You.

What a truly bloody day it's been. Everybody is fed up with it, packing up for the time being. It will all start again tomorrow at first light.

Tom and I enter the dispersal hut without speaking further. I hold the door open for him and motion him inside. Brian is standing waiting with the CO, who has just returned from a visit to Group. Tom Wiesse is on the phone, to Ops no doubt.

'Boy, where on earth have you been?'

The walk has done me good and I grin. 'Now, Brian, don't you start. I've been bollocked by my ground crew, I've been bollocked by Tom here and now you. I got a little carried away when I saw an 88 and I've been chasing the bastard all out over the North Sea.'

'Yes, Tom told me. He said that he saw you go up into cloud, he wasn't certain why, although he realized that there must have been a good reason. He also said that you had no R/T, is that right?'

'Yes.'

The CO looks at me earnestly. 'Well, Geoffrey, you're back and so we must give you the benefit of the doubt this time, but I have a strong feeling that the Hun turned away first before you followed him and, therefore, the pair of you had achieved the object of the exercise. To go up into cloud in the weather as it was with no R/T was not a very smart thing to do. Surely I don't have to point that out to a chap of your experience. You don't have to prove anything. I don't want to, indeed I cannot afford to, lose experienced fighter pilots because they get "carried away" as you put it. Understand, Boy? Don't feel you still have to prove something.'

'Sorry, sir, but you know how it is.'

'Yes, I know, Geoffrey, but do you understand what I am trying to put over?'

'Understood, sir.'

I ask Tom if he had managed to hear any of my transmissions.

'Barely, Geoffrey, you were terribly distorted and virtually unreadable. I heard something about "follow me", or "stay with me" and then a shout which I took to be "tally-ho". I saw a vague shape beyond you which you now confirm was an 88, then I saw you turning towards it. I think I also saw you firing, there were puffs of smoke behind, anyway, or it may have been cloud. Then I heard something about "below cloud" and that's about the lot. You did take a squirt at him, didn't you?'

'Yes, I did, and I'm sure I hit him. Did you notice his undercart drop down at all?'

'No, you both disappeared into cloud so quickly. Quite honestly, I couldn't see much at all. It all happened in a matter of seconds,' and then, turning to Brian and the CO with a look on his face that I hadn't seen before, 'the weather was atrocious; we were very lucky to get back, Boy in particular.'

'I know all about it, Tom, and I understand, but the important thing is that you turned the 88 away eastwards, is that not so?'

'Yes, sir.'

'OK then, that's all there is to it. The sortie, weather or no weather, was fully justified. I appreciate that it must have been pretty unpleasant.'

So ships *are* more important, just as I thought.

'Well, I'm pretty sure I hit him in the starboard wing and that as he went into cloud his right undercarriage leg dropped from the nacelle and was hanging down.'

At that moment Tom Wiesse comes from his office, a smile on his face in that slightly 'I know something you don't know' look. 'Have a good trip?'

Tommy and I say nothing. We're not falling for that one and in any case I suddenly feel sick of the sight of this damn dispersal hut. A cup of tea if there's one left, a hot bath and a quiet hour alone is all I want.

'What's the form, Tom?' asks the CO.

'Satisfactory, sir, Boy's 88 was the only one to persevere enough to get anywhere near the convoy as it turned out and, as far as Ops can tell, after the interception they plotted it back towards the Dutch coast before they lost it, flying at about 2,000 feet and rather slowly. Geoff, you fired, I'm told.'

'I did. I'm sure I hit him, Tom. I think his starboard undercarriage leg dropped clear of the nacelle.'

'You can't be more positive?'

'No.'

'Claiming a damaged?'

'I suppose so.'

'Good. Write the report later and let me have it. On second thoughts, I'll write it, you'll forget all about it. I'll tell Group in the meantime that we are claiming a damaged. Everything ties in with the Hun's behaviour: low height, low speed. It rather fits, doesn't it?'

Tom returns to his office seemingly content with the afternoon's work.

'Well, that's that,' says Brian. 'I could do with some tea, jump in the brake and we'll all go up together. You coming, sir?'

'No, thanks all the same. I've got my car and I'm off to see the Station Commander. I'll see you all later for a noggin.'

'Right, sir, see you later then.' The CO smiles at Tommy and me in an entirely 'for you two' sort of grin.

'Good effort. Well done, you two, and thank you.'

That's about enough. I go outside and survey the dispersal area, now deserted and lonely. We pile into the transport and the journey back to the Mess is done in silence except for Brian, who is humming very quietly. I glance across at Tom but no response. He just stares out of the window, tired.

I don't feel in the least like talking; the unwinding process.

Arrive at the Mess and, as we walk up the short path, I notice Wimpey standing at the window. Good God, he's awake! He turns and says something to someone behind him. We go inside out of the rain, have a wash together and wander into the warm room, friendly and hospitable. What a change from half an hour ago. What a lot can happen in a short time.

The room is the same as we left it. Our two chairs are vacant and to round it off Wimpey comes up to me with a steaming cup of tea. Bill Watling does the same for Tom and we sit and stretch out as a waiter enters the room.

Trevor looks up and turns to me. 'Toast?'

'Thanks.'

We relax, gaze into the log fire and sip our tea, hot and sweet and refreshing. I'm beginning to feel sleepy and content.

Tom asks quietly, with a lovely peaceful look on his face, 'Wimpey, you haven't bloody moved the whole afternoon, have you?'

'No, Tom, someone had to organize the tea for when you returned.'

'Of course, how stupid of me. Thanks very much, old lad, very thoughtful. I'm certainly enjoying this cup.'

10. Over There

January 1941. Deep winter: mist, that horrible thick drizzly sea mist, fog, frost, low cloud. You name it and we get it. Flying greatly restricted. With Goering's mob having been repulsed at least until next spring, England seems to be drawing a deep breath and unwinding, and 92 Squadron with her. How long will our respite be? Here at Manston we are based in the very forefront of the defences of the United Kingdom. You can't get much closer to France than the North Foreland.

Little enemy activity and with the unwinding a more relaxed atmosphere prevails. There are days when the squadron is released soon after breakfast and then we all pile into the available transport and motor into Canterbury and look around the shops. Rendezvous is at the sign of the Fleur-de-lis at midday sharp. There, in our favourite hostelry, we gather in front of the large fire. A cinema in the afternoon and then back to the pub in the evening for more beer and some food. The buzz of conversation, laughter, good company and great contentment.

The squadron are all there, the two Tommys, Wimpey, Tony, Brian and the rest. Smartly dressed women, perfume, jewellery and blue uniforms, pints held firmly in the fist and tobacco smoke drifting lazily about the ceiling. How the absent friends would love to be here. I'm glad I am, but I don't really deserve to be. For the life of me I just cannot think how I got away with it last summer but, looking around me in the relaxed and comradely atmosphere, I am truly thankful.

Pleasure in this company, reciprocated. I feel a warmth of

security. It might sound strange but these men mean a great deal to me. They are important and this way of life is important. At one time joining the RAF and becoming a pilot, preferably a fighter pilot, was the only thing that could possibly matter and once achieved nothing would ever, could ever, mean so much to me again. Now the achieving of an ambition has been replaced by the importance of a bunch of men from all parts of the country, and indeed the world, melded into the specialist team that goes to make up a fighter squadron. Times just move on, I guess. These chaps are all tested and hardened fighter pilots and presumably I can be included in the set-up. I still get teased about my age, 'the Boy'.

What we are asked to do these days is chicken feed when compared with the battles of last summer. Thank the good Lord for the lousy weather. Standing patrols, mainly in squadron strength. Long periods at readiness if the weather is anything like acceptable and an odd convoy patrol here and there. Very rarely do the Huns interfere. They seem to have gone to ground to lick their wounds.

We gave them something to think about during those long summer days, the first time they had ever really met determined resistance in this war. Mind you, they made us think a bit as well. It was a close shave but we won the battle; the Germans aren't here in England and that's all that matters to me.

German activity is still mainly confined to hit-and-run stuff on the seaside towns along the south coast. Sling a bomb or two on their 109s, come in very low under the radar, drop their bomb any old where as long as it's over a built-up area and then hare off back across the Channel before we can get them. This comes under the heading of total modern war, I shouldn't wonder. Low cloud, of course, suits their purpose and there is plenty of that around these days.

During the more reasonable days people go about their

various and sometimes self-appointed tasks. At dispersal, if your flight happens to be at readiness, maybe an air test or a gun test and now and again local flying just for the hell of it. It gets dark shortly after four o'clock these days and then it's teatime, tea in our very comfortable little Mess. It is becoming a ritual, a meeting with hot toast and unlimited cups of tea as we all sit around the fireside, a couple of devoted stewards to look after us. We are very spoilt and, of course, revel in it. Relaxed, one gazes into the fire and perhaps tries to read in it signs for the future and what 1941 will bring.

Over a period of about a month, the squadron has taken over some fresh aircraft. We have some ex 19 Squadron Spitfires armed with 20 mm cannons. 19 Squadron experienced a great deal of trouble with these aeroplanes, or rather their armament. They were withdrawn from service, modified in some way or other and then sent to us. There is still trouble with the 20 mm cannons, so the armourers turn the whole gun on its side and thereafter things work. Funny things, guns. At the same time, we are in the process of flying the aeroplanes up to the Rolls-Royce works at Hucknall where new and much larger superchargers are fitted to the engines, giving a great deal more power.

This power plant is now called a Merlin 45 and the Spitfire a Mark VB. Increase in all-round performance is truly tremendous and perhaps most important of all it gives us a much higher ceiling. Only the other day I was a member of the squadron patrolling North Foreland to Dungeness and our entire formation was flying at just a fraction under 40,000 feet. The view was breathtaking. A clear, cold day and I gazed in wonderment at the coastline as it swept right round the bulge of East Anglia to where it curves away westward into the Wash. To the west, the Isle of Wight stood out so plainly that I felt I could put my hand out and almost touch it. Way beyond was Portland Bill. It was a great experience and the sheer beauty of this fantastic panorama had a great and lasting effect on me. I got a feeling of remoteness and unreality, almost lethargy. Pilots understand, it's awfully difficult to describe.

When I shook myself free from my daydream, I noticed that my oil temperature had climbed very high indeed and was climbing even as I watched and waited, now thoroughly alert to the problem. The pressure had also dropped to about 15 lb. Something was getting bloody hot somewhere, no sense in hanging about up here. Nothing for it but to get down on the deck as soon as possible. What a shame; I was enjoying the scenery even though I was bloody cold. I went in to land at Lympne and allowed everything to cool down. A quick phone call to Manston to let everybody know I was safe. Later, with things in a more normal state, I took off and wandered quietly back to base.

Five others had been affected in the same way, so the powers that be decided to enlarge the oil coolers, a mod that was done in a remarkably short space of time. Thereafter, we have had no more trouble as far as oil cooling is concerned. These high patrols are in the form of a proving trial so we are told. It's always the same old story. The phone will ring and it's the Controller.

'Patrol Maidstone patrol line or, Dungeness to North Foreland, maximum height.'

In fact, the height and results we achieve astound even the boffins. Something about the cold winter air giving greater volumetric efficiency. All very grand and technical. It is bitterly cold and we experience snags with hoods icing up on the inside, especially when we descend to a lower altitude. Vision is totally restricted and as you scrape the ice off with your gloves it re-forms almost immediately. Air jets are incorporated to spray air directly on to the glass. It helps, but not all that much. No, the main problem is the intense cold and the difficulty I personally experience in talking at heights around 38–40,000 feet. I always have the oxygen turned on to maximum and my voice gets very husky. I have to try two or three times before I can get any sound out at all and then it feels as if someone is using a rasp on my throat. As for clothing, I find, through trial and error, that the best thing is to wear silk underclothes and generally loose-fitting garments. Presumably you don't restrict the circulation that way. Wearing silk inners with tight gauntlets over the top one day I go through sheer hell. With the feeling coming back to my fingers on the descent it was all I could do not to yell out; when I realized that nobody would hear me, I yelled out anyway. Never worn gauntlets after that, only silk inners. Another time, I was stupid enough to take off one of my silk inners to alter an altimeter setting and the wretched glove had to drop into the bottom of the cockpit where I just couldn't reach it. It was all I could do to hang on to the end of the patrol. It was misery.

We were all shattered the other day, however, when a pair of 109s described a couple of wide circles round our formation about 1,000 feet above us. We were at the absolute limit of our ceiling and could do sweet damn all about it. I bet that they in turn were surprised to see a whole squadron of Spits patrolling in good order at only just below their height. They made no attempt to attack and the thought was that they might have been unarmed photo recce aircraft.

The cannons, being new to us, are exciting. The first time I fired them on an air test I was amazed at the noise and the recoil and at the damage the shells did to the ground target. That in itself, of course, gave food for thought. Fancy hitting something for a change, even if it is only a ground target. First burst as well. A section of ours got caught up with an He 111 recce kite a week ago. Tony had a go at it and it quite literally broke up when it was stupid enough to get in the way of an accurate burst of cannon fire.

The cold days of January 1941 seem slow to pass. It appears that winter is determined to linger as long as it can. One late afternoon, with everybody huddled round the red glowing dispersal stove whilst at readiness, a rumour infiltrates, nasty habit rumours have (presumably it arrived artfully concealed in a blast of cold air) that 'something is up'. Nobody knows exactly when or how it starts circulating; it is a feeling really. One just senses that something is in the offing, something strange and new. The CO is called away to Group for two days and this merely adds fuel to the fire.

Now, when you really want to find out what is going on, there is only one sure way to go about it: ask the erks, preferably the most junior on the squadron, who in this case is AC2 Webber, our telephone orderly. Just the chap, we all decided.

'We're goin' ter drop bombs on the 'Uns in Frogland in daytime,' he says with a pained expression. 'Everybody knows.' He looks at us pityingly in our ignorance. You can almost hear him thinking, 'Bleedin' pilots, don't know nuffin', all glammer.' He's probably dead right.

I think of AC2 Webber about ten days later as I look around at the assembled company in an improvised briefing room in the intelligence section and I smile to myself. Everybody is here, even the Station Commander. He is talking to the CO and Brian when I arrive and take a seat on my own at the back of the room. Sixteen pilots of the squadron in attendance, although only twelve are to fly, of which I am one. Am I pleased or not? This is something new. We're going over to the other side. Bail out over France and it's 'good night, nurse'.

The intelligence section is a Nissen hut. Hanging from the ceiling are black model aeroplanes, recognition models. Rows of chairs face a raised platform that runs the full width of one end of the hut and covering the whole wall behind the raised platform is a vast map of the south-east corner of England, the Channel and northern France. On the map are pins and linking the pins red string. The strings come from the fighter airfields around London and the south-east: Tangmere, Kenley, Biggin, Hornchurch and North Weald. With one exception, they all meet at one focal pin, a nice large pin, at Canterbury. From there one thin red line reaches out across the Channel as far as Boulogne, round another pin and back to Dungeness. The odd string sweeps down mid-Channel; that looks like Tangmere's job. What's all the fuss? It doesn't look all that far, but there is all that water, of course.

Tables along one side of the room carry intelligence information, something all good pilots should read. I've got a feeling that during the course of the coming summer we may well experience an awful lot of briefings in rooms like this. Back at Biggin, and it's reckoned that we are going to return there soon, there must be a much bigger and better one. That's the one we shall all get to know. I get a dig in the ribs.

'Geoff, do pay attention or at least show a modicum of interest, the big men are about to hold forth.' Tommy Maitland-Thompson is sitting beside me, a totally false and serious look on his face.

'I'm all ears.'

'I know, I can see, but use them to listen.'

The Station Commander and the CO are on the raised dais facing us. The one with the more stripes will speak first, have his little say as it were. He does.

'Well, chaps, this is the day we have all been waiting for . . .' Now, who would have guessed that he was going to open his little pep talk in that manner? He goes on and the remainder is just as predictable ·. . . carrying the war to the enemy, throwing down the gauntlet and so on and so on. I don't hear it all. Am I too young to be cynical? Probably just plain unreasonable, or could it be that I am a little on edge? Rubbish, of course not. The talk approaches its end. '. . . So give good account, hit him hard, that's the only thing that the Hun understands and good luck to you all.'

Hey, Guv, we're off to Boulogne, not Berchtesgaden.

I turn to Tom. 'Now wasn't that sumpin'?'

'Boy, do please behave. Give the poor chaps a hearing and have some respect.'

'Right, so sorry.'

'This is a most important occasion and don't let me have to tell you again.'

'Right.'

'Have you two quite finished?' the CO asks. 'I would prefer it if only one person spoke at a time, preferably myself.'

Tommy gets to his feet. 'Sorry, sir.'

I follow suit, playing it safe, 'Sorry, sir.'

'Right, let's get on then.' He turns to the wall map.

'Right.'

Tom treads on my toe hard and the look on his face could do me an injury.

The CO starts off and his talk is far more down to earth. Twelve Blenheims, heights to fly, positions, speeds, intelligence situation, ME 109 dispositions, bombers' turning point after bombing, all good stuff.

'Keep the 109s from getting at the bombers, that is your primary and indeed only task. Press tits at forty-five minutes past the hour and synchronize your watches with the clock on the wall, OK? That's the lot, then, off you go, see you all later.'

I leave the room with Tom, our flying boots clumping on the ground. The transport waits.

'There's plenty of time, Boy, let's walk.'

'If you must.' Actually, it's a good idea.

It's a pleasant sort of morning, little wind and the gulls gliding about making their plaintive cries. Shades of holidays in Cornwall. They were good days. Tommy and I walk steadily. We have little to say.

At dispersal, before we enter the hut, he says, without turning his head, 'That's it then, see you later, Geoffrey.'

'See you, Tom, take care.'

'And you.'

As the whole circus of aircraft heads out over the coast, England and its white cliffs have never looked so friendly. We climb away and keep station on the twelve Blenheims.

Below is the sea; can't stop gazing at it. Behind, just, England and ahead France and the Germans. The wind is north-westerly, blowing across the Channel and urging us on to the battle. The sea glinting in the sunlight looks almost welcoming but I bet it's not so friendly when you are up to your neck in it supported only by an inadequate Mae West or in an exposed one-man dinghy. No mercy out there, just cold, exhaustion, exposure and final oblivion.

I look around at the Blenheims and the escort of Spits and Hurricanes. We of the Biggin wing are the close escort. A couple of thousand feet above is the escort cover wing and again on top of that lot the high cover. Another two or three wings are sweeping the Channel for twelve small bombers. The 109s shall not have them, chaps.

If one is at all cynical it is difficult not to poke fun, to a certain extent, at the importance attached to this 'offensive' of one and a quarter hours. Anyone would think the target was Berlin, not Boulogne. However, at least we are going over there and taking the war to the enemy, which makes a change. Nevertheless, Boulogne is a bit of a pinprick. Anyway, what am I worrying about? When we do turn back after the bombs have been dropped, I bet the Hun has a quiet smile to himself. We can't compete with their penetrations of last summer. London is a long way for them to have flown.

Boulogne is only a start, of course. I bet we'll end up a long, long way further before this year is out. I look back at the receding English coast and the countryside beyond. It looks a secure and friendly place. There she is behind us and getting farther away each second. I suppose that is what it's all about, what we are fighting for.

The sky seems full of RAF roundels as we reach the bombing height of 12,000 feet. The Blenheims level off and close into a good tight formation. We of the close escort weave gently, partly in order not to overshoot them but mainly to search the sky. One weave takes me over the top of the bombers on the outside of the formation and I clearly see the air gunner wave to me as I pass. Good luck, mate. I'd sooner be in my aeroplane than yours.

France is no longer far away and I can clearly see a largish town and harbour directly in our path, presumably Boulogne and the target.

I start to wonder with a feeling of commitment and resignation what reactions we can expect from the Hun. What's his radar like? Is it as good as ours? Hope not. As if in answer, the Controller comes over the ether.

'Gannic leader, this is Sapper. Twenty plus bandits over Abbeville.'

'Sapper, received and understood. How's it looking generally? Anything near us?'

'Nothing too serious at the moment, Gannic. Six plus just appeared over St Omer heading for Gris Nez.'

'Thanks, and the Abbeville lot?'

'Still over Abbeville gaining height. They don't seem to be going anywhere at the moment.'

Abbeville. Twenty plus. Well, that's not too bad; after all, Abbeville is quite a way away and if things get no worse that's not too serious a reaction. We shall be in and away before they know what's hit them this time; not really a penetration at all.

Weaving and searching in case the Abbeville lot decide to join forces with the St Omer crowd, I find my mind still wanders, which is no doubt very naughty. I wonder just what this summer will bring. I'm sure this sort of operation is going to be developed. During the last war the RFC were always on the offensive and now it seems we must do the same. Things will build up slowly and for some time to come our efforts will only be a mere irritation, a prick in the side of the mighty Third bloody Reich. They won't just sit and let us come, of course. Everyone thought that they would renew their offensive with the arrival of another spring, yet, here we are going over the Channel to meet them. Cynicism or not, it all seems to fit. Intriguing thought: if we mounted an offensive operation at the same time as did the enemy, and we both met in mid-Channel, bombers, the lot, what a battle there would be.

A black inky-looking thing like a chunk of dirty cotton wool brings me back to the reality of the present. What on earth is that? Another one appears and, as if by magic, a whole lot more. They are pretty close as well, not far away at all. How interesting. Two more puffs happen to be nearer than the others and a batch is right among the rear vic of Blenheims. Finally, it dawns on me. It's flak, that's what it is, anti-aircraft fire. I'm being shot at and there's not an awful lot I can do about it.

Dreaming as I was, it's with something of shocked surprise that I see the French coast almost underneath our noses. The Blenheims have their bomb doors open, their course straight and steady as they complete their run in. Down there someone is going to get hurt and, presumably, it doesn't matter who. What a funny war. Don't like the idea of bombing much. At least the role of fighter pilot seems cleaner somehow. Makes you wonder what life is all about. It must be a lousy way to get yourself killed, to have a bloody great bomb dropped on you. In any case, the Huns started it all, so it serves them right. Hard luck on the French, though. They didn't want to fight anybody.

'Three 109s, three o'clock, climbing up from below.'

'This is Gannic leader, who's talking?'

'Yellow 4 leader.'

'Then for Christ's sake, say so. OK, I can see them at about 2,000 yards, keep your eye on them, Yellow 1.'

'Will do, Gannic leader. Another four bandits, twelve o'clock high and crossing starboard to port.'

'Got 'em Yellow leader.'

'The bombs have gone.'

'That's the whole object.'

'This is leader, keep off the air, you are jabbering like a lot of old geese. Now wrap up.'

I can see the enemy. Those out to the right could be troublesome because at the briefing it was clearly stated that the bombers would be turning port after bombing and that would place our antagonist behind us, an ideal situation to dive down and come in underneath the escort and so up into the bombers.

Geoff, you're a proper little strategist. A glance to the ground below and except for a bit of smoke and dust in the dock area, there's nothing much to be seen. A bit disappointing, that, but at least the Huns haven't stopped us from bombing our target, even if it was on the coast. As far as I can ascertain, nobody has been actively engaged. Perhaps our gaggle of aircraft presents a pretty formidable sight to the relatively few 109s in the vicinity. We, as yet, have heard no more of the Abbeville lot. In any case, we can safely leave that to the Controller. He'll let us know the moment they start to make a move.

Now where the hell are we all off to? The Blenheims continue their straight course followed by literally hundreds of flak bursts. I guess that someone in their formation must be taking photographs or something but it's about time we got the hell out of here. The bombs have been dropped so please Mr Bomber Leader, let's go home. It looks a long, long way and I'm beginning to get homesick.

At long last and oh so slowly, the Blenheims start their long turn to port. It seems to go on for ever. The whole circus turns with them. I search around. Spits everywhere and I find reassurance. We're all in it.

'Yellow 1, this is leader. Can you still see those 109s?'

'Yellow 1, yes I can see them.'

'They're diving away, going away from us. I'm sorry, Yellow 4 here; sorry, leader.'

'OK Yellow 4, I can see them also. Let me know if they change their mind and decide to return.'

'Will do, leader.'

At least the whole formation is now pointing in the right direction, the only really sensible direction for any self-respecting fighter pilot, back home. Boulogne is just off to port and the flak still trails us round the sky. The French coast is just coming below us. Once over the sea, the bombers start to lose height, just a slight depression of the nose and the speed builds up as the whole formation of Spits, Hurricanes and Blenheims dive away towards England. What a jolly good leader that bomber bloke is.

We get well out over the Channel and the thought of Webber and his astonishment at our ignorance when he told us exactly what was going to happen makes me laugh outright into my oxygen mask. I can almost hear him when we get back to dispersal, 'Told yer so, sir, didn't I? Any time, sir, I'll let yer know.'

Once over England, the circus disperses. The Blenheims, all twelve, fly away to the north. We split up and dive away to our bases. It's not far to Manston and 92 Squadron forms up in proper order for a stream landing and we then taxi into our dispersal points. I pick out Bevington and Davy and experience a peculiar sense of achievement of which I'm more than a little ashamed. We really haven't gone all that far or been all that brave. Bevington greets me as I switch off and undo my straps.

'Everything OK, sir?'

'Yes, fine.'

'How did it go?'

'Nothing to it.'

11. White Cliffs

Outside, the steady summer rain has been falling since 5 p.m., blanketing the surrounding countryside in a saturating misty vapour. The weather has clamped; a fighter pilot's dream.

It started to rain as I was settling down to enjoy my toast and a cup of tea. An hour previously we had just returned from the afternoon's sweep but now I am comfortable and strangely content sitting in my big armchair; a wonderful feeling of drowsy tranquillity, not all that easy to define or, I suppose, find. However, be that as it may, it's teatime. Around me are the rest of the squadron. I can sense their relaxation as if sharing my mood. The rain, heard through the open window, seems to bring a totally relaxing background noise to the ante-room, but why do I notice it particularly today?

God knows, it has just been a day like any other for the last three or four months . . . rendezvous Dungeness. Two offensive sweeps or escorts over northern France and sometimes three has been the order of the day and most of them have been pretty hectic to say the least. I don't think that it is the pressure alone that has made us all that tired today, I just reckon it's the sound of steady rain and the smell of the wet dust and grass. It is a pleasant feeling. You are sitting warm and dry in a comfortable Mess and some poor bloke having to work outside or guard something isn't so lucky.

I haven't done any writing for months and now, later, as I sit at the writing table in my room the table lamp shines and its yellow light reflects down on the paper. A bath, shave and a change into clean clothing; I have a most pleasant fresh feeling and one also of great composure. Again, difficult to explain or put down in writing, but the main reason for my relaxed frame of mind and my great content is because, among other things, I have overcome the fear of dying. It no longer concerns me.

There is an hour before I need to go down to dinner and I feel I want to convey thoughts to paper.

I write a sentence, perhaps two, on this piece of paper and a month has gone by. How quickly a pen going back and forth across a page consumes time. I try to put the events of the past few months into some sort of order but I find it very difficult. Things, incidents, people and visions pass through my mind; faces too. A lot of those faces aren't around any more; I've lost track of how many. They are blurred faces. I knew them well and I should be able to see them clearly but, somehow, I can't. Some shot down over France and some posted away. Tony was posted to command a flight in 74 Squadron, Wimpey shot down and wounded and is in hospital. Roy was posted to command a flight in another Spitfire squadron but was lost over the sea. Johnny Kent, the CO, was posted on rest, as was Bob Holland after being wounded. It's all very strange, yet one adapts to this sort of life, for a period at least. God knows what happens if you survive and suddenly don't have to bother any more. Our new CO is Jamie Rankin, a Scot; I get on well with him and I feel he is going to be a top-class leader and fighter pilot. This is his first tour. He is still with us.

There are times when one ponders and when that happens everything seems unreal. Men come and go, characters, but men to the very last one. They are comrades during the making of history and those of us who survive, if any of us do, will never forget them, not ever. Yet in spite of all that has happened I am more at peace and ease at this moment than I can recall being for many months. I am, thank goodness, totally reconciled to death. No doubt my turn will come one day and there is nothing I can do about it. I can only trust that God is with me when I go; something quick perhaps. Let Him be with all pilots who catch it, friend or foe.

Often, after take-off and on the climb up, especially if we are top cover at 25,000 or more, a wonderful remote feeling of unreality seems to come over me. It's almost like a drug. Complete freedom from earthly worries or fears for the battle that will almost certainly develop after we cross the French coast. I just can't be bothered to get scared any more. Maybe it's confidence because, I suppose, I can be considered to handle a Spit with a certain degree of competence by now. It's taken time, of course, because I was always slow to learn.

It might also be something to do with the steady noise of the engine working well and hard on climbing power. Warm sun through the perspex and the rest of the squadron in close company with noses pointing up into the blue sky. I find it an environment of great beauty. It brings on a happiness and, almost, I look forward to the next operation before the one I'm on is finished. It's like gettting your second wind. I can lose myself for these few personal, precious and peaceful moments whilst on the climb.

Thoughts of the days when as a small boy I lived with happiness, love and family security. A stream in Surrey, the river Wey and my cousin and me sitting on the bank with our tins of sandwiches, rock cakes and bottles of orange squash, fishing for crayfish and minnows; as happy as the day is long. Warm sun on our backs, rushes, swaying reeds, water iris and all the other river plants. Always the slow meandering little stream, ripples and soft gurgling noises, running water. Occasionally, the leap of a trout and the blue-green flash of a kingfisher. No noise except that of the river, buzzing of bees and that funny noise that grasshoppers make. I wonder if any kids sit in what we considered to be our place these days. It was so peaceful and natural.

Being in the cockpit of a single-seater fighter at 20–30,000 feet can do strange things to a man and give him strange thoughts. In a way it's like the stream: it's peaceful and you just can't be bothered to worry. Is it a case of being nearer to God?

Time consumed by the movement of a pen. How quick and easy it is just to sit and write about everything. Oh, yes, one other thing, the King has given me a medal. Couldn't give it to Roy or any of the others of course so, obviously, he had no bloody option but to let me have it. On second thoughts, most of the others already have one.

Were it not for the companionship of the two Tommys, life would be pretty lonely, but the Big Man especially is a tonic not only to me, his friend, but to the whole squadron, especially when the chips are down. Dear 'little Tom' is very quiet these days.

I recall one day on the way home from Lens or somewhere, anyway, a deep penetration, and things were a bit fraught to say the least . . .

Our circus is being molested by 109s from all sides. Everyone seems to be weaving violently and all of us are a little edgy, what with watching the Stirlings and protecting our own tails. The action seems prolonged, the French coast still a long, long way ahead and seemingly getting no closer. It is also very hot as usual; most uninviting. Then up pipes Big Tom on the R/T with his best old-world Victorian politesse:

'Gannic leader, this is Blue 2. Six 109s at five o'clock, level climbing and I do declare coming round behind us even as I speak.'

'Thank you, keep your eye on them, Blue 2.'

'Certainly, Gannic leader. It is my belief that they are bent on mischief.'

'OK, Blue 2, I can see them now.'

'Quite capital.'

This is beginning to get amusing and amidst the turmoil and the tenseness I can't help chuckling to myself. I feel much better. Up pops Tom again.

'Gannic leader, do you not think that we should apprehend the enemy? My purpose holds to dissuade them from their intentions as I consider that if we do not the outcome could be most detrimental to our cause.'

'OK Blue 1, you've heard Blue 2, take your section and see what you can do to fend them off. We'll watch the bombers.'

'Excellent, leader, a capital idea, I declare; proceeding directly.'

'I wasn't talking to you, I was talking to Blue 1, so wrap up for just a second.'

'Your humble servant.'

Another time I recall our big fellah got himself shot up by a stray 109. He managed to stagger back across the Channel but his engine seized and caught fire and he had to bail out. Anyway, we had a phone call to say he was safe and unhurt. Much later in the day a noise like an express train passing through a station comes from the hall of the Mess and a loud voice proclaims, 'Stand back, I say, well back, slightly to one side and make way for he who cometh.' Obviously Big Man is back in the fold. There follows a heavy thump on the ante-room door, which, had it not burst open, would surely have come off its hinges. Through the portals Tom appears, looking more huge than ever. His face is flushed, wispy hair all over the place, muffler around his throat and wearing his rather muddy extra-large flying boots.

He is as tight as a tick! Tucked under his arm is the silken canopy of his parachute. Trailing and strung out behind him are the shrouds. He strides in like the leading bull in a herd of elephants and stops, looking at us as we sit around in the ante-room talking. Turning and swaying slightly he looks at the parachute shrouds trailing out behind him through the door.

'Heel, heel I say.' He pulls the remainder of his chute until it is piled at his feet. 'Now sit and stop making all that bloody noise.'

Dear old Big Tom, how pleased I am to see him back safely; can't imagine 92 without Tom around. Brian speaks:

'Hello, Tom, nice to see you. What on earth happened to you?'

'I've just been shot down.'

'So it would appear, dear chap.'

'I don't altogether recommend the practice as it is a truly bloody silly thing to do and getting oneself involved in such an escapade I would assess as being highly dangerous.'

'Quite understand, Tom, but that was at ten o'clock this morning and it's now teatime.'

'Not ten o'clock but 09.50 hours, to be quite precise.'

'Have it your way. Are you OK?'

'Oh, yes, quite well in fact, except that I am very drunk.'

'Well, I suppose that answers the question as to where you've been.'

'No, it doesn't. You don't know where I've been, in fact you haven't the foggiest idea.'

'Now, Tommy, don't be flippant. What happened?'

'I'm not going to bloody well tell you.'

'*Tom!*'

'Oh, very well, but what do you require to know, how I got myself shot down or how I arrived at my present disgusting state of inebriation?'

'How did you get shot down?'

'I don't know.'

'Come on, Tom, we might all profit and learn something.'

'I very much doubt it.'

'Well, just try us.'

'I'm sure I shall.' A large, satisfied grin. 'It happened very quickly. There was a flash and a very loud bang. The noise was quite deafening, lots of smoke and general corruption and a smell of glycol. It really was all most tiresome. In fact, the situation was obviously not one in which a gentleman should find himself placed, especially as we were heading back out across the Channel and with sparks flying out of our arse to boot. Anyway, I managed to get back over the coast when everything stopped and we caught fire. I decided to abandon the aeroplane with as much dignity as it is possible to muster in such circumstances.'

'Don't blame you, mate. Did you have any trouble getting out?'

'Knew little or nothing about it, can't even recall getting rid of the hood. I remember opening the door and as soon as I thought about the straps I seemed to be plucked from the cockpit like a feather on the wind. We were going downhill a bit, and bloody fast by that time.'

'Some feather! Plenty of wind, though.'

'Was that a typical Boy remark?'

'Sorry, Tom, I didn't mean it.'

'Tom, why don't you put your parachute outside in the hall for the time being? Here, let me give you a hand.'

'Stand back! Do not approach me, sir.'

'Christ, you're a funny bloke. What do you hope to achieve by standing there swaying around as tight as a fiddler's bitch and clutching the damn thing as if it will run away?'

'Gentlemen, this piece of equipment and I are very closely attached and it is my intention to see that no harm comes to it and, by the way, whilst I remember, there is the rip cord so nobody can sting me ten bob for not bringing it back. Not that I've got ten bob, anyway.'

'OK, well it's good to have you back in one piece.'

'It was rather a pleasant sensation, floating down, and I landed in a ploughed field quite comfortably.'

'It must have absorbed the weight, I suppose.'

'Now you are being rude again. Bert, Sidney and Percy wouldn't like to hear you talk to me in that way.'

'Who on earth are Bert, Sidney and Percy, in that order?'

'They are real gentlemen. Bert and Sidney picked me up just after I landed and when it appeared that I was in one piece we three trooped off and knocked up a Percy Crisp, Esq., landlord of a most excellent hostelry, the Horse and Plough. It didn't take me very long to realize that, early in the morning or not, there was a move afoot for everybody to get pissed, me in particular, and that's exactly what happened. We all had rather a lot of rum, I do declare, and then of course Captain Wainthorpe came along. He turned out to be a dear considerate chap and he said he would give me a lift all the way back here but we had better go and clear it with his boss first. So we went to what he called his battery, anti-aircraft guns and soldiers and things, and with their help, of course, I got pissed all over again.

'However, be of good cheer, I took two of those Pongos with me. The gallant Captain couldn't drive himself, not in his condition, so they arranged a driver for me and here I am, finally. Gosh! I've drunk enough to float the Home Fleet.'

'Didn't the army have any work to do with their guns?'

'I don't think so but, in any case, they assured me that success only seems to come when they can't see straight. Do you think they spoke the truth or were they pulling my leg? Oh, Christ, I feel terrible; cold and sick. I'm going to try and find my way to bed, now stand well back and slightly to one side.'

So saying, the Big Man turns and, still trailing his beloved parachute, sweeps with one mighty lurch out of the door.

'I'll follow him up in a minute,' says Brian, 'and see if he's all right. I think our Tommy the Large had a bit of a shaking today. Better let Doc know he's back, Boy. Ring sick quarters will you?'

Cryptic entries in my log book as I rapidly scan the pages. I really must enter it up to date some day. A great many trips that I really can't recall but I must have been there. I see that I have flown a total of forty-seven sweeps and escorts and, as I haven't entered up my log book recently, it must be well over fifty by now. That's probably as many as most people. Anyway, here it all is: escort cover Blenheims St Omer; top cover Lens; close escort Abbeville, Béthune, Lille, Mazingarbe and Lille again, this time the first escort of Stirlings. Stirlings first light, twelve Blenheims St Omer, rear cover sweep, Lens and out at St Valéry, attacked heavily by 109s . . . and so it goes on.

Some incidents stand out clearly. Coming out over the French coast having been to Béthune as close escort to a squadron of Blenheims. One is lagging behind badly, smoke from the starboard engine clearly denoting the cause. The CO details me to take my section to cover it. I do as I am told, no option, must do as the man says. Feeling just a little bit naked, we cross out from France at 8,000 feet, way behind the rest of the circus and losing height steadily. Ahead and in the distance, I can see the white cliffs. I reckon the poor old Blenheim might just make it, always providing the lot of us aren't shot down in the meantime.

The airscrew on his gammy engine seems to be windmilling but, a good sign, the black smoke has turned to a faint light grey and almost disappeared. We attract some flak; one or two bursts get rather on the close side but we get away with it and head out over the Channel and to home.

The cliffs of Dover get closer, but oh so slowly. I search the sky behind my number two flying wide from me but, search as I may, I can see no signs of any pursuing 109s, for which praise be to Allah or whoever is looking after our luck.

As we get lower, for some reason I feel compelled to close in on the stricken bomber. Somehow, it makes me feel as if I am being more protective. The gunner in the mid-upper turret I can see quite plainly. He waves and gives a thumbs up. I ease slowly ahead and the pilot, hunched forward over his controls, also gives a wave and holds his hand to his head as if he's got his hands full of aeroplane and his mind full of problems. Keep going, lad. You'll make it.

I pull up and over the top of him and, as I do so, I look down and get a plan view when, just at that moment, there is a puff of grey smoke from the front of the ailing engine and the whole airscrew, together with the reduction gear, detaches itself and surges ahead of the Blenheim. It revolves in a horizontal plane down towards the sea, rather like the rotors of an autogyro or helicopter. From this moment onwards, there is no longer any doubt that my charge is going to make it safely back to England. With the windmilling propeller out of the way, there is far less drag and he holds his height quite comfortably on his good engine.

We finally leave him over Canterbury. I fly in close to him and give him a waggle of my wings and with that my number two and I push off back to Biggin, quite satisfied at having seen the Blenheim safely over the fields of Kent. At least he's home.

The coming of the Stirlings on the scene seemed to bring a new purpose and dimension to our offensive efforts.

Over a period of time we had developed the techniques of escort work and sweeping the skies of northern Europe but, after a while, one sensed a lack of the dramatic. We wanted something more. After all, the poor little Blenheims didn't carry a very big bomb load and the effect of the bombing, although pretty accurate, seemed to be very small, especially when one considered the amount of effort that went into every operation as a whole. Possibly the novelty of this new task that Fighter Command was now being called upon to do was wearing off. The Stirlings gave the whole concept the shot in the arm that we needed.

After the Blenheim, which was only a light day bomber in the first place, the Stirlings seemed huge with their four engines and utterly unstoppable. Trip after trip, there they would be in their rigid formation, first of all three of them and then later six, ploughing on through the flak, which at times was very heavy indeed, straight as a die up to their target. Down would go the bombs, a lot of bombs, with devastating effect and the slow unhurried turn of 180 degrees back towards the coast again. The only slightly disconcerting thing was that they flew mainly at about 8,000 feet, which didn't seem very high to us. Should you be in the close escort, you just had to wade through the flak with the bombers, although we of course were weaving about whereas the Stirlings pressed on straight and level regardless. Brave men, these bomber boys.

We almost take for granted the invincibility of the Stirling. One day 92 Squadron is close escort to three of the big bombers on an operation to Lens. The flak has been very heavy indeed and at times so close that not only can I see the angry red flashes in the middle of the bursts but on several occasions I actually hear the crack as it goes off above the noise of the engine. I find the situation somewhat disturbing.

It is just as we have completed the homeward turn after the bombs have gone and we are on the way back to the distant French coast that I notice the merest trickle of thin grey smoke coming from the starboard inner engine of the Stirling on my side of the formation. The smoke persists and he shows a tendency to lag a bit behind his two chums. I sense trouble and drop back with my number two to give him cover should any 109s decide to interfere.

I wonder why he doesn't feather that engine. Think I'll call up and suggest that I should cover the big brother. I do and get an affirmative. The smoke is quite definitely increasing in volume and density and not all that slowly, either. I don't feel happy with the way things are developing one little bit.

I fly over the top of the wounded bomber. Gosh, what a size. Didn't realize they were quite so big. I can just make out the figures of the tiny heads of pilots in the cockpit. Thank goodness I'm not in their predicament; not yet, anyway. Back across the tail, covering as best I can, and it's then that I notice at the very base of the smoke, where it comes out of the engine, a bright, white, magnesium light. Oh, Christ, I think the poor bastard's on fire.

The light gets bigger. Smoke is coming from all round the cowl gills of the engine. I just can't tear my eyes from this impending disaster, but I must. Enemy fighters could well be attracted to this little enactment like flies round a jam jar. It's all clear at the moment, thank goodness. Even the flak has ceased. Just as well, we're a way back from the main formation, straggling and horribly naked.

A look at the poor old Stirling and I'm horrified at the speed with which the fire has spread. Flame is pouring out from the gills all around the engine. The airscrew is windmilling and the fire encroaches over the wing itself. There's no stopping this one. We're going to lose one good Stirling. I feel so helpless and shocked at what I'm witnessing. The whole process is so deliberate. Flames steadily advancing along the wing and even as I watch the momentum speeds up and the fire gains rapidly. The huge aircraft rolls over to starboard, slow but relentless. Over still further, the whole wing now engulfed in an ugly, angry great mass of very dark red fire. Rolling over still at a slowly increasing rate the nose drops towards the ground in what is the start of its death plunge. Down it goes, the flames triumphant, the Germans no doubt jubilant. It's a frightful sight. Good God, what a way to die.

Over the R/T: 'Come on, lads, bail out of that thing. Let's

have some of you, at least.' I think it must be me saying that. As if in answer two small black dots detach themselves from somewhere down the rear end of the fuselage, now plunging vertically for the ground. The whole forepart of the Stirling is now an inferno of flames and smoke, both wings, everything. Two parachutes open, that's all . . . out of what – seven crew, eight, nine?

Down and down, leaving an inky trail of oily smoke, which is so dense it seems to hang in the sky, reluctant to disperse. I am transfixed and can't stop staring at the molten mass at the base of that inky trail. I was so close to the whole thing. I have never witnessed an aeroplane burn so quickly or relentlessly, an aeroplane of such size, in addition. The whole holocaust finally hits the ground going through the roof of a small factory in a massive explosion. I make tracks to rejoin the squadron. Shan't forget that little scene in a hurry, that's quite certain.

Long after, when over the French coast and well on our way home, I look back and imagine I can still see that thin black line reaching down out of the sky to fade in the haze near the ground. Never have I been so pleased to be back over the English coast. Home.

The two remaining Stirlings pull away to begin their flight back to their base in the north somewhere, Lincolnshire probably. I stare at the gap in their formation. We drop away, losing height, towards Biggin Hill, the whole squadron in good formation and in fine order. Nobody says a thing on the R/T. Who chooses which of us is to die? Those poor sods in the Stirling today, whose turn tomorrow?

Safely on the ground, people are subdued. NAAFI tea in dispersal; cigarettes light up, quiet chats with Tom the spy.

'You know, that was just bloody ghastly, wasn't it?'

I wonder who said that. Nobody seems to have heard. There is another escort to Béthune this afternoon, perhaps they are all thinking of that.

A few days later, a new target. We haven't been there before. Stirlings to the Potez aircraft works at Albert at a very early hour of the morning.

Only a few persistent stars linger in the ever-lightening sky. The early morning atmosphere is heavy with moisture; there is a dew and a nip in the air. A clear sky, just the sort of day to wage war over France. This, an early morning attack, just to keep the Hun guessing; I bet he's worrying himself sick.

A shiver runs through me as I sit strapped in my cockpit waiting for the exact time to start the engines. I bet the Channel is cold this morning. Suppose some poor bloke from some wing or other will go plop into it before this operation is over. Don't mind the waiting these days as much as I used to. No butterflies, just total acceptance. I figure out you've got to go and that's all there is to it.

There is a peace of a sort in our dispersal pen. Davy is sitting on the trolley ack obviously thinking of nothing in particular. Sometimes he just sits, does Davy. Bevington is crouched on his haunches teasing a scruffy little dog that's been around for a few days. The little chap was lost, no collar or anything, and so the troops adopted him. He seems attached to Bevington in particular.

Briefing was at some ungodly hour. It was dark, the briefing room full of pale-blue cigarette smoke and a little quiet chatter but, generally speaking, things were at a pretty low ebb. The usual procedure: 'Well, chaps,' always the same that bit, 'Well, chaps, new one this morning, Albert, close escort, three Stirlings and the target the Potez works, height to fly 8,000 feet.'

OK, so now I know. The briefing rambles on, all the usual rigmarole. I just sit and listen and it goes in one ear and out of the other. Hope I'm not getting too blasé. The only thing that occurs to me is the question of the sun on the return leg. It will still be rising and directly behind us at that. Just the ticket for the Hun. 'Beware of the Hun in the sun.' Albert is a bloody long way as well. However, in the event, it turns out to be a quiet trip. The whole circus goes in, the bombers bomb two lovely sticks right across the factory, turn round and come out again. I don't even see a 109, although I gather a few sections were around somewhere. The Germans were all probably tucked up in bed with their m'am'selles where every self-respecting fighter pilot should be at this time of the day. None of our men drop into the Channel to my knowledge, so all is well; another operation behind us.

Following Albert, the nastiest of all, as far as I am concerned.

The Biggin wing is detailed to fly rear cover to the bombers and escorts as they return. The object is to sweep the sky of northern France round behind the main force, thereby drawing off or intercepting enemy fighters, which would otherwise be free to harass and get at the Stirlings.

We are way inside France, just behind Lille, when we run into a mass of 109s and before we know what is happening we have just one hell of a dogfight on our hands. These bastards are asking no quarter and have no intention of giving any. Fighter against fighter and I find myself completely involved and heavily engaged. I realize that I am outnumbered and not only can I not get in a shot but I can't seem to break out. I reckon there are three of the sods on to me. I start to get a horrible sinking feeling. I throw the Spitfire around as never before.

I give a fleeting thought to the distance we are from those white cliffs and for some reason my room in the Mess and my personal belongings. A feeling of hopelessness and despair begins to make itself felt. I'm not going to get out of this one, this is it. Never a day passes when those white cliffs don't give relief and a haven for returning aeroplanes. Well, they're certainly going to be a haven today but, in the meantime, there's a bloke behind taking a pot shot at me. I see him in time and turn into him and he goes over the top of me. I don't think he hit me; at least, I didn't hear any hits.

The air is full of grey, dappled, black-crossed Messerschmitt 109s, the yellow-nosed brigade among them. There is little chatter on the R/T. We are a long, long way from home and everybody is too busy fighting for his life.

Tracers everywhere, mostly German. They had the jump on us, came in from above. Lucky in one way there were so many of them, at least they are not troubling the circus. We just saw them in time and turned into them, thereby at once committing ourselves to what has turned out to be a fight as hard, even after all these months in the front line, as ever I have experienced. More 109s drop into the fray. I just can't recall having to fly as hard as this before and for so long a period. No respite, I'm hot and tiring. I don't want to die!

The enemy are over their own territory, just as we were last summer. I'm still forced to go the wrong way. Must watch my fuel if I am going to get back. It's going to be bloody tight. We must have been in this fight for a good seven or eight minutes, which is a hell of a long time to be involved at this intensity. I ask the Merlin for everything she can give: 2,850 revs and emergency boost override. Must be literally drinking up the fuel. I also subject the Spit to stresses that I would not have thought possible for any aircraft to withstand. Most of the time I seem to be on the point of blacking out but my feet are on the raised extension of the rudder bar and that helps a lot.

Slowly I appreciate that I am being forced lower. Tracers from all directions it seems and I know I've been hit. Heard it. I don't know where. I reckon that's probably Béthune beneath but I haven't time to make sure as I have to break into yet another section of 109s coming in from port and yet another one is trying to tuck in behind me. He fires but misses, I think.

Occasionally I fire my guns but it is more to keep up my

morale than anything else. Don't seem to have time to think about targets, it's far more important to avoid being one myself. I'm beginning not to give much for my chances. Chuck the Spit around as I might I still cannot seem to get clear. God knows where my number two is, or any other friendly fighter for that matter. It seems to me that I have been on my own for some little time now. It's me against the whole bloody Luftwaffe.

The sun is hot and suddenly glaring. Perspiration gets into my eyes and they begin to irritate and feel sore. Oh, Jesus, I'm getting so bloody tired. My arms ache and my thigh muscles seem to be tightening up. By sheer luck the chap on my tail has to break away. He couldn't quite stay and he never really got into a good firing position anyway. There is yet another coming in from above and he may well be troublesome. Blimey, not any more, surely. Please leave me alone for a moment. Dear God, call them off.

Here he comes, in on a high quarter. I've shot my bolt. Let's just sit back and be shot down. Make it quick. It takes a tremendous effort to reverse my turn and go under him. I must make one more attempt to get away from this lot, to break clear, or I'll have had it. Laurie, Peter, Nick and all you others, won't be long before I join you. I shall be on my way in a moment, hang on mates, don't be impatient. Once again, asking everything the Merlin can possibly give, I pull up and try to gain a bit of height. Up we go using every last ounce of power. I can't at the moment see anything behind me. A quick wing over and I am pointing towards the coast. What must that be? Twenty or thirty miles? A few seconds' respite, thank the Lord. Weaving, I look behind again and, sure enough, coming up from slightly below are a pair of 109s, their yellow noses showing quite plainly in the clear air and strong sun. Oh God, no. Right, right you sods. I'm utterly fed up with this bloody party. If I've got to go I'll take one of you bastards with me, I'll be damned if I don't. Eddy Lewis, you're going to be proud of me.

Throttle back a very quick turn allowing the nose to drop. We have a slight judder. Near a high-speed stall there; ease the stick. I find myself pointing straight towards them and my guns are firing, don't remember opening fire. Throttle wide open and go straight at 'em. The closing speed must be in the region of at least 600 mph. That's what they didn't expect me to do. They break, thank Christ. Hope it bloody well shook them.

I'm almost beyond feeling. A quick glance at my airspeed . . . well over 400 on the clock. OK, Geoff, one more effort and if this doesn't throw them off I'll bail out of this bloody thing and get a bit of peace and quiet at the end of a parachute. Be nice and cool as well. Pull back firmly on the stick and up we go into a roll off the top. Pray God there's nobody waiting up there for me. This will gain me height and point me back in the direction of the coast. Here we go then, up . . . up . . . put your head back . . . watch for the horizon to appear just like Eddy told you . . . there it is! Now roll out. Lovely! Now full bore for the Channel. I can't hang around any more.

What's my fuel? Fifteen gallons. Won't get to Biggin. No matter, anywhere will do, if I'm going to make it at all, that is. Keep your height for the moment, Geoff, there doesn't seem to be anything up here. If there is, I can't see them and that will mean curtains. There is something climbing up away out to port. I keep my eye on them. They are Huns, right enough. Subconsciously, I climb myself to gain yet a little more height and keep my advantage on them. I'm streaming with perspiration.

They're not going to get up to me. The French coast gets closer. Beyond I can see those white cliffs, home. Could I glide back to England if I run out of fuel? Who's to say my fuel gauges are accurate? With the French coast almost below, the urge to get back over home territory overcomes everything else. Dropping the nose so that I can see the English coast clearly over the cowling I leave the throttle wide open and dive for the white cliffs.

It can't obviously be very much later and I'm not sure what has happened in the meantime but, below me, is an aerodrome. It's Hawkinge, I'm back on our side. Fuel gauge reads something below five gallons. Hawkinge will do me. I go straight in and land, taxi up to the Watch Office where I can see a lot of petrol bowsers. This'll do here, switch off, helmet off and hang it on the stick. It's wet inside. Undo my parachute and Sutton harness and climb out. Nobody coming to meet me. I've just dropped in out of the blue.

Somewhere there is a skylark making skylark noises. The reaction sets in. I lie down under the wing . . . shade . . . coolness . . . green grass . . . Oh, God, thank You!

A voice from somewhere: 'Are you OK, sir?'

'Yes, thanks, just a bit tired.'

Throughout the spring and summer of 1941, offensive operations over France became a highly organized ritual. Biggin Wing consisted of 92 and 609 Squadrons at Biggin itself and 74 Squadron at Gravesend, our satellite. Sailor Malan was our wing leader with Jamie Rankin as our CO with 92, Michael Robinson with 609 and Mungo Park 74 Squadron. It was a very strong team and very few operations were put on without Biggin being heavily involved in the forefront of battle. I feel so grateful for being one of this band of fighter pilots in this hour of our country's history.

It is such a full and hectic life that I find it difficult, as I sit here writing, to set events down in any sort of order. The same applies to the many faces that came and went. Three of them were Neville Duke, Gordon Brettel and a Canadian named Dougal. Dougal was shot down over St Omer whilst trying to warn his section leader, whose R/T had failed, that they were being bounced by 109s. He pulled alongside his leader, waggling his wings and pointing. In so doing he became separated, thereby offering himself as a target. He was shot down in flames. Later we heard through the Red Cross that he managed to bail out at 2,000 feet, very badly wounded. It appears that the Luftwaffe looked after him as they would one of their own pilots and he survived. No doubt he will be repatriated. He lost an arm and a leg. We were all delighted when he was awarded the DFC but Doug paid an awful price.

Most operations that come easily to mind involve battles with 109s fought in difficult circumstances because those squadrons that were involved with the actual escort had to stick with the bombers – in other words, waiting to be attacked – and this is not what a fighter pilot should be asked to do. I have doubts about the tactics we employ, smacks of 1918 stuff; this is what our powers that be employed and so must we.

Sailor Malan is a magnificent leader. He was leading the wing as top cover to six Stirlings bombing the steel works in Lille when, coming towards us some distance ahead and slightly below, he saw a formation of aircraft.

Over the R/T: 'Hello, Michael, Jamie, Sailor here, about thirty aircraft plus, twelve o'clock low, coming towards us. I think they're Hurricanes.'

'Jamie here, understand, Sailor.'

'Michael here, I can see them, Sailor.'

'Sailor here, no they're not, they're 109s. OK, chaps let's bounce the bastards good and hard. A quick tonky-tonk first burst and away. Going down now.'

'Gannic Squadron, this is leader, follow me in now.'

92 Squadron plunges down as one into the 109s. I open fire on the outside one. I'm closing rather too fast but there is nothing I can do about it now. I see at least two cannon strikes

on his wing. I'm hitting him well and truly and as he tries to turn away I turn easily with him. I'm going to clobber this bastard. His nose drops as he tries to turn away and I follow, realizing as I do so that I'm getting a bit lower than the dogfight going on all around. A sixth sense, I look behind just in time to see a 109 nicely on my tail opening fire. Break, Geoff, for Christ's sake. Stick over and break hard starboard in an inverted climbing turn. His tracers flash by and just underneath but he doesn't try to follow. Gosh, that was a close call. Now what? I find myself milling around in a mêlée of tumbling aircraft and crossing tracers. To hell with this, this is unhealthy. Chuck her around, any bloody place and then, quite suddenly, I find myself going round in circles apparently on my own. Where on earth has everybody gone? How incredible.

Turning away in the direction of the French coast, I see about half a dozen Spits and I plunge after them to join up; safety in numbers. As I approach, I see it's Jamie and some of the boys going home.

'Gannic leader, this is Blue 1 joining up on your port side.'

'OK, Boy, I can see you.'

I'm a bit brassed off that I didn't see what happened to the 109 I clobbered but no matter; after all, I came out unscathed, got away with it again, and Tom Wiesse did allow me a probable.

A couple of days later, I am able to make up for my disappointment. Whilst escorting three Stirlings to Béthune, the escort cover become involved with some 109s that are milling about round the edge of the circus, making the odd dart and generally making a bloody nuisance of themselves. I am rather surprised when a solitary 109, with no number two that I could see, dives straight across the front of me heading in the general direction of the bombers. Where he appeared from God only knows. I call my number two to stay and cover

me and, flinging the Spit after the 109, I find myself astern at
fairly long range. The enemy aircraft is diving very fast indeed.
I've got to take a crack at him or else he'll get away. Putting
the dot of the sight on top of his fuselage I open fire with
everything I've got. Nothing happens for about half a second,
then there is a most satisfying explosion somewhere in the
centre section. A large puff of black smoke followed by an
angry tongue of red flame. He plunges vertically towards the
ground.

'Blue 2, did you see that?'

'Blue 1, confirmed.'

It's almost dark outside. I can still hear the rain. My table lamp
shines down on the paper but I feel I've written enough.
There is a soft tap on the door. It is Tommy Lund.

'Hello, Tommy, come in and take a seat, dear chap.'

'Sorry if I've disturbed you, Geoffrey, but I just popped in
to say that I'm keen to buy you a stoup of ale.'

'Not at all, Tom; I'd love one. Be right with you.'

'Having a quiet half hour?'

'Yes.'

'Nice, isn't it? I do the same.'

'Right, let's go get that beer.'

'My purpose holds, Boy, to have a quiet civilized sort of
evening consuming ale. I'll be your guiding light.'

'I've never doubted.'

12. Twilight

I would never have thought it but it's a most odd feeling when you are told that you will not be flying on the next operation. 'It's about time you had a trip off,' they say, 'a bit of a breather.'

I can't remember when I had my last breather. You feel neither one thing nor the other. It's idle to deny that there is a certain sense of relief, at least there is as far as I'm concerned. At the same time, however, your inner searching tells you that you should be going along. You get so used to the daily offensive escorts and sweeps over northern France that, when you unexpectedly find you are not flying, a guilty sort of 'not pulling your weight, somebody else doing your job' complex makes itself markedly felt. Possibly it's because you feel guilty at being relieved that you are not going.

Briefing is at 08.00 hours and I somehow find myself attending. God knows why. The cigarette smoke-filled room attracts me as a bee to a honeycomb. After all, somebody may have to drop out at the last moment and I might be called upon to go. Just as well, therefore, to know what's going on.

Food for thought: if I feel like this when I have a trip off, what's it going to be like, I wonder, when I'm finally pushed off the squadron? I might not live long enough to see that day, of course. The thought of being posted from 92 Squadron does not recommend itself.

I suppose some bloke in his little den in Air Ministry, wherever that is, will just pick my name out of a bloody great hat they have for the purpose. Then he will take another ticket from another hat, not such a big hat this time so as to make it easier for him to tell which hat is which. Mistakes have been made. But this ticket will tell him where to send the poor chap whose name came out of the first hat.

Whatever comes of it, I most certainly won't want to go so I'll argue and bitch and try and phone somebody up to get the whole thing cancelled. It will all be a wretched waste of time and I'll end up by losing out and doing just as I'm told. It's the system, the bloody system, and you can't beat it, you cannot win, it's too bloody big and the individual's too small.

This question of being posted on the excuse of being tired has been more on my mind of late. With the exception of Mac the Adjutant, I have been on the squadron longer than anybody else, beating Brian by a few days. My turn for a rest must surely be coming. Everybody in immediate authority has been so nice to me recently, or so it seems. Only the other day I happened to meet the Station Commander in the main hall of the Mess. It had been a pretty busy day and I was gasping for a pint before going to bathe and change.

'Good evening, Wellum,' the great man said. 'Going to the bar for a quick one?'

'Yes, sir, I had such a thought in mind.'

'So am I, let's go in together.'

We make our way to the bar.

'What will you have?'

'A bitter will save my life, sir, thank you.'

'Two pints, steward, please.'

'Sir.'

'Busy day?'

'Yes, sir, Béthune this morning and we're now just back from Lille.'

'Not very nice, this last one, I'm told.'

'Well, sir, Lille is a long way, of course.'

'Yes, I know.'

The bar is starting to fill up but the others stand clear, leaving the Station Commander and me to ourselves.

'It wasn't too bad really, sir, there have been a lot worse by far.'

'Yes, maybe, but bad enough by all accounts. How are you keeping these days? You've been on the squadron for some considerable time now, have you not?'

'Feeling fine, sir, could go on for ever.'

'You didn't really complete the answer to my question.'

'Yes, I have been on the squadron for some time, I'm becoming a sort of fixture, I hope.'

'Had any leave?'

'I had a week, last March I think it was.'

'Not exactly overdoing it, are you? Ah, here we are. Thank you, steward.' The pints arrive and he signs his wine book.

'Cheers.'

'Cheerio, sir.'

The scraping of chairs and the buzz of conversation snaps me out of my reverie. The briefing must be over and I didn't hear a word of it. Presumably nobody has dropped out. I shall not be going.

'See you later, Boy. Don't get into trouble while we're away.'

'Cheers, Brian. Good trip.'

I wait until the room has cleared. Everybody has gone to the waiting transports. What a very strange and lonely feeling to be left behind.

Outside it looks like being a nice day. If I walk down to dispersal the long way round the peri track, I should arrive there about the time they are due back. It should be quite pleasant over by the woods that flank the far side of the aerodrome. Setting off and not hurrying, I rather enjoy being alone for once. When did I last go for a walk in the country on my own? Not the faintest idea, not that an airfield is exactly the country, but the far side of the airfield is seldom used. Be honest with yourself, Geoff, you're not sorry to be left on the deck for once.

As I stroll quietly along it is impossible not to reflect on my conversation with the Station Commander. It looks as if I might be moving on soon. I don't want to. Why can't they leave people alone? I'm happy on the squadron.

My thoughts are interrupted by the noise of the wing taking-off. I watch them as they form up and head away towards the south coast and the Channel.

Along by the woods the trees rustle in a light breeze. Very few people about over this part of the airfield and even a rise in the ground blocks out the hangars and buildings. A cock pheasant calls from concealment in the woods; a skylark is making himself heard and there appears to have been a hatch of butterflies. I lose myself.

How nice it must be for men whose jobs keep them close to nature, farmers, naturalists. Perhaps a bit of leave would be a good thing, then I could go away into the country and have a long quiet walk in the rain – or sun, it wouldn't matter which. I'll ask Grace along.

I suppose I am a bit tired . . .

13. Beyond the Hill

Taxi slowly back to dispersal. No point in hurrying.

That's another sweep over, the second today. Nothing terribly hectic so it's strange that I should feel so bloody tired. Must be about teatime.

Let's see now, that last trip should take my total number of sweeps to something well over fifty. One day I'll count up, if I can be bothered.

The Spitfire waddles its way slowly over the bumpy grass. I am not conscious of controlling it, not conscious of guiding with just a little throttle and a touch of brake here and there. Looking along the side of the long nose in order to get some idea of where we are going I am even immune to the smell of the pale exhaust gases as the smoke is blown aft by the slowly revolving airscrew.

There's something rather pleasant and comforting about the smell of the fumes and the buffet of the slipstream as, safely on the ground at the end of another day, one somehow seems to wander in the general direction of the squadron dispersal, still in the land of the living.

It's been a long time now. What is it? September 1941, and the squadron has been hard on the offensive since that first tentative effort to Boulogne in January.

Even now an autumnal evening haze is unobtrusively encroaching over the airfield. The sun, a large fiery red orb, is descending down the sky. Hope we are released until the morning, we should be. Then, of course, it will be the same old routine. That same sun will rise a pale fresh yellow. Those on readiness will see it, then the Form D briefing and the operation itself with a better than even chance that somebody will get the chop. Might even be me but, somehow, it's always the other bloke up to now. In any case, I would not change places with anyone else for the world. This is my destiny. I know of no other way of life.

I can't even be bothered to consider the possibility of not coming back. I also find that I lose all track of time. Don't even know what day it is, I really don't. Doesn't matter two damns anyway, and for God's sake pay attention to where you're going, Geoffrey. You've only about thirty yards to go to the dispersal pen and aircraft seem to be taxiing everywhere.

A bit of brake, swing the nose to get a clearer view, ah, yes, there we are, there's my perch and Davy and Bevington waiting for me as ever. Throttle back, just rolling as they each grab hold of a wingtip to guide me in, bless 'em. This'll do. Just here. Starboard brake, a burst of throttle and we swing round and stop, tail towards the bay. A thumbs up from Bevington, that's it then, really home. Pull the cutout, the airscrew jerks to a stop, switches off, fuel off; gosh it's quiet.

'Brakes off.'

'Brakes off.' The ground crew push on the leading edge of the wings and the Spitfire rolls back into the protection of the blast walls.

'Brakes.'

'Brakes.' Lock them on.

'Good trip, sir?'

'So-so, as usual. The aircraft's fine. I didn't fire.'

'OK, sir.' They turn away absorbed as the petrol bowser chugs up and they prepare to refuel. I clamber out on to the wing and jump to the ground.

Made it again.

Unfastening my parachute I sling it over my shoulder, push back my helmet, good old pal that helmet, walk out of the bay and turning left down the peri track stroll towards the hut.

Be in time for tea in the Mess if we're released. I could do with a cup. It'll brace me up a bit.

As I walk slowly along, not hurrying, I can't help noticing even after all this time the ground crews as they go about their work every time the squadron returns from an operation. Totally preoccupied with readying their charges for the next sortie. Except those who are still waiting for their aircraft to return, but even they have no time for any sort of diversion, for if those who are waiting have to wait for any length of time they turn to and give a hand to the others, while constantly watching the sky towards the south-east. Presumably they feel a sense of loss as well as we pilots. Quite honestly, I've never thought of it in that light before. Why today? I watch them as I near the hut. A wonderful bunch, drilled in their various jobs and calling to each other amidst the clink and clank of spanners and the constant chug-chugging of the petrol bowsers.

'Chiefy, we're pissing glycol out of this header tank. It's leaking along that seam. Look, just there.'

'Where's that oil bowser? Come on, Lofty, hurry for Christ's sake, smack it about.'

'Dusty, how many bleedin' times do I have to tell yer, get them bloody chocks positioned right for Gawd's bloody sake.'

Brian and Mac the Adjutant are standing outside the hut talking earnestly. A lot of water has passed under the bridge since I first presented myself in Mac's office. He looks up and sees me approaching. Saluting the boss man, he turns and gets into the little Hillman car, waving to me as he does so. I wave back.

Brian walks a couple of paces towards me, then stops and waits for me to arrive. Now what on earth does he want? Not another trip this evening, surely. He looks at me as I approach and he speaks quietly.

'Hello, Boy. Good trip? Any luck?'

'Same as usual, Brian, no, I didn't get near anything.'

'Nor did I, Boy, one of the quieter ones. Look, Geoffrey, that's about enough for you old lad, you're off ops. We'll all be very sorry to see you leave us. You've done bloody well. You've been posted to an OTU to instruct, teach the young ideas.'

'I beg your pardon, Brian?'

'You're off ops. It's all over. Finished.'

I stand before him, parachute slung over my shoulder, map stuffed in the side of my flying boot and helmet pushed off my head, hot, sweaty and undignified.

Christ, I'm choking.

This is just a bad dream. It's a nightmare. I shall wake up in a minute.

'Why, Brian? Have I put up a black?'

'Good Lord no, my dear young Boy, very far from it. You've come to the end of the line, over the hill, you're finished.'

How I've dreaded this day, this bloody day. What on earth am I going to do, for goodness' sake? Easy to answer, right now I'm going to be sick and I am in sight of everybody.

Sod it!

In dispersal I hang up my parachute in what has been my locker for the last time. Full of luck, that locker. Other things as usual, familiar faces and habits, cigarettes being lit, the smoke curling to the rafters as usual. Rush, bustle and laughter and the general air of relief as another trip and another day is over. It'll be the same for them tomorrow but not for me. I'm no longer a member of 92 Squadron. It's all over, I've been posted. As the man said, I am over the hill, finished. I look around, none of the old lot left and now I'm on my way. This is the only life I know, I don't want to go.

Utterly miserable and feeling totally empty, I find myself walking slowly on my own towards the Mess, trying to collect my thoughts and think sensibly about things. As I pass near the camp buildings I meet up with Mac coming out of the Squadron Office, a smiling Mac. He seems to look at me in an almost fatherly way.

'Well, Geoffrey, how does it feel?'

'Bloody terrible.'

'Do you know, Boy, I was never more happy than when I saw you landing safely. Your posting came through just before you took off. It was too late to stop you but, as I say, when I saw you land ... well, my goodness, I felt a load off my shoulders. At least, I thought, Geoffrey Wellum has made it and lived. God only knows I've written enough letters to the parents of those who didn't.'

'Well, I suppose there's that side to it. I bloody well knew that something was afoot when you waved to me back there. I felt it in my water.'

'I was so relieved. I really mean it.'

'Thanks, Mac, it was nice of you to feel that way.'

'I feel for everybody the same, take it from me, but there was a little something about you. I'll never forget the look on the CO's face when he called you a cocky young bugger after your interview. Do you remember your arrival day? I do.'

'Yes, Mac, I remember. I'm not cocky now, though. Why should I be here and not all those others?'

I must have answered in a pitiful self-sympathetic sort of voice because Mac turns quickly towards me and puts his arm through mine.

'Now that's quite enough of that sort of balls. Come on, Geoffrey, snap out of it, laddie.' He is deeply sincere. 'In any case, the bar is due to open very soon and if it's not open then we'll bloody well open it and have the most enormous Scotch each that you have ever seen in your life. What do you say?'

'That's a very sensible thing you've just said.'

★

I turn my little £5 car out of the gates for the last time. A has-been. No further use to anybody. Merely a survivor, my name no longer on the Order of Battle in the dispersal hut. A worn-out bloody fighter pilot at twenty years of age, merely left to live, or rather exist, on memories, reduced to watching from the wings.

Will I ever know quite the feeling of trust and comradeship as experienced in a front line Spitfire squadron, and in such a period of our country's history, ever again? Nothing can possibly quite rise to such heights, at least not in my personal life, that's very certain.

Ask yourself, what's the use of anything any more? Far better to be with Peter, Nick, Laurie, Roy, Butch, Bill, John and the rest. There is just no purpose left now. How can anything replace or even approach the last eighteen months?

I stop the car by the side of the road under some trees. This is just not good enough. Really must take a grip. I feel quite wretched and emotional and, for the first time in my life, I'm in danger of breaking down completely and losing my self-control. I know this is stupid behaviour but I just can't help it. You see, I'm finished.

> But now discharged I fall away
> To do with little things again . . .

> Rudyard Kipling, 'The Return'

14. Return to the Fray

February 1942 and the conclusion of a miserable train journey from a grimy and dejected Liverpool Street station.

Audley End station seems to secrete moisture, enveloped as it is in a dull canopy of steady drizzle. The world looks grey and the surrounding countryside of rural Essex bedraggled, saturated and deserted. I take advantage of what limited shelter the archway leading to the entrance of the station affords, the stone of which, in the late twilight and dampness, has taken on the colour of lead.

The dirty, tired and resigned-looking locomotive seems to arouse itself to an exteme effort. Wheezing and puffing it labours and tugs at the carriages as it leaves the station, continuing its journey to Cambridge. The sound of its exhaust gradually recedes into the distance to be replaced by the steady relentless sound of water dripping from the eaves and gutters. Nothing seems to stir, the only movement being the patterns made by the raindrops on the all too familiar puddles.

I stand and quietly survey the scene. There's no rush. Once I've passed through the main gate of RAF Debden I've not the shadow of doubt that I will become totally involved in the atmosphere of an operational fighter squadron. Debden is the home of three Spitfire squadrons, 65, 71 Eagle and 111, so there will be all the rush and bustle anybody could possibly want.

At the age of twenty I have been posted to 65 Squadron as a Flight Commander.

In spite of my greatcoat, I shiver in the dampness of this February evening. The whole atmosphere reflects the sombre mood of a Britain that has been fighting on her own for over two years against the might and aggression of Nazi Germany.

The Duke of Wellington knew what the score was and what he was talking about. 'A damn near-run thing.' That is exactly the situation as it is, the only difference being that the Germans were on his side at Waterloo, though admittedly they had arrived rather late in the day.

It was five months ago, near enough, that I drove my little £5 Ford Ten through the gates of Biggin Hill for the last time and away from 92 Squadron.

Following 92 Squadron and Biggin Hill, life as an instructor at No. 52 Operational Training Unit at Aston Down, flying Hurricanes initially, was almost unbearable. Indeed, it would have been, were it not for Grace. To make things even worse, it was at Aston Down that I got news that Tommy Lund had been shot down over the Channel and was lost. Without Grace I think I would have broken down. So many friends lost and now dear old Tommy was on the bottom of the sea, still in his Spitfire, alongside Peter.

Grace came down to visit me whenever possible just so that we could be alone together, as we so often wanted to be in the Battle of Britain days, and it was at a quaint little inn where we used to stay that we first slept together and learned about loving. Slowly I found a new peace and fighter squadrons and combats fell into perspective as, gradually, I seemed to unwind. I even began to enjoy giving pupils dual in the Master and then getting them off solo in a Spit. Formation, battle climbs and gunnery followed. Eventually, I was flying all I could, often very early in the morning or late evening when the air was still and I seemed to have the sky to myself. It was an environment I understood.

During this period, I received a summons to attend an investiture at Buckingham Palace. It was a very moving occasion and one which I shall always cherish. The quiet dignity and protocol made a tremendous impression. His Majesty was softly spoken, sincere and quite charming as he pinned what appeared to be the biggest medal in the world on my chest. All the while a military orchestra played quietly in the background. And I became Flight Lieutenant Geoffrey Wellum, DFC.

Mother absolutely lapped it up but Dad was quiet and composed. It was only when he shook my hand after the ceremony and looked me in the eyes that I understood.

Old friends from Biggin Hill days were there, their best blue uniforms in marked contrast to how I last remembered seeing them. Firm handshakes, 'Well done old boy. Jolly good show.' The whole thing was so very British and I was very proud of the fact. To hell with those who sneered at our behaviour and way of life in Fighter Command.

Whilst waiting my turn I couldn't help thinking of absent friends. All the best ones seem to go first. Presumably, the gods consider that they have more than justified their time in this life and so take them back. The rest of us leave something to be desired; we have not fulfilled what is intended for us and so we remain.

Enough of this musing, phone for transport.

The narrow lane leading off the main A11 Cambridge road leaves the whole length of one side of Debden airfield on its left. As the little Hillman car breasts the rise and the airfield comes into view, the windscreen wipers click-clack backwards and forwards with a regularity that is almost hypnotic. I gaze through the window out over the expanse of green grass which blends in the distance with the misty grey of low cloud sitting on the deck. We are on top of a rise here, highish ground. Must remember that if ever I'm trying to get my flight back home in bad weather. Round the perimeter I can see the Spitfires and some Bostons parked, some in their blast pens and others on the grass in the open. There is little activity.

My driver seems to know exactly what the form is. No messing about with Station Headquarters this evening, straight to the Mess he says.

'On posting, sir?'

'Yes, 65 Squadron.'

'They have been as night fighters, sir, up to about a week ago that is.'

'Really?'

'Yes, so has the whole wing. Converting back to ordinary like now, sir, painted all black, they were.'

'What were?'

'The aeroplanes, you know, sir, night fighting, like. Spitfires were all black; 'orrible, they looked.'

'Yes, I follow, how did they get on?'

'Weren't arf some bleeding prangs.'

'Broken aeroplanes all over the place, eh?'

'Yes, and pilots, most of 'em killed, sir.'

'Spits are not the easiest at night.'

'Yes, sir, that's what we all thought when they kept on crashing, like. Wouldn't get me in one of them things any time, let alone at night.'

'Yes, I understand your viewpoint.'

'You bin on this lark before 'ave you, sir?'

'What lark's that?'

'Operations, like.'

'Yes, I've done a bit.'

'Thought so . . . Right, 'ere we are, sir, I'll give you an 'and wiv yer luggage.'

'Thank you very much.'

The car has stopped outside a building not unlike the Mess at Little Rissington but somewhat smaller. They are putting the blackout up but, from some windows, the lights shine brightly. The Mess has a friendly appearance and I can't wait to get inside.

'Thanks again, driver.'

'OK, sir. I've put your baggage in the 'all, like. Good luck, sir,' and he is gone.

I push open the swing doors and enter into a spacious hall. It's beautifully warm after the cold drizzle of what has been a truly lousy afternoon. I sign in the signing-in book, put 'on posting' in the remarks column and I'm about to put down the pen on the silver inkstand when:

'Hello, Geoffrey. Welcome aboard.'

Turning, who should I see of all people but Tony Bartley, grinning all over his face.

'Tony, my dear chap, what a sight for sore eyes. How are you?'

'Fine, Geoff, and you? You're looking well.'

To meet up with one of the old crowd again makes a happy ending to what has been a pretty dreary day of travelling, even more so when Tony tells me he is also a Flight Commander in 65 Squadron. It's somehow comforting to have him around and to know that we will be doing our second tour of ops together as Flight Commanders.

Our CO is Humphrey Gilbert, who is a great friend of Tony's and whom I'd met on a couple of occasions when he dropped into Biggin in a Defiant to see him. A nice chap; his greeting is typical:

'Hello, Geoffrey, nice to see you again. You can have no idea how good it is to have you join Tony and me.'

'Hello, sir, it's wonderful to be here.'

The following day I am introduced to my flight by Humphrey. Three of the officers are from Southern Rhodesia, Freddie Haslett, Tommy Burke and Flying Officer Grantham. The remainder are Pilot Officer Vic Lowson and two NCO pilots, Stillwell and Smith. They look a well-selected bunch, good material, but only three of them have operational experience and Freddie Haslett seems a little unsure of himself. The CO had warned me and said I would have to nurse them along, which gives me much food for thought and some concern. I am, in fact, beginning to realize the responsibilities of being a Flight Commander.

During the next ten days I fly with my flight twice a day unless we have a squadron practice and, at the end of that time, I feel that we are becoming a pretty useful team. I have a personal problem, however, in that I am not at all happy with my Spitfire. In vertical turns or when pulling out of a dive it tends to tighten up on itself to a very dangerous degree. It is not altogether easy to recover from these situations, especially as more often than not they black you out. It also has a nasty tendency to drop the starboard wing on landing, something Spits never do, and I begin to suspect that somewhere the airframe is twisted.

Other aircraft are also afflicted and, at Tony's instigation, Geoffrey Quill, the chief test pilot for Supermarines, comes up and flies one of our Spitfires, which he promptly takes back to the factory for evaluation and intensive testing.

Our first operation is a North Sea sweep, looking for ditched bomber crews. It is a good mission with which to open the batting, as it were, because, after that, 65 Squadron re-enters the war in real earnest.

Fighter sweeps and bomber escorts over France, Holland and Belgium are almost daily routine and, more often than not, twice daily. It doesn't seem as if I've ever been away; the same feeling of being a long way from home and trying to dodge the flak. Also we have to contend with a new German fighter and a most formidable opponent, the Focke-Wulf FW 190. Quite simply, the FW 190 outclasses our Spitfire VBs. It is 40 mph faster, has very good armament and a very high rate of roll.

65 Squadron moves from Debden to the grass satellite

airfield at Great Sampford and, as we are the only squadron there, we become a little community on our own. I enjoy being out in the Essex countryside and often go for walks in the fields when I want to forget the war and unwind. We take-off, rendezvous with the two Debden squadrons in the air and then off on our sweeps or escorts. Places so well remembered from 92 Squadron days, St Omer, Lille, Lens, Flushing, Zeebrugge and so on ad infinitum. It is hard fighting all the way and the 190s give us trouble. We suffer casualties, but it is towards the end of April that 65 Squadron has its hardest battle of all.

It is on a perfect spring morning that we make rendezvous with six Bostons as escort cover to St Omer. Since St Omer is not all that deep a penetration the bombers start to gain height as soon as we meet up, crossing the enemy coast at 12,000 feet, the bombing height. As escort cover, the Debden wing is at 15,000 feet, and of that wing 65 Squadron is the right-hand squadron. I had noted at the briefing that, after bombing, the Bostons were to turn away port and, therefore, our squadron will be on the outside of the turn; a most vulnerable place to be.

The whole circus crosses in at Gris Nez to be greeted by some fairly accurate flak; the little black puffs, just like cotton wool, appearing all around. Some of them have angry red flashes of flame in the middle, which shows that the bursting shells are very close indeed. I watch the bombers and the close escort below pressing right on through and, as I do so, the Controller comes on the air reporting forty plus bandits approaching from Abbeville and a further thirty plus dead ahead at thirty miles gaining height. A feeling of unease and foreboding comes over me. I don't much like the way the situation is developing. This looks very much as if we are in for another one of those battles when far from home, shades of 92 Squadron days; oh, God, please not. Please!

Think of something else. I wonder what Grace is doing. Right now I'd rather be with her than in this bloody aeroplane. Automatically I look to see if my flight is in position and there they all are, bless them, weaving gently with Freddie Haslett, my number two probably a little too wide but fairly well positioned. Humphrey must be having the same thoughts as me because he comes up on the R/T.

'Doily Squadron, this is Doily leader, keep a sharp lookout and watch the sun, especially on the turn.'

Freddie is still too wide so I give him a call.

'Yellow 2 from Yellow 1, not too wide, Freddie; in a shade.'

'OK, Geoffrey. Understood.'

The Controller continues to report the movements of the enemy aircraft as they home in on us. Everything inside me seems to turn itself into a knot and a stark fear grips me. Will it be my turn today to get the chop? Please God, help me to cope.

Am I as good a fighter pilot as I was during my first tour? I don't know, possibly not. I don't think anybody could ever reach quite such peaks and be the same quality of fighter pilot as when they were new pilots, keen, adventurous and eager to mix it with all who flew against them. One gets over the top of the curve and down the other side. One lives with fear, especially at night when sleep comes with difficulty and when it does then so do the dreams. Continual operational flying saps at reserves of strength and determination until you are reduced to a wreck and things come to a standstill. However, when you are not on ops you feel you are not pulling your weight, you're not at the sharp end, an operational fighter pilot, and so you move heaven and earth to return. I'm so afraid of being frightened. Anyway, as far as this situation is concerned, for Christ's sake bombers, bomb your bloody target and let's get out of here.

'Doily Squadron from Doily leader. Bandits twelve o'clock level, climbing.'

'Doily leader, Blue 1, Bandits three o'clock, above.'

'OK, Blue 1, watch it, Doily, the bombs have gone.'

I have a very quick glance downwards just in time to see the Bostons start their turn to port, no time to look for the bomb bursts. We are well into the turn when I glance behind and to the left to see a bunch of 190s slicing into our escort. Where the hell's the top cover? To the right and behind I see another bunch of FWs coming straight for us. Oh, God, we're being bounced.

'Breaking starboard, Doily Yellow. Bandits five o'clock above and coming down.'

I turn my flight into the attackers just in time but there are even more 190s coming down at us from behind and one of them is on to Freddie Haslett, who is too far out and weaving away.

'Behind, Freddie; break hard, Fred,' I yell on the R/T, but it's too late. Freddie Haslett's Spitfire explodes.

Two other Spits have collided and go spinning down, both out of control. Dear God, this is ghastly. Taking a quick look behind, a dappled grey FW 190 sits on my tail at less than 100 yards. Breaking hard I pull round in a climbing over vertical turn and as I do so there is a white flash and loud explosion just behind me followed by the hiss of passing tracers. Instinct makes me duck as I keep pulling like mad on the stick. Another muffled bang and the Spit judders as I continue to pull and then I begin to black out. I know what's happening, ease the stick and vision returns. I know I've taken hits but at least it would appear that my controls are still intact.

I lose all track of time as I fight for my life on my way out of France. Never have I had to fly harder. I can't see anything but my cockpit and tracers everywhere. I just recall hamming the stick around the cockpit, perspiration, throwing the Spit all over the sky without really looking round; fear giving way to anger and resignation. I hear hard breathing and groans. That can only be me. Tracers still continue to flash past. I can even hear the bloody things. The 190 pilots are relentless and determined opponents. Well, sod it! If I'm killed then I'm killed. I keep taking quick shots but I've no chance of hitting anything. The speed that things keep happening at is tremendous. So keep hamming about, Geoff, for God's sake. Then, quite suddenly, I find myself at 4,000 feet with Dunkirk just down there on my port side and quite alone.

This fight started at 15,000 feet and those Krauts have forced me down a good 10,000. Well, at least I gave them a fight for their money all the way down, but where on earth has everybody gone? Over the sea now and going like a bat in the general direction of Dover, I begin to feel not too good. I keep swallowing into my mask and my legs are trembling on the rudder bar. Everything feels heavy and, in addition, I have a splitting headache pain across the top of my eyes. Jesus, I feel dreadful. I slide open my hood and take off my mask and feel a little better. We are low over the sea and not wasting any time. Pulling up over the white cliffs I am home over friendly countryside. Gaining height, I set course for Great Sampford where I thump the Spitfire on to the ground. The silence when I switch off at dispersal is deafening. My God, it's good to be back in rural Essex.

We lost four during this show and Tony has crash-landed at Biggin, so a phone call tells us. Humphrey is waiting for me. He looks as knackered as I feel. It would appear that the squadron has been given a forty-eight hour stand down for replacement aeroplanes and pilots to arrive. My Spit has to go away for a new monocoque to be fitted. Feeling totally drained, I don't want to talk to anybody so I go to my room. I'm not what I used to be. Never have I experienced such a reaction. Haslett, Grantham, Davis and a new chap who only lasted two days are no longer with us. Haslett my number two shot out of the sky and I feel a terrible sense of responsibility.

Is it my fault Freddie has gone? Should I have seen those Huns a fraction earlier? Questions pump through my head. I've just got to snap out of this so I go to the Mess where I manage to scrounge a very stiff Scotch.

The following day Humphrey Gilbert kills himself and the Controller. He died trying to take the Controller to a party at White Waltham sitting on his knees in a Spitfire. How truly bloody stupid. What is happening to us?

Tony is devastated at the loss of his close friend. He goes away for twenty-four hours and, whilst he is recuperating, replacement men and machines arrive. Four of the pilots are Czech, fine young sergeant pilots but with no operational experience. On his return, Tony Bartley is given the squadron and I am now Senior Flight Commander. Colin Hewlett takes over Tony's old flight.

On the day of Humphrey's funeral, Operations require 65 Squadron to do a single squadron feint at the French coast to try to get the Germans into the air so that a three-wing fighter sweep following can engage them and shoot them all down. Tony asks me to take the squadron, which I do to Sangatte and down the coast to St Valéry. Moderate flak follows us all the way but mostly behind. My new Spitfire is straight from the factory and is a beauty. Apparently, our feint is successful but it was good to get back to Sampford with the squadron intact and personally to feel back in harness again. We are released for the rest of the day to attend the funeral and after that it's back to normal. Most days over the other side and one op to Flushing. A long, long way across the North Sea. We act as close escort to Bostons again and the whole circus flies over the waves at nought feet to keep under the enemy radar.

I get a kick even after all this time to be with the Bostons and their fighter escorts all thundering along over the water, literally right on the deck, the RAF roundels standing out clear and bright. The quick climb up to bombing heights follows, through the accurate flak, both light and heavy, bombs away and then turn back out over the sea again and down to nought feet, all the while listening to every beat of the engine and constantly scanning the instruments.

Tony, however, is very tired and has flown himself flat. The spark has gone. His lovely girlfriend comes to stay with him and it helps a lot; it is his retreat. He still feels Humphrey's death very much indeed. It has totally knocked him for six. He badly wants a rest.

I also get these headaches across the eyes much more frequently and am beginning to feel strain. I find I have to steel myself before every operation, on top of which I am sleeping badly. Only an almost daily evening telephone call to Grace keeps me going for, when ops are over for the day, there is always tomorrow. We manage to get one glorious twenty-four hours together, during which I am possessive and demanding but she is wonderful, understanding and so delicate. Afterwards, back to the war; offensive sweeps and more losses in the wing, including the Wing Leader, Pete Gordon. Pete is replaced by Duke Wooley, a very fine leader indeed.

In July, Tony is finally posted for a rest and a new CO arrives. I am still not twenty-one years old, so too young to take over the squadron. The new CO and I don't hit it off. I miss Tony very much and feel rather lonely. It is an unsettling time generally because the Debden Wing was destined for Russia but, when we return from forty-eight hours' embarkation leave, the whole thing has been cancelled and so it is, yet again, 'once more unto the breach'.

A week later I am posted overseas at twenty-four hours' notice.

15. Operation Pedestal

Within two hours of being told by the CO that I was posted overseas I was on a train bound for London. In my pocket I had a railway warrant for a sleeper on the overnight train from Euston to Glasgow for the following evening. I was to report in to the RTO Euston at 19.00 hours.

Somebody had moved very fast indeed and unreasonably I thought it might well have been the CO who wanted one of his chums to take over my flight. The Adjutant, however, assured me that this was not so and as we were good friends I accepted what he said, although the boss did nothing to stand in the way of my departure.

Apparently, there is a 'Top Secret' flap on and I'm part of it. I spent my last night with Grace and the war was forgotten.

Morale at a low ebb. Euston is dirty, grimy and busy. Seldom have I felt so miserable. Not only was my goodbye to Grace distressing but the speed of events that ended with me being dumped on this train has totally knocked me off course. Had I been new and fresh to operational flying I might be excited, but this upheaval comes when I am somewhere near the end of my second tour and, here I am, night train, Euston to Glasgow non-stop, no restaurant car and no bloody arguments.

I travel with a flight lieutenant I met at Aston Down. His name is Woods and everybody has always called him Timber. Sharing our four-berth sleeper are two naval officers on survivors' leave and they each have a bottle of Scotch. Without these two bottles our journey would have been sheer purgatory. As it was, they helped somewhat to allay the misery of Glasgow station at six o'clock on a dull grey misty drizzling morning. I think this is what they call Scotch mist.

Dishevelled RAF officers are met by the service police who escort us to waiting buses and, before one can say 'what a perfectly bloody situation', we are sitting down to breakfast in the Mess at Abbotsinch.

'Scotch porridge for breakfast, chaps, and you are all confined to the station.'

It would seem that a jolly time is going to be had by all.

There are about forty fighter pilots involved in this obviously important operation and of those forty, four are flight lieutenants: Timber Woods, a delightful Scot named McGruda, another named Wilkins and myself. In charge is Group Captain Walter Churchill, whom I met at Debden when he was due to take the wing to Russia. A highly decorated fighter pilot in his own right, he is a splendid leader and a very charming person.

For the remainder of the day we are left to ourselves to speculate as to our fate. The betting seems to be odds-on in favour of Malta with the Middle East a weak second favourite.

The following afternoon finds us piling into buses, bag and baggage, and an hour later we are deposited on a dockside in Greenock alongside which is a naval trawler. Without preamble we are ushered aboard. I can't help feeling unsettled by all this secrecy routine. Too much of the cloak and dagger for my taste. I like things to be straightforward and open, then we know who we're fighting. I wander on my own up to the bows of the trawler. The Clyde is full of ships, both RN and merchant, silent at their moorings. The hills of Scotland seem to brood over the scene and the whole environment is made all the more sinister by the wheeling gulls and their plaintive cries. The scene, I admit to myself, is not without beauty. There is strength in the atmosphere and a distant bugle note from one of the cruisers only adds to the solemnity of the occasion.

A shudder goes through the trawler and slowly the gap between the boat and the dockside widens. We head out into the stream straight towards an aircraft carrier, which grows huge as we get nearer. A short time later we are aboard, returning the salute of the Officer of the Watch. I note that her name is *Furious*.

The dignity and tradition together with the events of the last twenty minutes create a deep impression on me. I've read all about this sort of thing in the Senior Service, of course, but what I didn't cater for is the feeling of pride that one gets when one becomes involved for the first time. Of course, I'm not going to tell them that.

The RAF is made to feel at home and tea in the wardroom, all worn leather armchairs and polished mahogany, is a revelation. Loaves of freshly baked bread, bowls of various jams and as far as I can see about a pound of butter for every two people. No rationing aboard ship it seems.

Furious is obviously a happy ship. She has a good wardroom with a warm and friendly atmosphere. It doesn't take much to imagine this Mess in the piping days of peace. Our naval hosts display immaculate manners and I begin to feel better. Whatever is in store for us, this is a damn good team to be with.

Walter Churchill takes the four flight lieutenants into a corner after tea and informs us as to what this operation is all about, telling us to keep our mouths shut for the moment. Each of us is to lead up to ten Spitfires to Malta. That's all we need to know for the time being. There will be a full briefing later.

'However, gentlemen, there is a snag, follow me.'

He leads us on a tour of the ship and ends up in the hangar, a massive steel echoing barn of a place that is full of Spitfires. The Spits are painted in desert camouflage and have large tropical Vokes air filters under the nose.

'Notice anything else?'

'Yes, sir, they have the old-type De Havilland airscrews.'

'Precisely. No more than 2,650 revs for take-off and the flight deck is not only short but it's got a bloody great ramp in it about two-thirds of the way along. It was put there to throw the old biplanes into the air on take-off and to slow them down on landing before the days of arrester wires. Men used to run out and grab the wingtips. It therefore should not have been beyond the powers of comprehension of the planners to have appreciated that with these old-type airscrews this wretched ramp will throw you and me into the air before we have anything like flying speed. It will, in fact, merely slow us up.'

'Has anybody had a go at this?'

'Yes, I have, early this morning.'

'Well, sir, you obviously made it.'

'I started with just over 30 knots of wind over the deck and parked right down aft to get the longest run I possibly could. Take it from me, I made it, but only just. I was right down on the surface of the water and for a moment I was quite certain that I was going to end up in the drink with the added prospect of a bloody great aircraft carrier thundering over me.'

'Food for thought, sir.'

'Indeed, indeed. So, gentlemen, if each of you is spotted at the head of your ten aeroplanes and, therefore, not right aft on the blunt end as I was, added to which you each have a ninety-gallon overload tank on, there is only one way you and the rest of your aeroplanes are going to go and that is splash over the sharp end.'

'Can't say I'm altogether in favour of that, sir.'

'No, I don't suppose you are. So, the form is that tomorrow we put to sea and will fly off a Spit using 18 lb of boost; in other words, the tit pulled and wooden wedges of 25 degrees stuck in the flaps.'

'Good God, who thought that one up? What actually happens, then?'

'What happens is that before you take-off you lower your flaps and then some poor little junior rating holds, neatly between forefinger and thumb, the bit of angled wood in just the right place and then you select flaps up and, hey presto, you've got 25 degrees of flap and possibly, of course, a forefinger and a thumb. Gentlemen, this high-tech thinking is enough to turn one to serious drinking so let's go and make a start. The bar in the wardroom has been open for two whole minutes.'

'I wonder why I find this amusing, Timber?'

'I can't think, Geoff. What the hell will we have to do for them next? This is a typical British remedy to a typically British balls up that might just work.'

That night in my cabin I try to put the last two or three days in some sort of perspective. It's left me feeling cut off and lonely. Nobody knows I'm here and I'm not allowed to tell them. I'm cut off from the life I understand: fighter squadrons and local pubs, home and family, Mother and Father and, of course, Grace. I don't know if I'll ever see them again, or even see England again for that matter. I find these thoughts disturbing. I've never felt quite like this before. Eventually, thank God, the alcohol takes over and I sleep uneasily.

At sea the following morning in the Firth of Clyde we are steaming at 30 knots into a 10-knot wind – 40 knots over the deck. The pilot in the Spitfire ranged right aft on the flight deck opens the throttle steadily, holding the aircraft on the brakes. As soon as the Spit starts to edge forward, the brakes are released. Full power, the deep throaty roar of the Merlin blotting out all other sound as the aircraft thunders along the deck and up the ramp, which throws her into the air without anything like enough flying speed. It then thumps down on its undercarriage right on the forward part of the flight deck, bounces into the air again and falls off the front end of the ship. The poor bloody pilot, who is by now, I imagine, rather concerned at events, just manages to hold the aeroplane off the water in a semi-stalled condition and then, as the speed slowly builds up, climbs away to safety.

'Well,' says Timber Woods, 'those bloody little bits of wood did little to help that bloke and, if they want me to try, I'm going to jump overboard tonight and swim ashore to desert. To hell with that for a game.'

'You know, what we really want are revs, not necessarily power. We want 3,000 revs to get off this deck, then I reckon it should be fairly straightforward but, until we get 'em, we're just not going to make it,' observes Mac.

'You're very quiet, Geoffrey.'

'I feel it, dear chap. I'm going to the bar, it's open in five minutes or so and I intend to be waiting.'

That evening, Walter Churchill, Mac, Timber and I are taking a pre-dinner stroll up and down the flight deck. We are back at anchor off Greenock again. It is a peaceful evening, the wind has dropped and, apart from the gulls, everything is very still. The conversation obviously centres around our take-off problem.

'Well, sir, what's the form?'

'I've discussed the situation with the captain and the outcome of that was that I've signalled Air Ministry requesting that hydromatic airscrews be made available at once or else the operation will have to be called off.'

'But hydromatic airscrews are very few and far between, aren't they, sir? In fact, are they in full production? I mean, our squadron had one for trials.'

'Really, Mac? I'll tell you what, I bet your squadron hasn't got it by this time tomorrow; the whole country is being scoured for them. So, that's the form, chaps. I can see no alternative to being cooped up in *Furious*, swinging around our buoy for two or three days whilst they rake around for these bloody propellers. I would, therefore, suggest that the only answer is to patronize the wardroom bar. There's time for a couple of quick ones before dinner.'

Two nights later we slip moorings and, together with our escort, head out into the Atlantic at 25 knots. In the hangar are forty-five hydromatic airscrews. A Spitfire is prepared with one of the new propellers fitted and successfully takes off at first light, no trouble at all. It is to land at Aldergrove in Northern Ireland. That, I reckon, leaves thirty-eight to fly into Malta.

A leisurely breakfast follows in a subdued atmosphere, everybody with their private thoughts. Now that the chips are down and we are at sea and really on our way one can almost sense the drama to come.

I take a stroll on my own on deck and the scene that greets my eyes is totally new to me. There is quite a sea running but *Furious* is pushing ahead, shouldering the seas aside almost with disdain. Astern is our escorting cruiser, the *Manchester*, pitching into the swell with a massive bow wave and throwing the spray back over B turret and sometimes up to the bridge itself. She makes a magnificent sight, a lovely looking ship with graceful raked funnels. Everything is grey and white. Grey seas, grey skies, grey ships and white crests to the breaking rollers. A shaft of sunlight appears momentarily through the overcast sky and shows that lovely ship in the environment she knows. If only I was an artist. The sun shows up her grey paint clear and bright with her ensign streaming to the wind. *Manchester* has a clean, powerful, purposeful look about her and I wonder to myself what it is in my make up that finds beauty in powerful things.

On either quarter, two little destroyers, lithe and brave, pressing on regardless through the waves, sometimes disappearing from sight in a smother of blown spray, then reappearing on top of a wave crest before plunging down almost out of sight again. Terriers of ships. There is a certain cheekiness about them and all the time good old *Furious* thunders along as steady as a rock.

In the afternoon there is a general briefing in the wardroom. We are due to meet up with the convoy in the morning at 11.00 hours and the aim is to relieve Malta, which has been cut off and virtually in a state of siege over the past months. The island has been subjected to constant and relentless air attack, more in fact than London during the blitz. The code name for this operation is 'Pedestal'.

Malta is important to the Allies as a base from which attacks can be made on the Axis supply lines to Rommel in North Africa. We are told that there is a submarine flotilla operating and, apart from the remnants of the day fighter squadrons, there are some Beauforts for maritime strikes, Beaufighters for night fighting and a few Wellingtons for night bombing. The main snag is that petrol stocks are very low on the island and, although there are not many aeroplanes left on Malta at the moment, things are very tight indeed.

We are required to fly off from *Furious*, thirty-eight Spits in four formations at intervals. I am to lead the third formation. On take-off, our position will be south of the Balearic Islands and about sixty miles off Algiers. Our aircraft will carry ninety-gallon overload tanks and the flight to Malta should take something over three hours.

There are two routes to choose from, one going round Cap Bon and the other cutting inland across Tunisia to the Gulf of Tripoli. Both routes meet again over the island of Linosa, which will be a good checkpoint for the final leg to Malta. Finally, we have to obey the flight deck crew's orders implicitly.

The Germans have some ME 109s on the island of Pantelleria and this factor decides us to take the route across Tunisia and Cap Bon, thus keeping well to the south and out of harm's way. There may also be some 109s in Tunisia, so we are briefed to go over high at a minimum of 20,000 feet. Our job is to get Spitfires to Malta come what may.

All pretty heady stuff. I get together with the pilots who will make up my formation, take them to a quiet corner of the wardroom and conduct my own private briefing. I explain my intentions and route. Across Cap Bon making landfall at about Bizerta, then Tunis, Hammamet and out across the sea, keeping well to the south of Pantelleria, until we pick up Linosa. We might be able to see the island of Lampedusa to the south of Linosa as an added check. Thence straight for Malta, taking care to come in from the south. Our airfield is to be Luqa.

'R/T silence unless an emergency. We will listen out on the Malta frequency, which we shall be given later, and I will only call up Luqa when I first catch a sight of the island, after which we will let down to 10,000 feet and from then on we will be under their control.

'We will fly fairly wide formation. Less stressful, keeping a good lookout. As for height, well, I certainly won't go over Cap Bon at less than 20,000 feet, I may even edge a bit higher, so keep a constant watch on me, OK?'

They all seem happy enough and so now it remains up to me to get them there, but all I have is a scroll map, a compass and my watch.

Meeting up with the convoy is yet another moving and unforgettable experience. I think to myself that this is history in the making. As we approach the lines of ships all in perfect formation, *Furious* makes her number, signal lamps flash and we take up our position with our faithful watchdog *Manchester* still in position astern.

This is truly a mighty force consisting of fourteen large

merchant ships including one tanker, the *Ohio*. She is heavily laden and steams alongside us. There are also, as far as we can make out, thirty-eight ships of war. Two battleships are in the middle of the convoy, *Nelson* and *Rodney*, four aircraft carriers in addition to ourselves, *Victorious*, *Indomitable*, *Eagle* and *Argus*, seven cruisers including *Manchester*, of course, *Nigeria*, *Kenya* and *Cairo* an anti-aircraft cruiser. Surrounding this lot, dashing around the place and being very busy, are a couple of dozen destroyers. It is a truly wonderful spectacle and to somebody such as myself, not really versed in naval matters, something to stir the soul, a sight never to be forgotten. It is the greatest concentration of aircraft carriers the Royal Navy has ever mustered; in fact, they haven't any more and I suppose this is one of the biggest shows of naval strength in war since Jutland.

The fleet does a practice AA shoot and lets off every gun they have, including the sixteen-inch guns of *Nelson* and *Rodney*. I've never heard such a racket, but then I've normally been on the other end.

On the night of 9/10 August, the convoy enters the Strait of Gibraltar. We are due to fly off on the morning of the 11th. For some odd reason it occurs to me that seven days ago was my birthday. I am now twenty-one years old and hadn't even realized it.

Our Spits are brought up on to the flight deck to have their engines run and new airscrews checked, also to ensure that fuel flows from the overload tanks; they have been known to give trouble in this respect. All is bustle and rush but the jobs seem to be getting done.

I am allocated Spitfire EP465 and, after lunch, I go into the hangar to generally look her over and place my parachute and helmet in the cockpit ready for the morning. All the others appear to be doing the same thing. It's good to have an aeroplane to muck about with again, concentrates the mind.

Whilst engrossed in my self-appointed tasks some RAF

armourers turn up and proceed to take all the ammunition out of the ammunition boxes. I can't really believe this and it takes but a few seconds for curiosity to get the better of me.

'What's going on here, corporal?'

'It's all about cigarettes, sir, and I think weight is coming into it as well.'

'Cigarettes and weight?'

'That's right, sir. Short of cigarettes on Malta, they are.'

Whilst absorbing and appreciating this reply a voice from behind me says: 'Everything all right Geoffrey?'

I look round to see Walter Churchill, who is obviously generally keeping his eye on things.

'Yes thank you, sir. I'm still learning. As you can see, I'm watching my guns being loaded with cigarettes.'

'Bloody marvellous, isn't it? Actually, to make absolutely sure of this take-off, it has been decided to take all the ammunition out so as to save considerable weight. After all, the overload tank and ninety gallons of fuel weighs in at 750 lb so we're already overloaded. It will also help with your range, although we should have a pretty good fuel margin I imagine.'

'I see. So cigarettes are the order of the day?'

'Well, yes, that's about the size of it. I agreed because fags don't weigh very much and things on Malta have been pretty tough. It'll do the troops' morale a power of good to get some cheap smokes.'

'That's very kind and considerate of us, sir. I hope the Germans and Italians don't know.'

'What if they do? You couldn't hit any of them even if you did have ammunition, Geoffrey.'

'I know you to be right, sir, but it would be nice to be in a position to keep on trying.'

'Oh, by the way, Geoff, what I really came round to say was don't jettison your overload tank unless you have an emergency. They want them in Malta, apparently. Tell the rest of your chaps, will you?'

'Certainly, sir, I'll go and rake them out right away.'

So the final preparations continue. On the forward aircraft lift, which is in the lowered position, the Royal Marines band plays popular tunes, one of which is 'Happy, Tell Yourself That You're Happy'.

As we stroll down the deck to our waiting Spitfires I can't help wondering if I shall ever see my luggage again. All we are allowed to take with us is our shaving tackle and a spare tropical shirt, shorts and stockings. Somehow, the rest will follow us on, possibly by submarine.

The first two formations bound for Ta' Qali, which is just a few miles west of Luqa, got away safely. Now it's our turn.

Arriving at 465, I walk round and automatically do the external checks, with the addition this time of the wedges of wood in the flaps and the overload tank tucked up as it is between the undercarriage legs. Patient little Spit, we've got a job to do today. Already I feel a sort of affection for my aeroplane. Two sailors are standing by to help me into the cockpit.

'You checked the fuel flow from the overload tank, did you?'

'Yes, sir. All OK and . . . Christ, what's that?'

'What do you mean?'

'Something has happened to the *Eagle* . . . I think she's been torpedoed.'

'Are you sure?'

'See for yourself.'

I manage to twist far enough in my seat and see that grand old ship already taking on a list. There is a plume of smoke around. People are staring and pointing, then a sharp word of command and discipline and purpose take over.

The flight deck officer gives me the start-up signal; a bit

early, according to my watch. They must be keen to get us off and away in view of what's happened to *Eagle*. My radiator temperature is right down to cold and so I prime on the Ki-Gas six strokes. Hope the bloody engine starts. I'd put a right spanner in the works if the gallant leader blocked the flight deck because he made a balls up of the start.

Press the starter button and the booster coil and the Merlin fires and bangs into life first time. Looking behind I am gratified to see that the others have also started, blue exhaust smoke dispersing on the wind. I settle down and check the gauges. Come on, hurry and warm up. Already *Furious* is turning slowly into wind and working up to full speed. The deck officer climbs on to the wing beside me. 'You'll be getting about 35 knots of wind over the deck. Good luck.' I nod my head and he takes up his position on the edge of the deck where I can see him easily. Check that the brakes are firmly on and wave away the chocks. The drill of the flight deck crew is exemplary. These boys really know their job. Meanwhile, *Furious* has stopped turning and is steaming flat out dead into wind. The old girl is really gathering up her skirts and working up speed.

Now that I'm in the cockpit I have the feel of the aeroplane through the seat of my pants. I am relaxed, I think, and ready to go when they give the word. Check again the airscrew control, in fine pitch, yep, that's OK. This flight deck looks bloody short from where I'm sitting.

As I keep my eye on the flight deck officer he raises both his arms above his head. In his right hand is a green flag, his left hand has its thumb up, an enquiring look on his face. I give him a quick thumbs up and drop my hand on to the throttle again.

Here we go, Geoff, this is the *moment critique*. This take-off has got to be right, with no swings. There is little margin for error.

The deck officer rotates his flag and I slowly open the throttle. Come on, more yet, the little flag rotates faster. I can feel the Spit wanting to go against the brakes and then the flag falls. Brakes off, full power, all she's got and 3,000 revs, coarse rudder, keep her straight, Geoff, for God's sake. Immediately we start to roll I have feel on all controls thanks to the 35 knots over the deck. The Spitfire accelerates and charges towards the ramp straight down the centre line of the flight deck. Here's that damn ramp coming . . . up we go and I'm thrown into the air. Catch it on the stick, don't let her sink too much if you can avoid it, and then we're off the end, sea below. Come on, little Spitty, build up speed. Undercarriage up and we start to climb away. Don't forget the wood blocks, I've got enough height, OK now, flaps down, braking effect, flaps up and we are back to normal. Phew!

Once I've got things settled down, I do a slow turn to port in an orbit of the carrier, wide enough to allow my pilots to cut the corner and join up as quickly as possible. As I do so I switch over to the overload tank and am relieved when the engine keeps running.

Looking below, I can see *Furious* still steaming full ahead with the last of my formation just leaving her deck. She looks so small, her white wake stretching far behind her. Fancy having to land back on that thing for a living. The boys are forming up nicely so I continue the turn and set course due east for Cap Bon and Malta.

Just as I come round on to course *Furious* breaks R/T silence.

'Keep clear, keep clear of the carrier, air attack.'

I am only too happy to comply. I double check and there they all are, my eight Spits nicely in position in wide formation. Continuing in a steady climb up to height, the convoy is now well behind.

Looking back I can see a colossal amount of flak being hurled up from the convoy at the attacking aircraft, which appear as gnats on a summer evening. They seem to be bombing from high level. I look above and all round but there are no enemy aircraft bothering to take any notice of us, which is just as well, seeing that we haven't a bullet between us. It seems to me we got out of there just in time.

The sun is high in the sky and still climbing. Being bang on the nose it streams in through the perspex and thick bulletproof windscreen, the heat even as we gain height making things uncomfortable and sweaty in our confined cockpits. There is quite a thick haze which reflects the sun and all around is very bright and the glare disconcerting. Like an idiot, I have left my sunglasses on *Furious*, which is not a very sensible thing to do when you've got to keep a good lookout in conditions like this. I chastise myself, for such forgetfulness smacks of irresponsibility. This haze is thicker than I thought and even as we top out at 11,000 feet I am unable to see the peaks of the mountains along the Algerian coast to starboard.

At 20,000 feet I level off and throttle well back, bringing the revs back to 1,950. I remember that in the old days, before Spitfires had constant-speed airscrews, the variable-pitch propeller in coarse pitch gave something between 1,900 and 2,000 revs and Merlins run smooth at these settings.

I settle down for our three hour plus flight. Now we are really on our way. It was reckoned that the distance was about 650 miles. Allowing for take-off and climb we have something approaching 900 miles' range, possibly a bit more if we were to jettison our long-range tanks, so I'm fairly happy about the fuel situation. Now all I've got to do is to keep my concentration going and navigate this bunch safely to Luqa.

If this haze were not so bloody thick those mountains would have made a useful check for navigation but, as it is, there is nothing for it but to continue on compass and timing. Shades of my cross-country to Netheravon. God, that seems years and years ago.

The even beat and smooth running of the Merlin together with the warmth of the sun make me feel drowsy and it takes a mighty effort to maintain concentration. I turn up the oxygen a fraction, although I'm already getting plenty.

After what seems an age a reddish brown smudge eventually shows up ahead and slightly off to starboard, just where the North African coast should be, in fact. I can't quite make it out yet but Bizerta should be down there somewhere; unfortunately, it's still very hazy. As we approach the coast of Tunisia I take a look for the umpteenth time at the rest of the boys. They are all there, and have closed in a bit now that a change of course is imminent. This turning point and the one at Hammamet are terribly important in giving us a good known position from which to start our last two legs to Linosa and Malta. As I strain my eyes into the glare trying to pick up the salient features on the approaching coast, I experience this horrible ache across the top of my eyes again. It hadn't happened in *Furious* and I thought that the rest from daily flying had allowed me to get over what was merely a passing phase. No matter, there's too much to think about at the moment. It's not long before I spot a sizable town. That must be Bizerta, it's surely got to be, so turn starboard now on to 120 degrees for Hammamet.

Overland now and I can see Tunis and Cap Bon coming into view off to the left. I glance around the cockpit to check the instruments just in time to see a bright red warning light flicker and then stay on steady. Now what the hell's gone wrong? Fuel pressure, of course, the drop tank must be empty. Quick, Geoff, change over to main tanks and for God's sake don't let her airlock whatever you do. Switching over to main and turning off my overload it is to my intense relief that the dear old Merlin continues turning smooth and unworried.

I now keep a pretty smart lookout. This is possible 109 country and, once, I think I see movement far below which could denote aircraft. I can't be sure, but even if they were there's no chance of them catching us up here.

I'm delighted to note that the haze has thinned considerably and ahead I can see the distant coast of the Gulf of Tunis. A little later and a small town shows up just slightly off to my left. That can only be Hammamet. As we pass directly overhead I alter course to port and out over the sea again for Linosa. About an hour and a bit to go. An oxygen check shows that I have used just over half. Should be sufficient to get me to Malta but, just in case anyone is a bit short, I decide to let down to 15,000 feet as soon as I sight the island; then, if somebody does run out, it shouldn't be too serious.

Everything goes according to plan. Linosa is where it should be and I let slowly down to 15,000 feet. Looking out to my right I can faintly discern the loom of Lampedusa. Last lap, Geoff, nearly there. Just keep steady as you go.

Not long after, our destination appears looking like a brown leaf floating on water. As we approach I can see no sign of dust, so presumably there is no air raid at the moment. Dropping down to 10,000 feet I call Malta on the R/T, getting an immediate response. We are now under their control and they say that the island is clear of enemy activity. I can now relax and merely follow their instructions.

As my wheels touch down safely on Luqa, I can't help but feel a sense of satisfaction. I have helped to deliver a formation of nine Spitfires to Malta intact and in good order.

At the end of my landing run a jeep is waiting, out of which descend a crowd of RAF people. The driver of the jeep beckons me to follow him and he guides me to a blast pen where a crowd of airmen and soldiers are waiting. Glancing behind I see that all the others have a chap sitting on their wing guiding them into similar blast pens where ground personnel also wait. They are certainly on the ball and organized here.

Even before I've had time to switch off and the airscrew has jerked to a stop, a mass of bodies swarm all over EP465. Armourers clamber on top of the wings, unload the cigarettes and replace them with cannon shells and bullets, and the soldiers are already helping to refuel from four-gallon petrol tins. Getting out of my cockpit I jump to the ground and stretch. It's good to be able to walk around. I'm not sorry that little escapade is over.

Whilst the work of rearming and refuelling goes on without pause, I am in the act of taking off my parachute when an open MG drives up. Behind the wheel is Air Marshal Keith Park, who is now the AOC Malta. Following up is the jeep that led me to my dispersal pen containing Wing Commander 'Prosser' Hanks. I've never met him before but I know of him. He is a well-known fighter pilot, having been with No. 1 Squadron in France before the evacuation of Dunkirk. With him is Squadron Leader Stanley Grant, another Battle of Britain pilot. At that time he was with 65 Squadron so, although I don't know him well, we have something in common. As all the pilots who flew off *Furious* are experienced, it would appear that there is a pretty strong team building on Malta.

The AOC walks over to where I'm standing by my Spitfire. I admire this man tremendously. He is one of the few senior officers who lead from the front. He was in charge of 11 Group in the Battle of Britain and he flew his own Hurricane round to his stations at the height of the battle. Not only that; he was a fighter pilot in the First World War as well as this one.

'Have you just flown in with this lot?'

'Yes, sir.'

'What is your name?'

'Wellum, sir.'

'Have we met?'

'Yes, sir, Biggin Hill, 1940, September.'

'Of course. I remember faces. What squadron?'

'92, sir.'

'Splendid, it's good to have you here. Did you take-off before *Eagle* was sunk?'

'No, sir, we were sitting in our aircraft when she was hit.'

'Well, I don't want the word to get around just yet to the Maltese if it can be avoided. Their morale has taken enough knocks for the moment and I don't want things made any worse. They'll hear soon enough so don't talk too much about it, understand?'

'Understood, sir. How did the Ta' Qali chaps get on, sir?'

'All arrived except one who just seems to be lost without trace; no news at all.'

By this time the rest of my pilots have congregated and Keith Park and Prosser Hanks give us a quick general outline of the present situation.

At the moment there is a lull and things are pretty quiet, by Malta's standards. The Germans are fully stretched following up Rommel's successes in Libya and Egypt, so we have a breathing space. The convoy of which we were a part is vitally important. Everything is in short supply, petrol, ammunition, food, and the beer has long since run out. There are restrictions and strict rationing. It is forbidden to fly above 20,000 feet even on operations and no practice flying or testing of cannon or machine-guns is to take place. Even the anti-aircraft guns defending Valletta Grand Harbour and the airfields are restricted to a few rounds a day. Everything depends on some of the ships in the convoy getting through if Malta is to hold out and not fall to the enemy.

To help in this respect, the Spitfires that we have just flown in will be required to take-off at first light and patrol over the convoy in the Sicilian narrows and squadron will relieve squadron throughout the rest of the morning at least, bearing in mind the inroads such an operation is going to make on our dwindling stocks of petrol.

What the arrival of our Spitfires means is that we now, if this lull in enemy activity continues and petrol gets through with the convoy, will go over to the offensive and take the fight to the enemy over Sicily. All pretty gloomy stuff, but then we all realized that Malta would be no picnic.

Shortly after our situation report Wilkins turns up with his formation, having had his take-off delayed because of the air raid that we saw just after my lot got airborne. He is a quiet sort of chap but very pleasant for all that. It's good to see him safe and sound. He describes the ack-ack from the convoy escort as having to be seen to be believed and remembering the practice shoot I can quite believe it.

I am to join 1435 Squadron and the other Flight Commander is a chap I got on well with at Aston Down. His name is Basil Friendship. He takes me under his wing and introduces me to my new CO, Tony Lovell.

Tony Lovell I haven't met before. Quietly spoken, he is very correct in everything he does and even after a day at dispersal in the dust and heat, his appearance is one of neatness and tidiness. There is nothing dishevelled about Tony, no matter what's going on.

Every Spitfire that has ever been on Malta was flown in and with our arrival, so he tells me, we have an adequate stock of pilots. Therefore, he hopes to start a routine of one day on, one day off, especially if the enemy remains quiet. Most of our aircraft losses have been on the ground through bombing shortly after arrival. The Germans had seen them arrive on their radar. The squadron is due to fly the second wave to cover the convoy in the morning and I will be flying this mission.

'Sorry about this, Wellum. I was hoping to give you a breather after today's effort and a day or so for you to acclimatize but maximum effort is wanted for the morning.'

Our Mess is a large requisitioned house at St Julian's, right next to the sea. When we arrive those not on readiness today are having a swim in the calm clear water. I manage to borrow a spare pair of bathing trunks from Basil and join them. After today it is sheer heaven. I shall be doing a lot of this on any days off I get.

After a very sparse evening meal I go to bed early in view of the busy time today and the early start tomorrow, but I spend a sleepless night. My mind is too active, added to which it is very hot and sticky. I lie under my mosquito net wide awake and worry about the coming dawn.

There is just the faintest suspicion of daylight when the first patrol heads off to cover the convoy. I watch them go, their navigation lights bright and clear as they get airborne and join up. An hour later I am taking off from Luqa with 1435 Squadron and setting course due west.

On arrival in the area where the convoy should be, the haze is as thick as it was yesterday. In our position, the sky above is clear of enemy aircraft. To see anything below is going to be difficult with the rising sun reflecting on the haze, making it appear almost solid.

Directly below I can see a cruiser steaming at speed. She seems to be screening just two merchant ships which are pushing on independently in the general direction of Malta. It would appear that the convoy must be pretty spread out and it's becoming painfully obvious that somewhere along the line they have had one hell of a battle and taken an awful pasting.

This patrol is turning out to be anything but easy and, not being used to the conditions, I find the heat through the perspex and this incessant glare troublesome. The squadron spreads out to cover as wide an area as possible. There is some faint R/T in the distance. I think that someone is tangling with some Ju 87s but is having problems in the haze, which of course will also make bombing difficult for the Germans. How I'd love to get among some 87s. I turn towards where I think the engagement must be but nothing comes of it. There is nothing for it but to continue patrolling, which I do. Eventually, someone says he is returning to base and, as my fuel is getting on the low side, I dive away with my number two due east for Malta. All in all the past hour and a half has been very frustrating, but I suppose we can say that our presence over the area where the convoy was supposed to be kept the enemy from attacking, certainly in the case of the three ships I did manage to see.

On landing I am surprised to find that most of the squadron has already returned. As I get out of my aeroplane I am conscious of the horrible nagging ache around my eyes. It's a little disturbing but I suppose it will go away sometime. In our dispersal tent I see Tony Lovell and Basil.

'How did you get on, Wellum? Can't keep calling you Wellum, what is your Christian name?'

'Geoffrey, sir.'

'Right, Geoffrey, so how did it go?'

'A nonentity, really. I saw what I thought was a cruiser and a couple of merchant ships and I heard some distant R/T about some Ju 87s but, although I turned in what I thought was the right direction, I didn't see a thing.'

'Nor did I. I heard the R/T but that's about all. How many of our aircraft are still to come, Basil?'

'Two, I think.'

'Well, it might have been them, I suppose.'

The two finally land on the very last dregs of petrol and they had indeed seen some Ju 87s which split up when approached and went down into the haze. They only claim a damaged but at least the Germans didn't attack any ships.

In the afternoon, Basil and I fly a standing patrol over Grand Harbour until relieved by another pair. We see no sign of the enemy and no sign of any ships coming into harbour. It has been a hectic two days and I'm not sorry when the Luqa squadrons get an early stand down.

The following day, four battered but defiant ships enter Grand Harbour escorted by some destroyers. What a battle these boys have been through. We fly standing patrols of two aircraft at a time to cover any hostile action by the enemy, but for some reason they leave us alone; it's almost unbelievable.

I recognize three of the ships. They had been steaming close to the *Furious* and their names are the *Melbourne Star, Brisbane Star* and *Port Chalmers*. The fourth I don't recognize, but she's pretty big. Surely these four can't be all that's left of that proud convoy? The central figure of the whole saga is, of course, the tanker *Ohio* and she is still adrift somewhere.

The joy of the Maltese is total. They stand on the ramparts overlooking the entrance to Grand Harbour cheering, waving Union Jacks and pointing to the damage sustained by these dignified ships. I wouldn't mind betting there is a tear in many an eye and a lump in many a throat.

Unloading starts immediately and goes on throughout the night under floodlighting and still the enemy does nothing about it. Our few Beaufighters keep standing patrols through-out the hours of darkness and 1435 Squadron is on readiness from dawn to dusk.

It is whilst at dispersal that the news came through that another ship is in. Rumour has it that she is the *Ohio*. If true, Malta is saved. It was later confirmed that it was indeed the *Ohio* but so extensively damaged that two destroyers, one lashed to either side, brought her in at 3 knots. Their pumps are barely keeping the big ship afloat. She has been hit by bombs and torpedoes and it is said a Ju 87 crashed into her deck. Many of her crew have died and there are fires still burning. Her cargo of fuel is intact.

As the three ships come through the harbour entrance, just

about maintaining steerage way, the cheering of the Maltese who have come to welcome her in slowly subsides until there is absolute silence. Some of the men, mostly elderly, take off their hats and the womenfolk in their black hoods and cloaks cross themselves. From the fort a bugle sounds the 'Still' and not a soul moves.

Operation Pedestal has been a monumental and bitter battle fought by the Allies with a touch of desperation. Of the fourteen merchant ships, nine had been sunk and the navy had lost the *Eagle* and two cruisers, the *Cairo* and our chummy ship, the lovely and beautiful *Manchester*. Two of the other carriers, *Indomitable* and *Victorious*, were badly damaged and the destroyer *Foresight* was sunk by a torpedo.

At great sacrifice and suffering the navy had brought the convoy through and raised the siege of Malta. The enemy had failed to do what he set out to do: prevent the British from relieving a beleaguered and gallant little island.

16. White Clouds

The days that follow settle into the promised routine of one day on, one day off. The four ships brought in enough bottled beer for two litres a man. I find three non-drinkers after an extensive search and, as I am a non-smoker, swap my cigarettes for their beer. Later another two litres come my way through a new pilot being posted to my flight. His name is Walton, answering to Wally. We get on quite well together. He has an engaging way of not pronouncing his Rs. A fighter pilot of some experience, I might be pleased to have Wally around when the going gets tough again.

After about a week, I am agreeably surprised when my luggage that had to be left on *Furious* turns up, having been flown in by courier aircraft, a Hudson.

During my days off I swim in the warm Mediterranean and explore Valletta. It is very sad. Bomb damage and destruction everywhere and the lovely Opera House is now a shambles. Everywhere, however, is still busy and the whole place is working back to a more normal life now that the bombing has stopped and the people start to regain confidence.

On duty days it is a case of dawn to dusk readiness with the odd sweep over Sicily thrown in. There are escorts and fighter covers for the Beauforts on shipping strikes and we fly a top cover for the Ta' Qali squadrons briefed for a low-level attack on the enemy airfield at Comiso in Sicily. We have casualties. Walter Churchill takes a direct hit from a 40 mm and thumps straight into the deck. Mac McGruda also is missing on the same attack. So many friends and fellow fighter pilots have died. It's not as if these two met their end in air-to-air combat but on ground attack. You can't do anything about the flak. You just have to wade through it and trust to luck. What a bloody waste of two experienced and trusted comrades.

I am in a large formation that beats up some seaplanes at Syracuse. Low level all the way and the flak over the target is intense but we have surprise on our side and we are all amazed and cheered when everybody makes it back.

Very few Me 109s or Macchi 202s are encountered. They sometimes do very quick darts in and out over Malta but they are few in number and normally very high. Although we are scrambled as soon as they come up on our radar we can never quite get up to them. After one such sortie when we do manage to mix it a bit, albeit with a disadvantage of height, I take a hit in my radiator and lose all the glycol so I plough the thing in on Luqa.

All this time my headaches over the eyes are getting worse until one day I almost get tunnel vision and I start to worry. It so happens that a medical officer is having a post-dip glass of lemon squash in the Mess when I get back from readiness one evening. I'd been airborne a couple of times during the day looking for E-boats off Sicily. The glare from flying near the water and straining my eyes looking for the non-existent E-boats had brought on a great deal of discomfort and I wasn't feeling too good generally. It was nice to be able to flop down out of the sun in a shady room. The MO came up and sat with a bunch of us and must have noticed something.

'You're Geoffrey Wellum, aren't you?'

'That's right, Doc.'

'Thought so. I was at Biggin for a short while. You were with 92, weren't you?'

'Yes, that's right, nice to meet you.'

'You feeling all right? You look a bit knackered.'

'I'm OK, got a bit of a headache.'

'Get 'em often?'

'Now and then. Why, what makes you ask?'

'You are puffy round your eyes and they look inflamed.'

'Well, we had a couple of trips today over the sea and there was a hell of a lot of glare. Probably a bit of strain.'

'Are you on day off tomorrow?'

'Yes.'

'Right, I'll pop down after sick parade in the morning and have a look at you, see if we can do something about those headaches. I suppose you do a lot of swimming on your days off?'

'Yes, I do.'

'Well don't until after I've seen you in the morning. I mean it, Geoff, I don't like the look of your face at all.'

'Not many people do, Doc.'

'Very funny. Just be here tomorrow.'

True to his word, he sees me in the morning, the outcome of which is that in the afternoon I am in the nearby military hospital having an X-ray and the doctor there shows me the plates. It means little to me but he points to white smudges all around my eyes.

'See that? Fluid. Take this envelope and X-ray plate back to your MO and I want you back here 10.00 hours tomorrow morning. We have a good ENT man. He'll fix you up.'

I do as I am told but I'm quite determined to have a chat with the MO when I hand him this envelope. After all, he started all this.

'Now look, Doc, what's going on? I want to know.'

'Well, Geoffrey, these pictures are frightful. How long have you had this problem?'

'Oh, two or three months, on and off.'

'By the look of these pictures more on than off, I'd say.'

'I suppose so, but it's nothing I can't cope with.'

'Look, old boy. You have chronic sinusitis and they want you in hospital for a day or two to try and relieve the pressure round the eyes.'

'Hospital? I'm not bloody going. Just give me some aspirin or whatever, you must have something, Doc, I'm on readiness in the morning.'

'You most certainly are bloody going and I haven't any bloody something and you're not on readiness tomorrow morning, so get it straight.'

So that appears to be that and, once again, no bloody arguments. These medical chaps can be oh so masterful when they get the glimmer of a chance.

As bidden, I turn up at the hospital with a pair of pyjamas, a toothbrush and shaving tackle. What follows turns out to be four very unpleasant days. Firstly, within ten minutes of arriving I find myself in bed when I don't want to be in bed and, secondly, I have a long session with the ENT specialist that leaves me flat on my back and feeling like death.

He is an elderly grey-haired man who is polite, interested and very easy to talk to; a man with a clear conscience, a peaceful and gentle person. After half an hour's conversation, I realize that by his quiet and astute questioning he has found out all about my background, home life, school, how much operational flying I've done and so forth. He ends by looking at the X-ray plates of my sinuses.

'Well, old chap, we're going to have to clear that fluid as a matter of urgency, so we'll have a go at it right away. What I am going to do is cocaine the inside of your nostrils and then drill a hole through into the antrums.'

He calls to an assistant who has a tray of nasty looking instruments. I haven't a clue what an antrum is and I don't honestly give a damn because by this time I have reconciled myself to the fact that I have fallen into the hands of the medics. I am also terrified.

He removes the cocained cotton wool from my nose. My whole face tingles.

'Now, I'm not going to pretend that this is going to be pleasant, so just try to relax.'

So saying he picks up what looks like a long sharp knitting needle and the pair of them go to work. Everything suddenly becomes vague and dark, my head is being held, there is pressure and then I am jerked back to what is happening by an excruciating stabbing pain and an awareness of straw-coloured liquid pouring out of my nose like water from a tap. The room swims and I feel as if I'm doing a slow roll. I have lost all sense of balance and I can't orientate. I hear a voice a long way away saying, 'Good God, it must have been a cyst.' Hands are still holding my head.

'All right old chap, all right, it's all behind us now. Just hold still a moment. That's it, that's the idea. Now let's see if we can get you back to the ward right away . . .'

I don't know if I passed out completely or not. I don't think so, but I don't remember how I got back to the ward, either. Anyway, I'm damned if I'm going to pass out now. When things start to reorientate I am lying on my bed bathed in perspiration and then the bedclothes are pulled over me. I've had enough of this. I'm getting back to the bloody squadron. I'm not staying here, but at the moment I haven't the energy to lift a finger, let alone walk.

'I want you to take these pills, please. Shall I help you?'

I open my eyes and see a very pretty little nurse with an Australian accent.

'Do what you like, darling. I feel frightful.'

I take the pills and know nothing more. Fourteen hours later I return to the land of the living and what I hope will be a quick return to the squadron. At the moment, though, I feel thoroughly and totally drained. However, the one good thing is the feeling of relief around my eyes.

I recover some strength over the next couple of days, but a lot of the time I just sleep.

My specialist friend sends me to have a complete medical check-up, after which he invites me into his office. He tells me quietly and with obvious sincerity that I am seriously in need of a complete and prolonged rest from operational flying. My whole body, everything about me, has rebelled; it's had enough. My sinus trouble followed by the medical shows that I am absolutely played out mentally and physically; there are no reserves left. 'But you are young and will recover with time. You'll be back one day, don't worry. Young bodies have great powers of recuperation.' He goes on to tell me that he is sending me home to England and is getting me a place on the first available Hudson as far as Gibraltar. When I get home I am to report to the Central Medical Board in London with the full report he has written on my case and I'm sure I detect the ghost of a smile on his face when he says he has recommended that I be given a month's leave.

There is no point in pleading my cause to stay on the squadron so I thank him for all that he has done and leave his office clutching a sealed brown envelope. I don't see him again.

Before boarding the Hudson a couple of nights later, I go and see Tony Lovell and apologize because I consider I have let him and the squadron down. It is all I can do to prevent tears, which shows my emotional state, I suppose. He is very kind, tells me not to be bloody silly and is so charming that I can't wait to join the transport taking me up to the airfield. I am near to breaking point.

We land at Gibraltar after an eight-hour flight and I am given a room in the Bristol Hotel; no blackout, full shops, no rationing. It all seems very unreal. I don't want to eat, so after I've telegraphed Mother, Dad and Grace, I repair to the bar and there I tarry a while. Gibraltar is sheer bliss after the privations of Malta and I cannot help but feel rather annoyed at the complacency of everybody, which I know is stupid of me. However, when I think of how things were in the UK when I left, I realize that there may be some small justification for my anger.

I have made a friend of the Movements Officer and he telephones me one afternoon to say there is a Catalina going back to the UK the same evening, would I like to go on it? Yes, please, I would like to go on it and at eight o'clock we are airborne from Gibraltar bound for Mountbatten, Plymouth, where the aircraft is to undergo a major inspection.

The Catalina seems to do everything at 90 knots and it takes thirteen hours to reach our destination. Within a short time of arriving I have been fixed up with a first-class railway warrant and taken to Plymouth station where I catch the express to Paddington.

It is a gorgeous afternoon and the West Country looks lush and green. I am reminded of my walk down Kingsway for my interview to join the RAF when I look up and see white clouds. I close my eyes but I can't seem to rest. This is where I came in; my life has turned full circle. Looking up again and there they are, my little white clouds, drifting slowly across the sky, casting their shadows over green fields and grazing cattle. Surviving two tours of operations places a great value on life and I am grateful that I'm here to appreciate the beauty and tranquillity of the Devon countryside.

In most lives, I suppose, there comes a time when one has to make a supreme effort that calls for every morsel of endeavour and more often than not that effort has to be sustained. With me, I am certain that my time came with my three years as an operational fighter pilot in our country's finest hour. My only regret is that it had to happen so early in my life, but there it is. So drift on, little clouds, I know I'll be back with you one day soon.

Epilogue

Compared to the sleek beautiful Spitfire, the Typhoon looks a great hunk of an aeroplane.

I pause for a moment and take a long look at the brand-new Typhoon standing out in the sunlight waiting for me. I'm back with aeroplanes again.

It seems longer, but six weeks ago I landed back in England from Malta exhausted, both mentally and physically. I had no reserves left. I was sent home on sick leave and there was my room waiting for me just as I had left it over three years ago. Clean, dusted and polished, nothing out of place. Something inside me gave way and I stretched out on the same familiar comfy bed and broke down. I grieved for my lost friends in the squadron and I cursed that I had reached the pinnacle of my life before the age of twenty-two. I'd gone over the top. A medal and a royal handshake didn't seem important any more. Two full tours on Spitfires, the Battle of Britain and nearly one hundred escorts and fighter sweeps over occupied France and I felt destroyed by the war.

Slowly, however, rest and quiet helped a young body recuperate. I put on an old pair of slacks and an open-necked shirt and I went for long walks in the forest followed by a quick pint in the local. I found an old fishing rod and went down to the lake, nobody about, and I watched that little red float and relaxed. One day it bobbed under the surface. I pulled the line in and there was some sort of small fish on the end.

The improvement continued and I began to feel I wanted to fly again, so I went up to London and a medical board

passed me fit to fly. My old instructor from Desford was in
postings and I went to see him. It was a happy reunion, the
outcome of which was a secondment to the Gloster Aircraft
Company as a production test pilot, and here I am.

Without realizing it I have arrived at the Typhoon and after
a look around to see if it's got two of everything, I clamber
up the tall side and into the cockpit. Home again; the smell,
the instruments, they're all there to greet me.

Strapped in, I look up at the small white clouds against the
blue summer sky. I'm back. Hold on, little clouds, I'll be up
there in a minute.

Clear to start up . . . Contact.